'Read this ground-breaking collection—it will challenge you to think, read, talk, and think again about what you thought you knew of global migration! Grounded in serious considerations of the pluralithic perspectives of children and youth migrants, this book challenges us to reconsider who are migrants, what are the ideologies and politics which shape their lives, and whose perspective of migration counts. This analysis of young people's experiences of migration in the Global South and North opens new frontiers of for migration studies which will revitalise teaching and research on mobility, diversity, and integration'.

Khayaat Fakier, *Prince Claus Chair of Equity and Development, International Institute for Social Studies (ISS), The Hague, Netherlands*

'This is a much-needed book that focuses on children to challenge nation-centric epistemologies of migration and migrants. Strident nationalist politics often obscure the ways in which migrants are constructed as "the other" and blamed for a number of social problems. By bringing children to the centre, this book shows how states engage in the construction of ideologies against migrants through education systems, along with explicit policies and practices that violate the rhetoric about integration, equality and freedom. We learn from cases in countries on the edges of the Global North as well as the South so that the theoretical approach rests on a global array of cases. A significant effort towards decolonialising migrant-focused research'.

Bandana Purkayastha, *Professor, Sociology & Asian American Studies, and Associate Dean Social Sciences, University of Connecticut*

Global Migration and Diversity of Educational Experiences in the Global South and North

This book presents a child-centred approach to migrant children's experiences in education. Using a decolonising framework, the book interrogates the diversity of migrant experiences in the global South and North.

The book brings together researchers and practitioners from education, childhood studies, sociology, and linguistics to debate and theorise key methodological and empirical issues in migrant children's experiences through education. It focuses on how diverse forms of global mobilities are key to transforming educational experiences of children and considers the interplay of class, race, gender, geography, and learning settings. By doing so, the book uncovers particular challenges for addressing sustainable development goals relating to education and inclusive development. Diversifying the study of migration and development, the book challenges the Eurocentrism of the discipline and contributes to ongoing efforts to liberate the field from labels and discourses that further marginalise migrant children.

Using an intersectional and decolonising approach to address an important gap in the diversity of migrant experiences, the book will be of great interest to researchers, scholars, and students in the field of migration studies, sociology of education, intercultural education, and international development.

Shoba Arun is Professor of International Sociology, Department of Sociology, Manchester Metropolitan University, UK.

Khawla Badwan is Reader in Applied Linguistics, Manchester Metropolitan University, UK.

Hadjer Taibi holds a PhD in Applied Linguistics, Manchester Metropolitan University, UK.

Farwa Batool is a Research Fellow at Bradford Teaching Hospitals, NHS Foundation Trust, UK.

Migration and Education
Series Editors
Dympna Devine, University College Dublin, Ireland.
Nihad Bunar, Stockholm University, Sweden.
Halleli Pinson, Ben-Gurion University, Israel.

This book series examines issues of rights, (in)equalities, and social justice in the analysis of education, migration, and displacement. Set within the wider context of rising levels of global migration at a time of profound social, environmental and economic change, the series explores the reproductive power and positioning of education as a source of risk as well as opportunity for migrant and refugee children.

The series places a particular emphasis on the voices of those often marginalised in debates and policy analysis: migrant and refugee children, their families and educators across the education system. Through engagement with a range of theoretical and methodological frameworks, the series will explore these multiple dynamics and positionings both across country/educational contexts as well as within migrant/refugee communities in both the global north and global south.

The series welcomes authored or edited contributions in topics relevant to migration and education, including topics such as inclusion and exclusion, racism and privilege, lived experiences of migrants, educational policy, pedagogical challenges, and the role of schools as often contradictory sites in the realisation of internationally upheld rights for migrant and refugee children.

Books in this series:

Immigration, Integration and Education
Children of Immigrants in France and England
Oakleigh Welply

Global Migration and Diversity of Educational Experiences in the Global South and North
A Child-Centred Approach
Edited by Shoba Arun, Khawla Badwan, Hadjer Taibi, and Farwa Batool

For more information about books in this series, please visit https://www.routledge.com/our-products/book-series/MAE

Global Migration and Diversity of Educational Experiences in the Global South and North

A Child-Centred Approach

Edited by
Shoba Arun, Khawla Badwan, Hadjer Taibi, and Farwa Batool

First published 2023
by Routledge
4 Park Square, Milton Park, Abingdon, Oxon OX14 4RN

and by Routledge
605 Third Avenue, New York, NY 10158

Routledge is an imprint of the Taylor & Francis Group, an informa business

© 2023 selection and editorial matter, Shoba Arun, Khawla Badwan, Hadjer Taibi, and Farwa Batool; individual chapters, the contributors

The right of Shoba Arun, Khawla Badwan, Hadjer Taibi, and Farwa Batool to be identified as the authors of the editorial material, and of the authors for their individual chapters, has been asserted in accordance with sections 77 and 78 of the Copyright, Designs and Patents Act 1988.

With the exception of Chapters 1 and 6, no part of this book may be reprinted or reproduced or utilised in any form or by any electronic, mechanical, or other means, now known or hereafter invented, including photocopying and recording, or in any information storage or retrieval system, without permission in writing from the publishers.

Chapters 1 and 6 of this book are available for free in PDF format as Open Access from the individual product page at www.routledge.com. It has been made available under a Creative Commons Attribution-Non Commercial-No Derivatives 4.0 license.

Trademark notice: Product or corporate names may be trademarks or registered trademarks, and are used only for identification and explanation without intent to infringe.

British Library Cataloguing-in-Publication Data
A catalogue record for this book is available from the British Library

Library of Congress Cataloging-in-Publication Data
Names: Arun, Shoba, editor. | Badwan, Khawla, editor. | Taibi, Hadjer, editor. | Batool, Farwa, editor.
Title: Global migration and diversity of educational experiences in the global South and North : a child-centred approach / edited by Shoba Arun, Khawla Badwan, Hadjer Taibi, Farwa Batool.
Description: New York : Routledge, 2023. |
Series: Migration and education | Includes bibliographical references and index. |
Identifiers: LCCN 2022054331 (print) | LCCN 2022054332(ebook) | ISBN 9781032380315 (Hardback) | ISBN 9781032380322 (Paperback) | ISBN 9781003343141 (eBook)
Subjects: LCSH: Immigrant children—Education—Cross-cultural studies. | Children of immigrants—Education—Cross-cultural studies. | Home and school. | Multicultural education. | Emigration and immigration. | Third-culture children.
Classification: LCC LC3745 .G557 2023 (print) | LCC LC3745 (ebook) | DDC 371.826/91—dc23/eng/20230118
LC record available at https://lccn.loc.gov/2022054331
LC ebook record available at https://lccn.loc.gov/2022054332

ISBN: 978-1-032-38031-5 (hbk)
ISBN: 978-1-032-38032-2 (pbk)
ISBN: 978-1-003-34314-1 (ebk)

DOI: 10.4324/9781003343141

Typeset in Bembo
by codeMantra

Dedicated to all children who have had to move homes and lands, for their futures through an education without borders.

Dedicated to all educators who continue to challenge the status quo in education to make room, wrap arms, and foster migrant children.

Contents

List of Figures	xiii
List of Tables	xv
List of Abbreviations	xvii
List of Contributors	xix
Acknowledgements	xxvii
Foreward: Thinking Researchers' Positionalities about the Other and Opening to a Decolonised Research Gaze	xxix
FERNANDO HERNÁNDEZ-HERNÁNDEZ	

1 Introduction   **1**

SHOBA ARUN, KHAWLA BADWAN, AND HADJER TAIBI

PART I
Methodological, Conceptual, and Ethical Considerations in Child-Centred Migration Studies   17

2 Research with Migrant Children from Countries of the Global South: From Ethical Challenges to the Decolonisation of Research in the Sensitive Contexts of Modernity   **19**

URSZULA MARKOWSKA-MANISTA AND MANFRED LIEBEL

3 Reflexive Narrative on Identity and Exclusion of the Zimbabwean Child in the Diaspora: *'The Odd-Looking Fellow'*   **35**

SHEPHERD MUTSVARA

x Contents

4 Critical Decolonial Interculturality as a Tool to
Analyse Best Practices of Inclusion Centred on
Migrant Children in a Multi-ethnic Territory of São
Paulo City during the COVID-19 Pandemic   53
LUCAS RECH DA SILVA

PART II
**Intersectional Inequalities, Racism,
Stereotypes, and Discrimination of Migrant Pupils   71**

5 'Othering' and Integration of Migrant Children and
Young People of Albanian Ethnic Origin: Evidence
from Slovenian Schools   73
MATEJA SEDMAK, ZORANA MEDARIĆ, AND LUCIJA DEŽAN

6 Online Learning during a Pandemic and its Impact
on Migrant Children in Manchester, UK: "When the
School Closed...and being Isolated at Home I Feel
Like My Heart is Closed"   90
HADJER TAIBI, SHOBA ARUN, FARWA BATOOL, ALEKSANDRA
SZYMCZYK, AND BOGDAN NEGRU

7 Impact of the Pandemic on Refugee Education in Greece   109
NEKTARIA PALAIOLOGOU AND VIKTORIA PREKATE

PART III
**Well-being of Children in Migration Processes:
Case Studies   125**

8 A Profile of Well-Being among Children of Kerala
Migrants: Growing Up, Left Behind   127
S IRUDAYA RAJAN AND ASHWIN KUMAR

9 What do We know About Migration and the Role of
Education in Migration? The Case of Uzbekistan   145
DEEPA SANKAR

Contents   xi

10 African Migrant Children's Experiences in South African Schools   165

MARIAM SEEDAT-KHAN, ARADHANA RAMNUND MANSINGH, AND JOHN MHANDU

11 A Comparative Study of Language Learning Barriers of German Refugee and Cyprus Migrant Children   183

HRISTO KYUCHUKOV

12 Conclusion: Working towards a Hopeful Future through Child-centric Migration Studies Perspectives   199

Index   211

Figures

3.1	Writer's ZEP permit	36
3.2	Reasons for migration (n=77)	43
3.3	The age of the accompanying child in the country of arrival (n=100)	44
3.4	The effect of culture and peer interaction on social inclusion	46
3.5	Migration status in the country of arrival [South Africa]	47
6.1	Is a collection of words young people used in their interviews to describe their feelings during the pandemic	100
11.1	Total score of the short-term memory test as a dependent variable. Age group as an independent factor	188
11.2	Total score of the short-term memory test as a dependent variable. Ethic group as an independent factor	188
11.3	Total score of short-term memory test as a dependent variable. Interaction between the age and language as independent factors	189
11.4	Total score of short-term memory test as a dependent variable. Interaction between the age and language as independent factors	190
11.5	Total score of short-term memory test as a dependent variable. Interaction between the ethnicity and the language as independent factors	191
11.6	Total score of short-term memory test as a dependent variable. Interaction between the age, language, and ethnicity as independent factors	191
11.7	Total score of number repetition test as a dependent variable. Ethnicity as an independent factor	193
11.8	Total score of number repetition test as a dependent variable. Interaction between the language and ethnicity as independent factors	193
11.9	Total score of peabody picture vocabulary test. Verbs as dependent variable. Interaction between the age and ethnicity as independent factors	195

Tables

3.1	Demographic features of the survey (n=77)	43
6.1	Participants' Socio-demographic Information	97
7.1	Evaluation of Access of Refugee Children to Online Learning during the Pandemic	112
7.2	Evaluation of Access of Refugee Children to Specific Means of Online Learning	112
7.3	Prioritization of Funding Needs for Future Improvement of Refugee Access to Online Learning	112
7.4	Estimates of Refugee Population Percentage Aged 5–15 Participating in Online Education during School Closures in 2020–2021	113
7.5	Estimates of Refugee Population Percentage Aged 5–15 Participating in Online Education during School Re-openings in 2020–2021	113
7.6	Comparison of Refugee in-person Attendance after Re-opening of Schools Compared to Prior to the Pandemic	113
7.7	Reasons for Differences between in-person Attendance Before School Closures and after School Re-openings	114
7.8	Suggestions Regarding the Improvement of Refugees' Access to Online Education	114
7.9	Obstacles in Refugee/Migrant Student Inclusion in Class	115
8.1	Migration Status of the Surveyed Children in the Kerala Children's Survey, 2010	131
8.2	Profile of the Surveyed Boarding Schools in Kerala, 2010	131
8.3	Migration Status of the Surveyed Respondents in the Boarding Schools, 2010	131
8.4	Average Height-for-age (cm) of Children by the Migration Status of the Household	133
8.5	Average Weight of Children by Migration Status and Gender	133
8.6	Proportion of Respondents Reporting any Health Condition Necessitating a Visit to the Health Profession, by Migrant Status of Households and Boarding Schools, 2010	134

xvi List of Tables

8.7	Health Conditions/Problems Reported by Children among Households by Migrant Status, 2010	134
8.8	Health-Seeking Behaviour among the Children of Migrants, 2010	135
8.9	Enrolment Rates, Kerala, 2015–2016	136
8.10	Type of Institutions Attended by the Children of Migrant and Non-migrant Households in Kerala, 2010	136
8.11	Academic Performance Assessment of the Children of Different Households by Migration Status, 2010	137
8.12	Academic Performance Assessment of the Children in Boarding Schools by the Migration Status of Parents, 2010	137
8.13	Perceived Impact of Migration on Academic Performance of Respondents Residing in Households and Boarding Schools	137
8.14	Self-Reported Negative and Positive Aspects of Growing Up Without Parents	139
8.15	Response to Family Reunification among Migrant Children in Households and Boarding Schools	140
8.16	Response to Family Reunification among Migrant Children by Age in Households and Boarding Schools	140
8.17	Would You Like to Migrate in the Future? 2010, by Gender	142
8.18	Would You like to Migrate in the Future? Responses from Boarding Schools and Households By Age, 2010	142
9.1	Multivariate Analysis of the Characteristics of those Migrated within the Country and those Emigrated Outside the Country	155
10.1	African Migrant Children's Challenges in SA Schools	170

Abbreviations

ICDS	Inter-Censal Demographic Survey
SARS-CoV-2	Severe acute respiratory syndrome coronavirus 2
SLEI	Socio-legal exclusion/inclusion
ZEP	Zimbabwean Exemption Permit
DZP	Zimbabwean Special Dispensation Permit
RHC	Refugee Hospitality Center
REC	Refugee Education Coordinator
DYEP	Structures for the Welcoming and Education of Refugees

Contributors

Shoba Arun is Professor of International Sociology in the Department of Sociology at the Manchester Metropolitan University, United Kingdom, with research interests on global social identities and inequalities with a keen interest in migration studies and actively publishing in many academic journals, books and blogs. She is a Senior Fellow of the Higher Education Academy and member of the British Sociological Association and the Global Studies Association, UK. She serves on the Editorial Board of the Work, Employment and Society Journal. Her latest book, Development and Gender Capital in India: Change, Continuity and Conflict in Kerala (Routledge, 2017) adopts a feminist Bourdieusian approach to the gendered economy and society of the Indian state of Kerala in the global south. She has just completed her role as UK Lead and PI for the Horizon 2020 Project on MICREATE- Migrant Children and Communities in a Transforming Europe, (see www.micreate.eu). She is also Director of the Research Centre for Applied Social Sciences, and co-convenes the Migration and Interdisciplinary Global Studies Research Cluster.

Khawla Badwan is a Reader in Applied Linguistics at Manchester Metropolitan University, UK. Her work focuses on language education, social justice, sociolinguistics of mobility, new materialist approaches to intercultural communication, and literacy debates.

Farwa Batool is a research assistant at the Manchester Metropolitan University and King's College London. Her research interests relate to child and youth well-being and have now successfully completed several research projects within this area.

Lucija Dežan is a doctoral candidate of sociology at the University of Maribor and a young researcher at the Institute for Social Studies at the Science and Research Centre Koper, Slovenia. Her main research fields are migration, integration, gender studies and sociology of youth. Lucija has been a visiting fellow at the University of Oklahoma, USA, where she conducted field experiments related to US exit polls.

xx List of Contributors

Ashwin Kumar is currently a Graduate Student in International Migration Studies at the Graduate Center, the City University of New York (CUNY). Prior to this, he was a Research Associate at the International Institute of Migration and Development (IIMAD), Thiruvananthapuram, Kerala, India, under the supervision of Prof. S. Irudaya Rajan. He has worked extensively in the area of international and internal migration in the Global South and from India in particular. He has also previously worked with the Indian Centre for Migration, which is a think tank affiliated to the Ministry of External Affairs, Government of India. Additionally, he has also consulted on a research project commissioned by the International Labour Organization, New Delhi on the impact of COVID-19 on the Indian migration governance system, along with the Centre for Indian Migrant Studies (CIMS), Kerala.

Hristo Kyuchukov is a German scientist (born and raised up in Bulgaria), professor of Romani linguistics and Intercultural education at the University of Silesia, Katowice, Poland. He is known in Europe and worldwide for his research on Romani and Turkic (Balkan Turkish and Gagauz) languages, for his psycholinguistic research with Roma and Turkish children, for his research on human, linguistic and educational rights of Roma worldwide, for his research on intercultural education of migrant and refugee children and for his research on Roma history and culture. He is the Director of the Roma Research Centre at the University of Katowice, Poland, the President of the European Young Roma Scholars Network, based in Berlin and the Vice-President of the Gypsy Lore Society

Manfred Liebel holds a degree in sociology and a PhD in philosophy. He was a professor of sociology at Technical University of Berlin until 2005. Thereafter, he founded the MA Childhood Studies and Children's Rights (MACR) and was its director at Free University Berlin (until 2016) and is now at University of Applied Sciences Potsdam, where he was appointed honorary professor for intercultural childhood and children's rights studies. Outside academia, he holds the vice-chair of the council of the National Coalition Germany – Network for the Implementation of the UN Convention on the Rights of the Child. He did participatory field research with marginalised children and youth in Germany and different countries of Latin America, where he also was engaged as street worker and consultant of child rights–based NGOs and social movements of working children. Based on his research and experiences as educator and consultant, he published books in Spanish, English, German, French, and Polish. His latest publication in English is Decolonizing Childhoods: From Exclusion to Dignity (Policy Press, 2020), in German Unerhört: Kinder und Macht (Beltz-Juventa, 2020), in Spanish La Niñez Popular: Intereses, Derechos y Protagonismos (Los Libros de la Catarata, 2021).

List of Contributors xxi

Urszula Markowska-Manista holds a PhD in Educational Sciences. She is field researcher in education in culturally diversified environments, childhood, and youth studies concerning children's rights, postcolonial and decolonial perspective and participatory approaches. She was the director (FU Berlin 2016) and co-director (2017–2021 FH Potsdam) of the MA Childhood Studies and Children's Rights (MACR) international programme and is an assistant professor at the University of Warsaw (Faculty of Education). She is currently a researcher in international PATICIPA - Erasmus+ EU Project and researcher in an international research project about and with Ukrainian refugees led by Harvard University (USA). She has conducted extensive (community-oriented) field research in Central Africa, the Horn of Africa, the South Caucasus, and Central Europe. She is an author of books, articles, and chapters in international publications including by Sage, Springer, Routledge. Her latest publications are: Childhood Studies and Children's Rights between Research and Activism. (co-edited, Wiesbaden: Springer, 2020); Children and Childhood on the Borderland of Desired Peace and Undesired War – A Case of Ukraine. (co-authored, New York: Palgrave Macmillan, 2021).

Zorana Medarić holds a Master's degree in Sociology and is a Research Assistant at the Institute for Social Studies at the Science and Research Centre Koper, Slovenia. She conducts research in the fields of migration, intercultural studies and sociology of everyday life. From 2013 to 2020, she was the head of the Public Opinion Research Centre, which operates under the auspices of the Institute. From 2009 to 2021, she was a researcher and lecturer at the Faculty of Tourism Studies at the University of Primorska. She presents her work at scientific conferences and meetings and in guest lectures at various universities.

John Mhandu acquired his PhD in 2019 from the University of KwaZulu Natal. His research focuses on qualitative methods, sociological theory, and urban and rural sociology. He is an energetic and talented researcher with a strong desire to build a career within the research industry. He has written extensively on diverse issues of ethnography, migration, migration and informality, religion and migration, the politics of identity, and entrepreneurship and identity. He has published extensively in these areas and authored a number of book chapters, conference presentations, and papers in internationally acclaimed academic journals. His most recent publication is 'Navigating the Informal Economy: Social Networks among Undocumented Zimbabwean Migrant Women Hairdressers in Durban, South Africa'. He is currently a postdoctoral research fellow in the Department of Sociology at the University of KwaZulu-Natal.

Shepherd Mutsvara is a doctoral candidate at the Pedagogical University of Krakow, Institute of Political Science and Administration. His main research fields are refugee policy and protection, asylum procedures, and border externalisation. Besides being a member of the Kaldor Centre for International Refugee Law (Africa Research Group), Shepherd has been a visiting scholar at the Bremen International Graduate School of Social Sciences (BIGSSS).

Bogdan Negru is currently the Head of English as an Additional Language (EAL) at Cedar Mount Academy in Manchester, a role which he started since 2016. Previously to his current role, Bogdan worked with the local authority and different schools across Manchester in order to support the best practices for learners of English as an Additional Language (EAL) and those of Gypsy, Roma, and Traveller heritage. Bogdan previously also held various positions in management in different industries. Passionate about linguistics and semiotics, he holds a degree in Philosophy and a Postgraduate Diploma in Marketing Management from Manchester Metropolitan University.

Nektaria Palaiologou is Associate Professor at the School of Humanities at Hellenic Open University (HOU), former Assoc. Professor at the School of Social and Human Studies at the University of Western Macedonia (UoWM) until 2020. Since 2001 until today, she has taught Intercultural Education, Migration, and Refugee Education courses at six Greek and two European universities.

Nektaria has been participating as member of the scientific team at 10 international European projects in the past with UoWM as partner, in the field of Intercultural Education, Migration, Refugee Education Studies, in collaboration with European Universities and Organizations. Currently, with HOU as partner, she participates in three European projects: one HORIZON 2020 project and two Erasmus + projects.

Nektaria has published extensively at international journals (approx. 700 international references) on issues about Intercultural Education, Immigrant, and Refugee Education, Teacher Education.

Associate Professor, School of Humanities, Hellenic Open University, Director of LRM Programme.

Viktoria Prekate is a Secondary School Science Teacher and Psychologist, specialised in International Humanitarian Psychosocial Intervention (University of East London) and Language Education for Refugees and Migrants (postgraduate student at Hellenic Open Universities). She has extensive experience of education for refugee/migrant children, as a teacher, volunteer, and former Refugee Education Coordinator at Skaramagas Refugee Hospitality Center (hosting 2500 beneficiaries), facilitating access of refugees to Greek formal education and linking refugee and school communities. She also worked as psychologist with the International Federation of Red Cross and Red Crescent Societies at the Child Friendly Space of Skaramagas RHC.

LRM programme student, Secondary School Teacher, Former Refugee Education Coordinator.

S Irudaya Rajan is Chairman of the International Institute of Migration and Development (IIMAD), India and the Founding Editor in Chief of Migration and Development (Taylor & Francis) and the editor of two Routledge series - India Migration Report and South Asia Migration Report. He is lead editor of the new Springer series – South-South Migration. He also serves as the Chair of the KNOMAD (the Global Knowledge Partnership on Migration and Development) thematic working group on internal migration and urbanisation, World Bank. Earlier, he was a Professor at the Centre for Development Studies, Kerala and Chair of the Research Unit on International Migration (RUIM), funded by the erstwhile Ministry of Overseas Indian Affairs, Government of India (2006–2016). He is currently an editorial board member with Refugee Survey Quarterly (Oxford), Journal of Immigrant and Refugee Studies (Taylor & Francis) and Migration and Politics and has published with Routledge, Sage, Oxford University Press, Cambridge University Press, Springer, Palgrave, and Orient Blackswan. He is one of the expert committee members to advise the Government of Kerala on COVID-19.

Aradhana Ramnund-Mansingh acquired her PhD in 2019 from the University of KwaZulu Natal. Her study explored the link between institutional culture and career trajectories of women in academia. She is a prolific writer and has been acclaimed as an exemplary scholar, publishing a series of book chapters and five scientific journal articles within a year of completing her PhD. Her pledge to identify systemic gender impediments obviating women's advancement in the workplace is sacrosanct. Her research traverses decolonisation impacts on the socio-historical constructs of education in South Africa. She is a human resources practitioner with talent acquisition knowledge in human resources, and organisational transformation, talent management, and corporate culture have intensified her multidisciplinary gendered approach on the queen bee syndrome and the old boys' network. She is a member of the Association for Applied and Clinical Sociology AACS, the International Sociological Association and the South African Board for People Practices (SABPP), MANCOSA, Durban, South Africa

Postdoctoral Research Fellow, Department of Sociology, University of KwaZulu-Natal, South Africa xxiv List of Contributors

Lucas Rech da Silva holds a Bachelor's Degree in Social Science, Federal University of Pelotas (2015), Brazil, Master's Degree in Education (2018), Pontifical Catholic University of Rio Grande do Sul (PUCRS) – Full Grant CNPq/Brazilian Ministry of Education. PhD in Education at PUCRS – Full Grant CNPq/Brazilian Ministry of Education with a period abroad at Barcelona University (2020/2021).

Deepa Sankar is the Chief of Education, UNICEF Bangladesh. Prior to her current posting, she had served as the Chief of Education in UNICEF Uzbekistan. She holds a Ph.D in Economics from Jawaharlal Nehru University, New Delhi, Ms. Sankar had also served as a Senior Economist with the World Bank for more than a decade, leading and working on a range of education sector projects and analytical and advisory services in more than a dozen countries in Southern and Eastern Africa, South Asia as well as East Asia regions. She had also served as research faculty at the Tata Institute of Social Sciences, Mumbai and the Institute of Economic Growth, Delhi for brief periods.

Mateja Sedmak holds PhD in Sociology. She is Principal Research Associate and Head of the Institute for Social Sciences at the Science and Research Centre Koper, Slovenia. Her research interests include ethnic and intercultural studies, migration, mixed families and mixed identities, management of cultural diversity, and topics in sociology of everyday life and sociology of the family. She is the Head of the Section for Intercultural Studies at Slovenian Sociological Society and the leader of many national and international projects, including the Horizon 2020 MiCREATE project – Migrant Children and Communities and A Transforming Europe.

Mariam Seedat-Khan is a certified clinical sociologist at the University of KwaZulu-Natal. She is a member of the UKZN-Imbokodo, steering committee women in leadership programme. In 2020, she was named as a UKZN phenomenal woman by the Vice Chancellor. She is the founder and developer of SMART - Simply Managing Academic Related Tasks, developed to assist students with learning disorders and challenges. She is an active member of the International Sociological Association ISA RC-46 Clinical Sociology, South African Sociological Association-SASA-Working Group Convener Clinical Sociology; a board member of the Association for Applied and Clinical Sociology AACS and a member of the Canadian Sociological Association CSA. Professor Seedat-Khan is a visiting professor at Taylor's University in Malaysia and Covenant University in Nigeria.

Department of Sociology, University of KwaZulu-Natal, South Africa

Aleksandra Szymczyk is a researcher at the Policy Evaluation and Research Unit at Manchester Metropolitan University and a PhD candidate in

Social Anthropology at the University of Manchester. Her research interests include migration and transnationalism, right-wing populism, postsocialism, neoliberalism, and globalisation.

Hadjer Taibi holds a PhD in Applied Linguistics from Manchester Metropolitan University. She researches the sociolinguistics of globalisation and mobility, linguistic diversity, and social justice in applied linguistics. She is interested in decolonial approaches to language education and pedagogy.

Acknowledgements

The genesis of this book sprung during interactions as we met in an online conference during the COVID-19 pandemic to exchange findings from research on experiences of migrant pupils in countries across Europe. Many of us shared the glum experiences of children's education during the pandemic learning as they lost time from their precious childhood and learning at schools, but in particular struck by how migrant pupils faced a difficult time during this time, in much *shrunken bubbles*, not only separated from their friends, but extended families across borders who many lost, with more difficult living and learning spaces, severely affected by communication barriers with schools and migrant support service providers. As forms of lock down continued and with schools being closed in the grasp of the prolonged COVID-19, evidence was emerging from many countries on the 'lost generation' for many groups of children, many further affected by migration and displacement.

In this volume, we, as a team, have been able to bring together researchers, academics, practitioners, and teachers from many countries to discuss experiences of pupils in educational settings across a range of contexts, and engage in an interdisciplinary discussion grounded in debates on migrant integration, bilingualism, and interculturality, sociology of education as well influenced by recent calls for decolonisation and the epistemological considerations on framing migration studies in a global context. We express our thanks to the authors who contributed to this volume and for their continued commitment to the collective aspirations of the collection, we hope to continue our efforts for achieving an aspirational educational future of all children affected by the grand challenge of migration. We the editorial team share the challenges and thirst for a world that positively welcomes migration, given our own migratory backgrounds. Shoba was raised in the small hill town of Kotagiri in India before moving to the UK where her own experiences of regional migration as well as common wealth connections, which simultaneously ruptures and continually shapes her experience in both higher education as well as in everyday lived experience. Khawla lived her childhood years between Palestine and Saudi Arabia and experienced first-hand what it feels to be a migrant child longing to belong in education systems framed around stubborn national imaginings of the world. Like Shoba, these experiences led the path for her higher education trajectories where she became interested in, and then committed to, researching education as/for social justice. After moving from Algeria to the UK as a sojourner, Hadjer also became interested in how migration shapes individuals' lives and experiences especially in educational settings. Farwa was born and raised in Pakistan and moved to the UK at the tender age of 9. She experienced what it is like to move countries and lose all that was once familiar.

We are grateful to the financial support for the MICREATE project (funded by the European Commission's Horizon 2020 under the grant agreement number 822664). The editors acknowledge the support and role of the Commission and thank the Consortium team for their support in all stages of this work. The research findings, and their interpretation, included in this volume remain the responsibility of individual authors and the editorial team.

We acknowledge also the dedicated contribution of many researchers, expert advisors, and our teams who patiently reviewed these papers. Finally, we thank every one of the children and young people, teachers, and schools who participated in the various research activities for this collection. Without them, the research would not have been possible, but also helped create a vision of social justice *for all* through education.

Shoba Arun, Khawla Badwan, Hadjer Taibi, and Farwa Batool

Foreward

Thinking Researchers' Positionalities about the Other and Opening to a Decolonised Research Gaze

Fernando Hernández-Hernández

In 2018, I attended the 2nd Qualitative Inquiry conference in Leuven, Belgium. At that time, the movements of refugees, especially from the Syrian war, showed the true face of many European countries. In one of the sessions, a colleague from Ireland presented a refugee reception project that the European Union had funded. In the discussion, a participant in the conference asked the young researcher and activist who reported on the project: how do you deal with the contraction of receiving financial support from the European Union for the project when the same institution is putting up barriers for refugees to reach Europe? This question opened a debate that, in a way, runs through this book and the different chapters that make it up.

How to research the different realities that affect individuals labelled as migrants or refugees, with funds coming from institutions that stigmatise them and prevent their free movement? How do we relate to others in a situation of lack (of rights, language...) from the position of privilege of we who research Migrant Studies? How do we confront tensions and contradictions in researching about or with others situated on the margins of the positions we occupy as academics?

These questions are not rhetorical but affect onto-epistemology, methodological decisions, modes of relationship in research ethics, the political positions we face, and the research we carry out. This book addresses these questions and proposes some actions as an alternative to cope with tensions:

- 'Renewed conceptualisations and praxis around migration (...) that de-centre the nation-station and challenge the superiority of ethnic-based epistemologies and worldviews (...) break free from the colonial power discourses that reproduce "naturalised categories of difference"' (Dahinden, 2016, p. 13).
- 'To listen differently to the voices of migrant children, a doubly vulnerable group, so that we can shift the focus from broader political contexts to lived experiences'.
- 'To reimagine the integration of migrant children in ways that wrap arms around the vulnerable, rather than keeping them in an endless loop of

national expectations and gate-keeping processes that continue to other them and remind them that they do not belong' (all quotes taken from Chapter 1).

> It seems to me that the main contribution of this book to Migrant Studies in general, and in studies with children and young people, is to invite us to renew concepts, to learn to listen from another place (epistemic, ethical and political...) and to reimagine integration beyond colonising the Other. These aims align with the need to decolonise not only Migration Studies but also Childhood Studies, recognising the diversity of experiences (there are not childhood but childhoods) and knowledge researchers do not have. I could share these finalities, with nuances such as avoiding considering children as vulnerable (which implies making the subject responsible for their situation) but as vulnerabilised (by the prejudices and policies of the reception countries). But also 'engaging critically and reflexively with a child-centred approach, and (moving) away from a binary researcher-participant process'.
>
> (Chapter 6)

From this recognition of what the book contributes and invites, I will dwell on two of the questions presented here: how to think about the relationship with the Other whom we recognise, as Maturana points out, as a 'legitimate Other' (2001, p. 14), from our position of privilege; and how to decolonise our conceptual frameworks, modes of relationship and ways of presenting the Other in research from a decolonising position. Bearing in mind that although some authors of the book argue it is required to incorporate the visions and contributions of the Global South, most of the researchers involved in the book probably maintain the conceptual and political gazes of the Colonial North.

Approaching the Other from the perspective of the subaltern

Eduardo Viveiro de Castro (2010, p. 14) invites us, from anthropology, to strive for " the permanent decolonisation of thought" and thus to explore our relationship with the Other when it returns to us, as Maninglier (2005, p. 773–774) points out, "an image of ourselves in which we do not recognise ourselves". This statement invites confronting the camouflages and traps we project to evade what the Other gives us back about ourselves. This view makes us turn the migrant or refugee other into"fictions of the Western imagination" (Viveiro de Castro, 2010, p. 15). In this context, our imagination as university researchers runs the risk of projecting our "subjective phantasmagoria into the production of an Other that is alien to us but which reveals that we are heading towards more than what interests us, namely ourselves" (idem).

This tension places us in a back-and-forth loop in which the Other we approach also appropriates our culture and language in the same way that we appropriate theirs and leads us to engage in dialogue with some contributions from Spivak's (1998) perspective on subalternity. In doing so, we challenge our positionalities as scholars, the fantasies we project in our relations with the Other, and their historical differences and positions. Because as Spivak (1998) invites us to recognise 'the subaltern is necessarily that which always undermines (any possible) representation' (Beverley, 1998, p. 22).

The relation with the subaltern puts us in the position of having to recognise and confront the fact that, from the narratives in which we project representations of this Other that we approach with curiosity and a certain eagerness for salvation or social justice, the Other, as subaltern, by its very condition, always escapes us (Hernández-Hernández and Sancho Gil, 2018). Because the very idea of 'studying' the subaltern constitutes an internal contradiction in a sense that points to a new register of knowledge 'where the power of the university to understand and represent the world crumbles or reaches a limit' (Beverley, 1998, p. 14). Especially, when we do so without confronting the fact that a certain romanticisation of victimisation that nourishes our backgrounds as researchers

> [...] tends to confirm the Christian narrative of suffering and redemption tan underlines colonial or imperialist domination in the first place and to lead in practice more to benevolent paternalism, liberal guilt rather than solidarity, which presume in principle a relation of equality and reciprocity between the parties involved.
>
> (Beverley, 1998, pp. 28–29)

These contradictions brings us back as a boomerang, academically and politically. The boomerang is that those who are involved in the subaltern studies "are (mostly) white, middle- or upper-class academics working on research universities or in high culture institutions who want to represent ('map', 'let speak', speak for') the subaltern" (Beverley, 1998, p. 14–15 paraphrased).

This tension is revealed when we think that, because we listen to and tell the story of the Others, we are contributing to their 'coming out' of the situation of marginality. We will make our academic career, but will the Other be able to move away from their situation of subalternity? This brings us with the seemingly paradoxical situation posed by Gayatri Spivak (1998) when she states that the subaltern cannot speak, meaning that "the subaltern cannot transmit any kind of authority or meaning for us without altering the power/knowledge relations that constitute it as a subaltern in the first place" (Beverley, 1998, p. 13–14).

Facing Migrant Studies and childhoods as decolonisation of our thinking

In the book, some chapters are part of the European project Micreate, which is oriented on a child-centred approach. This project focused on generating evidence to provide results and recommendations for policymakers, administrators, and teachers. By taking this focus, the debate on concepts and the sometimes-contradictory positions we adopted took second place to the urgency of generating results. For this reason, in the group at the University of Barcelona, we decided to go further and find time to reflect on relational and performative ethics, intersectionality, cosmopolitanism, abjection, and decoloniality. On this last issue, given that one of the purposes of the book is to generate a mode of research that is not extractive and does not colonise the other, I will devote some paragraphs to our approach to decoloniality can contribute to this purpose of the book's coordinators.

In his comprehensive approach to a decolonial pedagogy, Andrés Argüello (2015) defines this tendency in contemporary social sciences on the assumption that coloniality is an unfinished historical process that has only undergone transformations over time and realities but has not been definitively overcome. Following this thought, Rivas Flores et al. (2020) point out that physical colonisation was replaced by ideological and epistemic colonisation through imposed subjectification. This is the premise on which the decolonial perspective is built on constructing a new world order. This order is based on the recognition of the different ways of knowing collectives traditionally annulled in the epistemology of what De Sousa (2019) calls the 'great north'; that is, the centre constituted by Western Europe and the United States.

Understanding coloniality beyond colonialism as a coercive structure, Argüello says, requires thinking about a definition beyond the episodic beyond the punctuations of the event that could eventually be considered as 'colonial'. In the decolonial perspective, this binding condition of history in its dimensions will be the weaving thread of the global coloniality of power, or as the Peruvian sociologist Aníbal Quijano (2000) would call it, the *colonial matrix of power*.

But decolonial thought is also born as a counterpart (Mignolo, 2007), as a way of positioning itself against what modernity represents, as thought based on universality, classification and hierarchy between different collectives and ethnic groups (Rivas Flores et al., 2000, p. 82). In this sense, Walter Mignolo speaks of paradigm-other, which is different from saying another paradigm. The paradigm-other is built on the awareness of the coloniality of power, of the inseparability of modernity/coloniality, difference and the relationship between the production of knowledge and processes of decolonisation and the socialisation of power. This paradigm-other contributes to "the right of existence of an 'other paradigm' in dialogue with the existing ones, as a paradigm that coexists in conflict with the existing ones" (Mignolo, 2003, p. 52 paraphrased).

Foreward xxxiii

According to this framework, decolonising research in the social sciences and education - and migration studies - involves reconstructing academic spaces as spaces of shared knowledge and scenarios of collaborative thinking (De Sousa, 2010). It means confronting the tension between the decolonial gaze that runs through university research to think beyond science. This position assumes that the university and research institutions incorporate a conditioning element as Quijano (2000) and Castro-Gómez (2007) point out: legitimising valid knowledge. This knowledge is articulated in a programmatic, ordered, linear way that generates categories in a vertical sense, which also disciplines the researcher, 'ordering him according to his fragmentary vision; forcing him to atomise reality and to unveil it for the objectives of those who hold power' (Castillo, 2017, p. 2).

In this research vision, the obsession with objectivity and objectification of the 'subject' plays an important role, negating both the research subject and the participant. The effect of this positionality is that, on the one hand, it annuls a way of thinking and producing as a whole, contributing only what an academic minority finds relevant. And on the other, it intensifies when it distances itself from the people, communities and collectives involved, even erasing the scenario, to discuss knowledge, categories, and meanings without the concurrence of the interested parties. In short, it is a matter of reducing the experiences given to us to how researchers think of them as measurable, countable or narratable data (Rivas Flores et al., 2000, p. 87 paraphrased). By raising these questions, the decolonial turn, in a transversal way, problematises what research can be, the research methodology, the politics of representation, interpretation, analysis and authorship of research (idem, 88).

As Mignolo (2003) points out, the decolonial paradigm is constructed from border thinking, rejecting any hierarchy or binary position. This paradigm seems relevant for Migrant and Children Studies because, as a local, contextualised way of thinking, it allows us to find stories with a multiplicity of temporalities and intersectionalities and other categories and ways of seeing the global world.

To continue the conversation

The reconfiguration of the Other and decolonisation of research places us, as Tuhiwai (2016) points out, on a path characterised by ethical-political reflection, horizontality, reciprocity, and dialogue between those who are different. This methodology-other can also be understood as a constant decolonising journey in research and our lives together. In this direction, Ortiz, Arias, and Pedrozo (2018) propose thinking about a 'non-methodology' that allows us to reinvent the processes of knowledge, representation and approach to reality. In this task, it is essential to decolonising the research subject, the processes, the academic contexts and the way of doing science.

From a decolonial perspective, research does not mean getting to know reality but letting it come, living with it in such a way that we do not question it, but rather it is the reality that questions us (Castillo, 2017). Every decolonial process is a self-decolonisation (Ortiz, Arias, and Pedrozo, 2018, p. 182 paraphrased). The 'decolonial doing' goes further in the decolonial process by recognising the participating subject as the other self in a dialogue between equals. It implies living in/by/for the community that seeks to decolonise itself.

We can bring these premises to research on childhoods and to projects such as Micreate that seek to rebalance relationships with groups placed in the position of subalterns. Specially to question our positionalities and, as Judit Butler (1993) proposes, to challenge what we see and do without questioning - for example, the child-centred approach (Stuardo-Concha et al., 2021) - and as something natural to generate subjects and regulate their behaviour.

Fernando Hernández–Hernández

References

Argüello, A. (2015). Pedagogía decolonial: Trazos para la construcción de un paradigma-otro desde la educación. *Revista Correo del Maestro*, 19(226), 28–37.

Beverley, J. (1998). Theses on Subalternity, Representation, and Politics (in response to Jean-François Chevrier). In: *Subculture and Homogenization* (pp. 11–51). Barcelona: Fundació Tàpies.

Butler, J. (1993). *Bodies that Matter: On the Discours Limits of 'Sex'*. New York, London: Routledge.

Castillo, D. G. (2017). Des-apreciaciones del método científico y la vacante en la metodología decolonial. *Hoja Filosófica*, 1(43), 5–19.

Castro-Gómez, S. (2007). Decolonizar la Universidad: la hybris del punto cero y el diálogo de saberes. En S. Castro-Gómez y R. Grosfoguel (eds.), *El giro decolonial* (pp. 79–92). Bogotá, Colombia: Siglo del Hombre.

Dahinden, J. (2016). A plea for the 'de-migranticization' of research on migration and integration. *Ethnic and Racial Studies*, 39(13), 2207–2225. DOI: 10.1080/01419870.2015.1124129

De Sousa, B. de S. (2010). *Descolonizar el saber, reinventar el poder*. Montevideo, Uruguay: Trilce.

De Sousa, B. (2019). *El fin del imperio cognitivo. La afirmación de las epistemologías del sur.* Madri:. Trotta.

Hernández-Hernández, F. y Sancho-Gil, J. M. (2018). When the *Other* arrives to the school. In E. Hultqvist, S. Lindblad y T. S. Popkewitz (eds.), *Critical Analysis of Educational Reforms in an Era of Transnational Governance* (pp. 231–244). Switzerland: Springer Nature.

Maninglier, P. (2005). Le parenté des autres. (À propos de Maurice Godelier, Métamorphoses de la parenté). *Critique*, 701, 758–774

Maturana, H. (2001). *Emociones y Lenguaje en Educación y Política*. Palma de Mallorca: Dolmen.

Mignolo, W. (2003). 'Un paradigma otro': colonialidad global, pensamiento fronterizo y cosmopolitismo crítico. In *Historias locales / diseños globales. Colonialidad, conocimientos subalternos y pensamiento fronterizo*, (pp. 19–60). Madrid: Akal.

Mignolo, W. (2007). El pensamiento decolonial: desprendimiento y apertura. Un manifiesto. In S. Castro-Gómez y R. Grosfoguel (eds.). *El giro decolonial: reflexiones para una diversidad epistémica más allá del capitalismo global* (pp. 25–46). Bogotá, Colombia: Siglo del Hombre Editores.

Ortiz, A., Arias, M.I., y Pedrozo Z. (2018). Metodología 'otra' en la investigación social, humana y educativa. El hacer decolonial como proceso decolonizante. *FAIA*, 7(30), 172–200.

Quijano, A. (2000). Colonialidad del poder, eurocentrismo y América Latina. In E. Lander (comp.) *La colonialidad del saber: eurocentrismo y ciencias sociales. Perspectivas latinoamericanas* (pp. 777–832). Buenos Aires, Argentina: CLACSO.

Rivas Flores, J.I., Márquez García, M.J., García López, M. Calvo León, P. Perspectiva decolonial de la investigación educativa y social. Rompiendo con la hegemonía epistemológica. In En J.M. Sancho Gil, F. Hernández Hernández, L. Montero Mesa, J. de Pablos Pons, J.I Rivas Flores, y A. Ocaña Fernández (Coords.), *Caminos y derivas para otra investigación educativa y social* (pp. 81–94). Barcelona: Octaedro.

Spivak, G. (1998). Can the Subaltern Speak? In C. Nelson y L. Grossber (eds.), *Marxism and the Interpretation of Culture* (pp. 271–313). Champaign, Ill.; University of Illinois Press.

Stuardo-Concha, M., Carrasco Segovia, S. y Hernández-Hernández, F. (2021). Possibilities, Difficulties, Tensions and Risks in a Child-Centred Approach in Educational Research. En M. Sedmak, F. Hernández-Hernández, J. M. Sancho-Gil y B. Gornik (eds), *Migrant Children's Integration and Education in Europe Approaches, Methodologies and Policies* (pp. 165–183). Barcelona: Octaedro.

Tuhiwai, L. (2016). *Descolonizar las metodologías. Investigación y pueblos indígenas*. Santiago de Chile: LOM ediciones.

Viveiro de Castro, E. (2010). *Metafísicas caníbales. Líneas de antropología posestructural*. Buenos Aires, Argentina: Katz.

Chapter 1

Introduction

Shoba Arun, Khawla Badwan, and Hadjer Taibi

Migration is arguably one of the key factors that shape global transformations. As a defining feature of the 21st century, migration can significantly impact the life, livelihood and well-being of migrating individuals, especially children and young people. Migration, as an important theme in social sciences, has been researched through a multitude of methods and approaches, bearing in mind the need for a multifactorial view of mobilities that takes into account complex processes of navigating power structures, national and international policies, local and global ideologies, and multiple histories linked to routes characterised by displacement, disadvantage, and disempowerment. That said, migration discourses continue to be dominated by nation-state and ethnicity-centred epistemologies that produce reductionist understandings of integration and migration. To address this epistemological pitfall, migration research requires renewed conceptualisations and praxis around migration, responding to Dahinden's (2016) critique which argues that, 'migration and integration research originates in the nation-state migration apparatus and is embedded in a corresponding normalisation discourse' (p. 2207).

This volume brings together a group of migration scholars committed to producing new conceptualisations that decentre the nation-station and challenge the superiority of ethnic-based epistemologies and worldviews. In addition, this work takes issue with methodological nationalism upon which migration studies are based and argues for the need to break free from the colonial power discourses that reproduce 'naturalised categories of difference' (Dahinden, 2016, p. 13). Central to the work presented here is the view that we need to listen differently to the voices of migrant children, a doubly vulnerable group, so that we can shift the focus from broader political contexts to lived experiences. As such, child- and youth-centred voices, methods, approaches, and perspectives become the new compass for a new migration praxis. The ultimate goal is to reimagine the integration of migrant children in ways that wrap arms around the vulnerable, rather than keeping them in an endless loop of national expectations and gate-keeping processes that continue to other them and remind them that they do not belong. As such, the work presented here speaks directly to the notion of 'foster-ship'

DOI: 10.4324/9781003343141-1

(Phipps, 2020; Badwan et al., 2021) that goes beyond entertaining the guest and offering aid and goodwill. This fostering takes a life of its own in the different chapters whereby different authors demonstrate numerous methodological and conceptual innovations to illustrate the educational experiences of diverse migrant children and young people across a range of contexts in the Global North and the Global South. These studies not only highlight a range of child/youth-centred methods but also shed light on the complexity of contextual factors that significantly impact on migrant children and young people's well-being and integration experiences. As a result, this volume challenges grand narratives and societal generalisations and pushes for an understanding that brings to the fore the individual, the lived, the intersectional, and the unrepresentational in order to allow us to collectively decreate (Weil, 2002) migration research, its language, categories, tools, and methods.

Child migrants and educational experiences: An overview

According to the latest available estimates, there are 272 million international migrants in the world, and 31 million of those migrants are children (World Migration Report, 2020). In an age of intense mobility and increasingly super diverse societies, there are growing calls for being more attentive to the voices and agency of migrants in conducting social research (Kosnick, 2021). We start with the premise that migrants do not move into and across empty and neutral spaces; instead, they move across spaces that are filled with 'racial power relations with a long colonial history, colonial imaginary, colonial knowledge, and racial/ethnic hierarchies linking to a history of empire' (Grosfoguel et al., 2014, p. 7). As individuals move, their languages, social connections, educational experiences, cultural backgrounds, religious beliefs, ethnic privilege (or lack of), and ways of living and becoming move with them and become 'resources' in a new metaphorical socioeconomic market that treats certain resources as valuable and others as less valuable or worthless in a world system that legitimises this sort of inequality. This process gives rise to hierarchies, othering, and exclusion for some migrant identity groups. We need this type of child/youth-centred research in order to understand how migrant children experience the processes of crossing borders and the challenges of dwelling in spaces filled with colonial hierarchies and predetermined expectations. Perhaps then, we can cease to see integration as a one-way process whereby migrant children simply learn to fit in the national moulds in which they find themselves.

Today, migration is much discussed as a process, policy, and practice. The chapters in this book weave together an understanding of migration as plurilithic experiences formed in interaction with, and as a result of, dynamics of power imbalances, policies, ideologies, and histories of conflict and control between and within the different parts of the world in the Global South and Global North (Kudakwashe et al., 2019). At the heart of researching migration as plurilithic experiences lies the need for a reflexive approach that takes account of dynamic social relationships and includes neglected meaning-making aspects (Ryan and Dahinden, 2021). This approach provides a flexible roadmap for methodological innovations that rethink 'matters of concern' (Latour, 2004) in migration research.

The project of listening differently to the plurilithic experiences of migrant children and young people entails focusing on how they exist in the world of education and how they navigate schooling requirements. Schools are important to the well-being of migrant children (Soriano and Cala, 2018) and to nurturing forms of societal integration (Tonheim et al., 2015). In fact, several studies provide recommendations on how to develop health and psychosocial well-being in school and through education for migrant children (Tonheim et al., 2015; Anastassiou, 2017; Mooren et al., 2019). Nevertheless, educational institutions such as schools, particularly, can be recognised as spaces in which hierarchies are reproduced and in which certain voices, groups, and knowledges are underrepresented or dismissed as problematic to, or at odds with, Western norms, worldviews and ways of being. In this book, we call for a wider decolonisation movement within migration studies through engaging in meaningful discussions with academics and practitioners from around the globe. Such a view of migration studies not only rethinks analytical categories within social research but also aims at decentring Europe through drawing on knowledges and perspectives from both the Global North and Global South (Heleta, 2016; Moosavi, 2020). In the context of the current widespread of colonial discourses, children with migrant backgrounds might find themselves at odds with what is presented to them in the curriculum and inside the classroom and their voices might not be echoed in what they are studying which might leave them feeling excluded through processes of othering and racialisation. Despite the centrality of children's experiences, in the process of policymaking and in the study of migration, children are often overlooked and are not regarded as autonomous, active agents (Medarić et al., 2021), we adopt a child-centred approach, which places children and young people at the centre of the decision-making and policy-making processes, which is elaborated next.

Child centredness in migration approaches

Migration scholars have called for children's experience to be the focus of research rather than through the voices of adults such as parents who are the primary migrants (see Doná, 2006). Thus, this perspective builds on research that moves towards social construction of childhood (following Ariès and Baldick, 1962; Christensen and Prout, 2002) embedded in relational processes. It views children as active participants and works in partnership with them to develop solutions. In social research, children are a valid source of information when it comes to expressing themselves and communicating about their worlds (Mayeza, 2017); thus, encouraging migrant children to take space, speak about their experiences, and make their voices heard would contribute to the creation of more inclusive societies. Drawing on projects related to child-centric approaches, Ozan and Arun (forthcoming) align with emerging discourse against the pitfalls of systematically including children in research (Kennan and Dolan, 2017) and acknowledge the need for outlining ethical dilemmas that may arise while offering guidelines for best practice, rather than relying on poor theorisations of participation that tend to become tokenistic (Fox, 2013), or participatory approaches that can bolster stereotypes and may not be able to reach groups often labelled as 'hard to reach' (McCarry, 2012; Fox, 2013; Ozan and Arun, forthcoming). Building on the sociology of childhood approaches, we not only consider children as competent social actors, but acknowledge that the diversity of such childhood experiences, such as migration renders them holding expertise about their own lives that is not available to adult researchers. Taking such an approach to the study of migrant children's experiences is important and timely given the ubiquity of migration levels around the world and the dominating adult-centred discourses. Such an approach acknowledges the cultural and linguistic diversity and richness of children's experiences and backgrounds. This diversity is often not reflected in the classroom because of the colonial, hierarchal, and overwhelmingly monocultural and monolingual schools' environments. In this book, efforts are made to prioritise migrant children's voices around the world and acknowledge their diverse, yet equal, linguistic experiences and trajectories through a child-centred approach. Moreover, the book champions work that legitimises the linguistic practices that have been supressed by linguistic colonialism and resists the prejudices migrant children face as a result dominant homogenising principles of education. Indeed, this book is a call to reflect children's diverse linguistic practices in the educational curriculum and pedagogy in order to create fair and just schools' environments. This is because 'when all children feel represented in the school life, they become empowered by and through the school' (Badwan et al., 2021, p. 707).

Structure of the book

As outlined, despite the centrality of children's experiences in social research, children are often overlooked in the process of policymaking in the study of migration. This edited volume draws attention to the experiences of children from migration backgrounds within educational settings. Accordingly, we strive to place children at the centre of sociological research, using an intersectional approach that give children from diverse backgrounds both the space and opportunity to express their ideas to inform child-centred narratives of migration studies. In related projects such as MICREATE (2019–2022),[1] research toolkits are expanded to give children spaces to communicate through a range of methods to provide rich qualitative data that are both traditional such as structured interviews and innovative such as artistic tools of expressions. This methodology allows for migrant child agency beyond dominant research cultures, often limited by measurement based on non-naturalistic variables, and encourage more participatory approaches that limit the overarching power dynamic between the children, educational structures, and the researcher so as to transform the research into a conversation rather than just a stimulus and response approach (Ozan and Arun, forthcoming). The main themes presented in the book relate to (1) Methodological and Ethical consideration within child-centred migration studies, including perspectives on research with children from the Global South and the need for decolonising migration studies and approaches in education (2) key issues in intersectional inequalities such as race, ethnicity, age, and spatial inequalities that impact on child and young people's migrant experiences within educational settings, including the impact of the COVID-19 pandemic and (3) case studies from contexts of Global South that reflect the impact of migration on child well-being. These are elaborated next.

Methodological, conceptual, and ethical considerations in child-centred migration studies

Any attempt to understand experiences of migration should place the research context in a frame that recognises political context, power, and culture. We draw on the Charter on Ethical Research with Children calls for respect for children, their views and cultures, as well as the requirement to treat all children equally and to prevent discrimination. Studies that outline the ethical considerations of working with children of migrant and refugee backgrounds (See Gaywood et al., 2020) acknowledge how these groups often live and experience two intersectional worlds: their old life and the potential of a new one. Hence, attending an educational setting is often a child's first experience of having to navigate the space between two cultures as children cross borders (Tobin, 2020). In Chapter 2, Markowska-Manista and Liebel write on ethical symmetry as a precarious challenge, as with the development of studies on children and childhoods that are oriented towards children's rights, subjectivity, and agency, the conviction has grown that only research *with* children is suitable for understanding the situation of children (Budde and Markowska-Manista, 2020) and also crucial for bringing children's diverse voices to the fore. As Articles 12 and 13 of the UN CRC clearly stress the right of all children to be informed, involved, and consulted in decisions that affect their lives. They discuss selected dilemmas arising from the epistemological environment of the researchers, question some of the attempts to give space and voice to migrant children from the Global South, and show why childhood studies especially as a part of migration studies need to free themselves from Eurocentric premises.

One of the issues that were encountered during the process of researching migrant children in UK-based schools during the MICREATE project was the stubborn insistence on equating the word 'migrant' with ethnic minority groups, especially the Black, Asian and Minority Ethnic (BAME) (See Syzmyck et al., forthcoming). In most cases, BAME children could be defined as local children. They can also be second- and third-generation migrants. To pay attention to the complexity of migrant histories across time, the distinction of new arrivals, long-term migrants, and local children was helpful for unpacking the term 'migrant', yet gate keepers often tended to exhibit a selection bias of children with migration experience from the Global South (Ozan and Arun, forthcoming), reinforcing a rather narrow interpretation of who a 'migrant' can be. Further, in most schools, access to migrant pupils was through EAL (English as other Language) definition, provision, and support and the research framework was confined to such classes rather than the general school setting (Syzmyck et al., forthcoming). This creates another layer of complexity whereby migrant children are entangled with deficient discourses due to their perceived linguistic disadvantage in comparison with their counterparts who are native or proficient in the national language.

Migration researchers need to question the ontological and epistemological basis of concepts and labels related to migration. For example, the uncritical use of terms such as 'others', 'integration', and 'immigrants vs citizens' leads to the social construction of migrants, asylum seekers, and refugees as homogenous social groups and contributes to the normalisation of discrimination through reinforcing binaries such as 'we' and 'them'. This could go as far as the justification of the dehumanisation of migrants (See Vanyoro, 2019). In a similar vein, focusing on the Zimbabwean diaspora, in Chapter 3, Mutsvara shows that while States have a sovereign right to choose who should come and reside in their territories, there is a need for a deliberate push towards humanising and amenable laws and policies that do not castigate a certain social group as undesirable and odd (Mutsvara, this volume). Such segregationist migration policies lead to stereotypes and prejudice, which is inimical to child development and can lead to family disintegration. Looking at the example of the diasporic Zimbabwean community, Mutsvara shows how socio-legal exclusion/inclusion (SLEI) affects social cohesion, assimilation, and a sense of belonging among diasporic children. To children, this may have a negative influence on how they grow and perceive society in general. This is because in trying to achieve inclusivity, the community and the institutions may exclude certain groups in society on the basis of their legal status (legitimacy) and level of assimilation (national belonging). This then borders on racialisation and may question the 'morality' of laws legitimately constituted but bordering on exclusion. In the field of migration, this creates a binary categorisation that pits desirable migrants against undesirable migrants. Children are then caught up in this socio-legal chasm, and their development is strictly curtailed thus affecting realistic chances for them to attain full self-actualisation. Subsequently, then, often, through a colonialist and nation-state lens, homogeneity, monolingualism, and monoculturalism are viewed as ideal as nation states are to be considered civilised and modern if they adapt the 'one nation, one language' European model (See Wolff, 2017). Thus, non-standard, vernacular, and minority languages are looked at as deficit and inferior. This line of thinking is based on symbolic domination, and it views plurilingualism as impure and dividing while monolingualism is regarded as neutral, unifying, and in fact 'desirable'.

The *monolingualising* discourses and policies of governments around the world (Heller, 1995, p. 374) often lead to exclusion and especially to marginalised groups, such as migrant group but also children who do have a central role in this migration process. Chapter 4 focuses on decolonising processes that dismantle colonial legacies and beliefs in education as it leaves deep-seated scars on both educational practices and mindsets (this volume, Rech da Silva). Rech da Silva notes that debates on interculturality in education in contexts such as Brazil in the Global South disregard cultural roots and ancestral knowledge and refers to a case study of an elementary public school recognised by UNESCO as an example of good practices in intercultural education and integration centred on migrant children. Through a decolonial approach, educational practices can address the needs of indigenous communities without nullifying their traditional knowledge.

With such ethnocentric bias in the classroom migrant, children might face feelings of exclusion, stigmatisation, and shame (Motha, 2016, p. 76) as existing, broader political, social, and institutional language ideologies that view certain language practices as normative and legitimate while others not (Bourdieu, 1977). Through these ideologies, nation states give privileges and promote for particular language practices in schools and educational institutions. This eventually leads to oppression and unequal access to life opportunities and chances (Badwan et al., 2021, p. 705), with speakers tending to adopt the normative ways of speaking, shun their own, and invest in the linguistic capital (Bourdieu, 1977).

Thus, practices and discourse need to focus on shaping the integration in a way that could eliminate the conflict and other problems caused by racism and discrimination, hierarchical power structures, and ideologies as these impact on social cohesion and well-being. Literature shows that across many immigrant groups, bullying and peer aggression were consistently significantly higher for non-official language speaking first-generation immigrant adolescents compared with third-generation and native-born adolescents (Arun et al., 2021). This suggests that risks related to violence are greater when an immigrant adolescent speaks a language other than the primary language of the host country (Pottie et al., 2015), and the experience of racism is therefore uneven. Visible difference in skin colour means that such issues extend to those who are not migrants, but have some form of migrant background (Åhlund and Jonsson, 2016; Priest et al., 2016; Johnsen et al., 2017). Studies note a distinction between the perception and racist behaviour in educational system between old and new EU countries. In Western discourse, we observe the denial strategies in reference to discrimination recognition. In Central and Eastern Europe, experience of racist behaviour is seen as common experience of migrants and minorities, something inevitably connected with their presence in the host country. In this collection, we have important insights into how socialisation processes in schools engenders processes of othering and identity. Based on in-depth study in Slovenian schools, Sedmak et al in Chapter 5 examine the othering discourses and practices towards children and youth of Albanian ethnic backgrounds. This study focuses on hierarchically characterised in-group and out-group binary opposition, exclusion, and segregation practices, and social distancing based on stigmatisation, symbolic degradation, and stereotyping, as well as the existence of discursive violence. For children, integration primarily means being accepted by their friends and teachers and being part of their class and school (Sedmak, 2021, p. 3). All of this could be identified in the discourses and practices of teachers and children in Slovenian educational settings, but also observed on the macro level through their accounts. Perceptions of the Albanian ethnic community as the definitive Other is reflected in their observation of a girl who moved to Slovenia from Kosovo four years ago: *Slovenians are open toward the foreigners, but not toward the Albanians (this volume).* This as more often cited in the literature, demonstrating the need for a strong integration policy, is prejudice, stereotypes, and discrimination at individual and institutional level (Fangen and Lynnebakke, 2014) and the issue of interethnic violence in schools often remains an under-researched and inadequately discussed phenomenon (Medarić and Žakelj, 2014), particularly in relation to cause for such violence (Eisner and Malti, 2012) as often the attitude of pupils towards their migrant peers is driven by wider societal context and prevailing media discourse (Medarić and Žakelj, 2014).

Intersectional inequalities, racism, stereotypes, and discrimination of migrant pupils

Intersectional inequalities often create unequal outcomes. The socioeconomic status of the migrant children is often categorised as one of the major sources of underprivilege and discrimination. Children are frequently excluded and marginalised, restricted from participating in activities and deprived from fundamental economic, social, cultural, and political rights (Medarić and Žakelj, 2014; Forbes and Sime, 2016). This affects mainly those groups classified as minorities with long-term history of social exclusion such as Roma people (Sime et al., 2018) or labelled as asylum seekers and refugees as we see in this volume too.

The heterogeneity of social groups is an important issue as not all social or migrant groups have similar learning experiences and outcomes. In some cases, such inequalities are accentuated during crises. In Chapter 6, exploring refugee education and digital divide in Greece during the pandemic, Palaiologou and Prekat find that young refugee groups, already underrepresented in Greece education, were disproportionately affected. Those living in large Refugee Hospitality Centres (RHCs) were even more disadvantaged, as camps were subjected to stricter lockdown rules than mainstream population. Shortage of digital connection, lack of digital competencies, long-standing malfunctions in the refugee education system, contributed to a deterioration of refugee access to education, as it happened for other disadvantaged social groups, like Roma children. Structural and material conditions such as lack of space, increased family violence, the stress, and trauma of the pandemic were in themselves aggravating factors, affecting refugee students' access and involvement in education. Such intersectional inequalities continue to be heightened during the COVID-19 pandemic in many ways. Evidence on learning and its impact on children show that socioeconomic status is key to the digital divide. Thus, children from middle-class families managed this transition much better in ascertaining access to both online learning and study spaces during the first lockdown in the spring of 2020 (Andrew et al., 2020; Benzeval et al., 2020). Migrant groups, with such intersectional inequalities, have been significantly affected by the global pandemic (Jourdain and Arnold, 2021), which then impacted severely in the ability to support their children's educational needs.

In the UK, research has shown that migrant children and families face many challenges at schools (Manzoni and Rolfe, 2019); including a lack of familiarity with the UK education system such as expectations around the level of parental engagement, feelings of isolation because of cultural differences, as well as language barriers. In the UK, in Chapter 7, Taibi et al (this volume) show that with the outbreak of coronavirus and the schools' closure, the challenges become heightened. The safety restrictions and social distancing measurements forced children to be separated from their peers who found themselves not only having to deal with the new threat of the virus but also having to adapt to different learning environments. In Chapter 8, Kyuchukov discusses how refugee and migrant children have to manage and adapt to challenges related to language, social environment, and often face bias and stereotypes, often with marked inter-group differences. For example, evidence comparing Arab refugee children and Roma migrant children shows that despite differences in learning attainment, school environments that support bilingualism are key to learning success and settling in educational settings.

10 Shoba Arun et al.

Well-being of children in migration processes of the global south

As migration is very much a global phenomenon, the recent trends indicate rising rates of human flows from the Global South, not only to the Global North but also within the Global South (as well as internal migration within the same nation state). The migration experiences from the Global South have been debated within transnationalism studies or within the migration-development nexus (Carranza, 2021). Thus, the focus on remittances and economic effect on family welfare does not look at the emotional implications for those left behind, particularly children (Castañeda and Buck, 2011; Vanore et al., 2015). Recently, evidence showed that the rising costs of such economic migration on child's well-being (Carranza, 2021).Two papers in this volume focus on this topic. Rajan and Kumar in Chapter 9, through a large-scale survey data, focus on the Kerala context of South India and show that education and health outcomes for children of migrant parents were certainly better than those of non-migrants, manifested in better anthropometric indicators, better access to healthcare facilities and overall better reporting of health issues. However, this does not automatically correlate the mental health of children in migrant households, with children feeling personal growth in the absence of their parents. However, these positive feelings were juxtaposed with negative feelings and anxieties, particularly with stress on many levels, which was exacerbated by the fact that they could not convey it effectively to their parents. They are also aware of the myriad pitfalls of migration.

In Chapter 10, Sankar (this volume) shows that in Uzbekistan, despite its systems of restricted movement within the country (*propiska* system), it has a large number of people (around 5 per cent) moving within the country (internal and in-migration) for economic opportunities as well as family reasons. Remittances contribute to improving food and housing among the receiving households and facilitating economic mobility to be among better welfare quintiles. Despite the benefits that remittances facilitate, studies show that children left behind by emigrating family members have socio-emotional challenges. A UNICEF (2020) study on Youth shows that young people perceive lack of work experience as one of the key factors impeding their employment after graduation. This shows huge disparities in young people (10–29 years) in digital skills across location, gender, and economic status of households. In addition, 'school-to-work' transition is challenging for most young people in Uzbekistan, resulting in a high rate of young people Not in Education, Employment, or Training (NEET).

While structural and material contexts in the Global South often lead to many forms of migration, racial and ethnic relations play an important role in the welfare of migrant children. Baak (2019) points out how visibly different minority group in a settler society such as Australia is shaped by a racialised history where for young former refugees, schools are a primary site in which they experience engagement with the wider society, but little attention has been given to students' experiences of exclusion, particularly through racism and othering. This leads to a breakdown in self-esteem from a distorted self-image, which is directly related to academic performance. Fuentes-Cabrera et al. (2019) posit that first-generation migrant children in general suffer higher abuse, bullying, and racial and ethnic harassment. Evidence from South Africa (Chapter 11 in this volume) shows that African migrant children in South African schools face considerable challenges resulting from pervasive xenophobic violence, hostile school experiences, and limited access to academic support services, thus negatively affecting assimilation and child development. Sustained post-apartheid segregation, palpable with xenophobic violence, bullying, and exclusion, perpetuates 'we -us' and 'them', impacting migrant children. First, it is noted that new arrivals, when negotiating their multicultural identity, try to avoid being positioned as victims, as vulnerable, or as exposed to cultural clashes and contradictions. Much like other migrants, the students can be seen to contest and renegotiate the ways they are categorised and labelled by the majority culture (Åhlund and Jonsson, 2016), and this may not always be positive.

Evidence from the EU context shows how migrant children adapt to the new situation, what psychological mechanism they are using or what kind of behaviour they perform, including violence in order to negotiate their statuses (Fangen and Lynnebakke, 2014; Åhlund and Jonsson, 2016; Priest et al., 2016). Most of the studies demonstrate that diversity education and real experience of engaging with and working with diverse individuals can allow children to become less prejudiced, more open to new ways of thinking and living and can also sensitise them to the value of difference while showing higher degrees of empathy (Priest et al., 2016; Panichella and Ambrosini, 2018). Similarly, the authors in Chapter 11 call for adopting the principles of *Ubuntu* to recognise the plight of migrants and to enhance migrant children's schooling experiences in South African schools.

Conclusion

Migration studies is indeed a burgeoning field in itself, but also within many disciplines as the very nature of human mobility is an inextricable part of broader processes of social change around us, constantly shaped by political, economic, and cultural forces. Often migration scholars have criticised the central importance given to categories created by the logic of the nation state premised on methodological nationalism. Others argue to 'de-migranticise' migration and integration research. As we see in this volume, migration studies within educational settings bring their own set of challenges both in terms of methods, ethics, and conceptualisations. Another challenge is living up to the focus on child-centred foci, which aim to provide a platform for a wider understanding of children's experiences. Children's voices provide key starting points for broader discussions between children and researchers, and as such it can be considered as an effective way to empower some children who are less eager to share their life experiences and make their 'voices' heard (Davis, 1998). The practice of reflexivity makes us be acutely aware of 'the need to reflect on the processes which produce children's voices in research, the power imbalances that shape them and the ideological contexts, which inform their production and reception, or in other words issues of representation' (Spyrou, 2011, p. 151). To illustrate diverse ways in which we represent 'children's voices' helps to move beyond positivist research culture while being aware of the analytical categories we impose on children's often complex and multi-layered stories, and incorporating decolonial scholarship from both the Global North and the Global South (Moosavi, 2020).

As we see in this collection, social research on migration involves many complexities, and methodological considerations. Different methods 'reflect and are imbued with, theoretical, epistemological, and ontological assumptions – including conceptions of subjects and subjectivities, and understandings of how knowledge is constructed and produced' (Mauthner and Doucet, 2003, p. 413). Research with young children in particular demands that we 'develop a much more critical appreciation of the power relations inherent within the research process' (Connolly, 2008, p. 123). This includes locating migration studies within the context of decolonisation of language, the mind and the heart (Phipps, 2019). As Åhlund and Jonsson (2016) point out the paradox of how newly arrived refugee and immigrant students are caught up in the institutional construction of an inclusive school that draws on a discourse of Otherness in which the student's voices are invited but seem to be ignored. This should invite us to rethink how migrant children are positioned in schools, by whom, and in relation to whom. These positionings need to be revisited in the light of recent calls for the decolonial paradigm, which challenge such colonial legacies of language, pedagogies, labelling, and categorisation, which among many things continue to support very rigid colonial and hierarchical structures that wound millions of individuals around the world. We invite our readers to join us in this quest to attend to children's words and worlds while being ready to listen differently and learn differently. The ultimate target is to unlearn the habits of marginalisation and exclusion that have continued to inform the language used to refer to migrants in general and migrant children in education in particular.

Note

1 The MICREATE is funded by the European Commission's Horizon 2020 under the grant agreement number 822664 and aims to stimulate inclusion of diverse groups of migrant children by adopting child-centered approach to migrant children integration on educational and policy level (see www.micreate.eu).

References

Åhlund, A., & Jonsson, R. (2016). Peruvian meatballs? *Nordic Journal of Migration Research*, *6*(3), 166–174.

Anastassiou, I. (2017). *Guidelines for Best Practice of Inclusion Based on Needs Analysis of Refugee Families*. Sofie, Sweden National Report. Accessed March 5, 2019. https://support-refugees.eu/media/io1-en-web.pdf

Andrew, A., Cattan, S., Costa-Dias, M., Farquharson, C., Kraftman, L., Krutikova, S., Phimister, A., & Sevilla, A. (2020). Learning during the lockdown: Real-time data on children's experiences during home learning. *Briefing Note*. Available from: https://www.ifs.org.uk/publications/14848

Ariès, P., & Baldick, R. (1962). *Centuries of Childhood* (p. 411). Harmondsworth: Penguin.

Arun, S., Bailey, G., & Szymczyk, A. (2021). Child migrants 'integrating': What do we know so far? In Sedmak, M. et al. (eds.) *Migrant Children's Integration and Education in Europe: Approaches*, Methodologies and Policies. Ediciones Octaedro SL, pp. 39–59. ISBN 9788418615375

Baak, M. (2019). Racism and othering for South Sudanese heritage students in Australian schools: Is inclusion possible? *International Journal of Inclusive Education*, *23*(2), 125–141.

Badwan, K., Popan, C., & Arun, S. (2021). Exploring schools as potential sites of foster-ship and empowerment for migrant children in the UK (Exploramos las escuelas como posibles centros de acogida y empoderamiento de los niños migrantes en el RU). *Culture and Education*, *33*(4), 702–728.

Benzeval, M., Bollinger, C. R., Burton, J., Crossley, T. F., & Lynn, P. (2020). The representativeness of understanding society. *Institute for Social and Economic Research*. Working Paper Series 2020–08.

Bourdieu, P. (1977). The economics of linguistic exchanges. *Social Science Information*, *16*(6), 645–668.

Budde, R., & Markowska-Manista, U. (Eds.). (2020). *Childhood and Children's Rights between Research and Activism: Honouring the Work of Manfred Liebel*. Wiesbaden: Springer Nature.

Carranza, M. (2021). The cost of "A Better Life": Children left behind—beyond ambiguous loss. *Journal of Family Issues*, *43*(12), 0192513X211044482.

Castañeda, E., & Buck, L. (2011). Remittances, transnational parenting, and the children left behind: Economic and psychological implications. *The Latin Americanist*, *55*(4), 85–110.

Christensen, P., & Prout, A. (2002). Working with ethical symmetry in social research with children. *Childhood*, *9*(4), 477–497.

Connolly, P. (2008). Race, gender and critical reflexivity in research with young children. In Christensen, P. & James, A. (eds.), *Research with Children*. London: Routledge, pp. 173–188.

Dahinden, J. (2016) A plea for the 'de-migranticization' of research on migration and integration. *Ethnic and Racial Studies*, *39*(13), 2207–2225, DOI: 10.1080/01419870.2015.1124129

Davis, J. M. (1998). Understanding the meanings of children: A reflexive process. *Children & Society*, *12*(5), 325–335.

Doná, G. (2006). Children as research advisors: Contributions to a 'methodology of participation'in researching children in difficult circumstances. *International Journal of Migration, Health and Social Care*, 2(2), 20–32.

Eisner, M., & Malti, T. (2012). The future of research on evidence-based developmental violence prevention in Europe–Introduction to the focus section. *International Journal of Conflict and Violence (IJCV)*, 6(2), 166–175.

Fangen, K., & Lynnebakke, B. (2014). Navigating ethnic stigmatisation in the educational setting: Coping stategies of young immigrants and descendants of immigrants in Norway. *Social Inclusion*, 2(1), 47–59.

Forbes, J., & Sime, D. (2016). Relations between child poverty and new migrant child status, academic attainment and social participation: Insights using social capital theory. *Education Sciences*, 6(3), 24.

Fox, R. (2013). Resisting participation: Critiquing participatory research methodologies with young people. *Journal of Youth Studies*, 16(8), 986–999.

Fuentes-Cabrera, A., Moreno Guerrero, A. J., Pozo Sánchez, J. S., & Rodríguez-García, A. M. (2019). Bullying among teens: Are ethnicity and race risk factors for victimization? A bibliometric research. *Education Sciences*, 9(3), 220.

Gaywood, D., Bertram, T., & Pascal, C. (2020). Involving refugee children in research: Emerging ethical and positioning issues. *European Early Childhood Education Research Journal*, 28(1), 149–162.

Grosfoguel, R., Oso, L., & Christou, A. (2015). 'Racism', intersectionality and migration studies: Framing some theoretical reflections. *Identities*, 22(6), 635–652.

Heleta, S. (2016). Decolonisation of higher education: Dismantling epistemic violence and eurocentrism in South Africa. *Transformation in Higher Education*, 1(1), a9.

Heller, M. (1995). Language choice, social institutions, and symbolic domination. *Language in Society*, 24(3), 373–405.

World Migration Report (2020). IOM UN Migration. Available from: https://publications.iom.int/system/files/pdf/wmr_2020.pdf

ISSOP Migration Working Group. (2018). Issop position statement on migrant child health. *Child: Care, Health and Development*, 44(1), 161–170.

Johnsen, A., Ortiz-Barreda, G., Rekkedal, G., & Iversen, A. C. (2017). Minority children and academic resilience in the Nordic welfare states. *International Journal of Migration, Health and Social Care*, 13(4), 374–390.

Jourdain, J., & Arnold, L. (2021) *Assessing the Socio-economic Impact of COVID-19 on Migrants and Displaced Populations in the Middle East and North Africa.*

Kennan, D., & Dolan, P. (2017). Justifying children and young people's involvement in social research: Assessing harm and benefit. *Irish Journal of Sociology*, 25(3), 297–314.

Kosnick, K. (2021). Decolonizing migration studies? Thinking about migration studies from the margins. *Zeitschrift für Migrationsforschung*, 1(2), 73–95.

Kudakwashe,P.V.,Hadj-Abdou,L.&Dempster,H.(2019). *From dehumanising to decolonising July 19th 2019.* Available from: https://blogs.lse.ac.uk/highereducation/2019/07/19/migration-studies-from-dehumanising-to-decolonising/

Latour, B. (2004). Why has critique run out of steam? From matters of fact to matters of concern. *Critical Inquiry*, 30(2), 225–248.

Manzoni, C., & Rolfe, H. (2019). How schools are integrating new migrant pupils and their families. *National institute of economic and social research*. London. https://www.niesr.ac.uk/sites/default/files/publications/MigrantChildrenIntegrationFinalReport.pdf

Introduction 15

Mauthner, N. S., & Doucet, A. (2003). Reflexive accounts and accounts of reflexivity in qualitative data analysis. *Sociology, 37*(3), 413–431.

Mayeza, E. (2017). 'Girls don't play soccer': Children policing gender on the playground in a township primary school in South Africa. *Gender and education, 29*(4), 476–494.

McCarry, M. (2012). Who benefits? A critical reflection of children and young people's participation in sensitive research. *International Journal of Social Research Methodology, 15*(1), 55–68.

Medarić, Z., Sedmak, M., Dežan, L., & Gornik, B. (2021). Integration of migrant children in Slovenian schools (La integración de los niños migrantes en las escuelas eslovenas). *Culture and Education, 33*(4), 758–785.

Medarić, Z., & Žakelj, T. (2014). Interethnic violence in schools: The case of slovenia. *Studia Migracyjne - Przegląd Polonijny, 40* (3(153)), 339–360.

Mooren, T., Bala, J., & Sleijpen, M. (2019). War, persecution, and dual transition: A developmental perspective of care for refugee adolescents in host countries. In Wenzel, T. & Droždek, B. (eds.) *An Uncertain Safety.* Cham: Springer.

Moosavi, L. (2020). The decolonial bandwagon and the dangers of intellectual decolonisation. *International Review of Sociology, 30*(2), 332–354.

Motha, S. (2016). The redundant refugee. *Law and Critique, 27*(1), 17–21.

Ozan, J., & Arun, S. (forthcoming). Child-centric approaches for migrant children: moving beyond consultation. In Gornik et al., (eds) *Handbook of Child Centred Approaches in Migration Studies.* Oxford: Oxford University Press.

Panichella, N., & Ambrosini, M. (2018). Between fears, contacts and family dynamics: The anti-immigrant attitudes in Italy. *Journal of International Migration and Integration, 19*(2), 391–411.

Phipps, A. (2019). *Decolonising Multilingualism: Struggles to Decreate.* Bristol: Multilingual Matters.

Phipps, A. (2020). Fostering integration: Making refuge real through the arts of justice and contemplative seeing. *A talk for the 4th Annual UNESCO Refugee Integration through Languages and the Arts.*

Pottie, K., Dahal, G., Georgiades, K., Premji, K., & Hassan, G. (2015). Do first generation immigrant adolescents face higher rates of bullying, violence and suicidal behaviours than do third generation and native born? *Journal of Immigrant and Minority Health, 17*(5), 1557–1566.

Priest, N., Walton, J., White, F., Kowal, E., Fox, B., & Paradies, Y. (2016). 'You are not born being racist, are you?' Discussing racism with primary aged-children. *Race Ethnicity and Education, 19*(4), 808–834.

Ryan, L., & Dahinden, J. (2021). Qualitative network analysis for migration studies: Beyond metaphors and epistemological pitfalls. *Global Networks, 21*(3), 459–469.

Sedmak, M. (2021). *Comparative report on qualitative research: Newly arrived migrant children: Migrant children and communities in a transforming Europe.* Available from: https://www.micreate.eu/wp-content/img/D5.2%20Comparative%20report%20on%20qualitative%20research%20NAM_webpage_final_feb.pdf

Sime, D., Fassetta, G., & McClung, M. (2018). 'It's good enough that our children are accepted': Roma mothers' views of children's education post migration. *British Journal of Sociology of Education, 39*(3), 316–332.

Soriano, E., & Cala, V. 2018. School and emotional well-being: A transcultural analysis on youth in southern Spain. *Health Education, 118*(2), 171–181.

Spyrou, S. (2011). The limits of children's voices: From authenticity to critical, reflexive representation. *Childhood, 18*(2), 151–165.

Tobin, J. (2020). Addressing the needs of children of immigrants and refugee families in contemporary ECEC settings: Findings and implications from the Children Crossing Borders study. *European Early Childhood Education Research Journal, 28*(1), 10–20.

Tonheim, M., Derluyn, I., Rosnes, V., Zito, D., Rota, M., & Steinnes, A. (2015). *Rehabilitation and social reintegration of asylum-seeking children affected by war and armed conflict.* SIK report 2015: 2, Misjonshøgskolens forlag.

UNICEF. (2019). *Building a Better Future: A Child-sensitive Social Protection System for Uzbekistan.* UNICEF Uzbekistan.

UNICEF. (2020). Youth of Uzbekistan: Aspirations, needs and risks report. UNICEF Uzbekistan. https://www.unicef.org/uzbekistan/media/3386/file/SitAn%20 -%20English%20-%20updated.pdf

Vanore, M., Mazzucato, V., & Siegel, M. (2015). 'Left behind' but not left alone: Parental migration & the psychosocial health of children in Moldova. *Social Science & Medicine, 132,* 252–260.

Vanyoro, K., (2019). *'Bringing Time' into Migration and Critical Border Studies: Theoretical and Methodological.* Migrating out of Poverty Research Programme Consortium. Available from: https://policycommons.net/artifacts/2178452/bringing-time-into-migration-and-critical-border-studies/2934430/ on 14 Aug 2022. CID: 20.500.12592/3nx4w7

Weil, P. (2002). Towards a coherent policy of co–development. *International Migration, 40*(3), 41–55.

Wolff, H. E. (2017). Language ideologies and the politics of language in post-colonial Africa. *Stellenbosch Papers in Linguistics Plus, 51*(1), 1–22.

Part I

Methodological, Conceptual, and Ethical Considerations in Child-Centred Migration Studies

Chapter 2

Research with Migrant Children from Countries of the Global South

From Ethical Challenges to the Decolonisation of Research in the Sensitive Contexts of Modernity

Urszula Markowska-Manista and Manfred Liebel

Introduction

Ethical standards are at least as important and necessary in research with migrant children as in any research on or with humans. And it is to be welcomed that interest in ethical aspects of research has increased in the last two decades and has even led to agreements that go beyond national borders and see themselves as a worldwide professional commitment (Liebel & Markowska-Manista, 2022). Articles 12 and 13 of the UN CRC clearly stress the right of all children to be informed, involved and consulted in decisions that affect their lives. The Charter on *Ethical Research with Children* (ERIC), which came about under the umbrella of UNICEF's Innocenti Research Centre[1] is an important document in this area. It underlines that:

- Children, their views and their cultures must be respected;
- All children must be treated equally and obstacles to their participation based on discrimination must be challenged;
- The benefits for individual child or children as a social group must be maximised;
- The results of the research must benefit children;
- Possible harm resulting from children's participation must be prevented;
- Children must agree to their participation, as must their guardians;
- The researchers must constantly reflect on the impact of their own assumptions, values, beliefs and practices on children (summarised from Graham et al., 2013).

But as meritorious and plausible as children's rights from CRC and these general principles may be, they are not beyond doubt, and cannot eliminate all the problems, ambivalences and contradictions that arise in research practice even with the best will of the researchers conducting research with migrant children. Their apparent plausibility may even contribute to concealing such problems and contradictions. This seems to be especially true

DOI: 10.4324/9781003343141-3

in the case of problems that arise from different life situations in different contexts, interests and unequal power positions of the persons (location of positionality) and institutions or other actors involved in such research. At this point another important factor needs to be added, namely the need for researchers to understand that due to the nature of their experiences, migrant children live between two worlds: their former life and their life here and now (Dwyer & Buckle, 2009). Understanding this duality and being aware of the multiplicity of difficulties they face (e.g. negotiating their position, social anchoring) is crucial for finding ethical solutions in designing research with migrant children.

In this Chapter, we would like to draw attention to the necessity of participation of crucial actors – migrant children, and to contribute to change, to expand academic, research-related and practical activities in which they can and will be able to participate. Thus, we will indicate selected problems that arise in research with diverse groups of migrant children from the Global South, insofar as it is conducted by adults in countries of the North, especially in the European Union. We identify some reasons for these problems and ask to what extent ethical principles can be of help in dealing with and overcoming these problems in such a way so as not to do harm and to do it well. We first ask about the possibilities of adopting ethical symmetry (Christensen & Prout, 2002) in childhood research. Then we discuss selected dilemmas arising from the epistemological environment of the researchers, question some of the attempts to give space and voice to migrant children from the Global South, and finally show why childhood studies especially as a part of migration studies need to free themselves from Eurocentric premises and decolonise themselves as well as in what way this can be achieved.

Migrant children from countries of the Global South

Migration is a very broad subject. We hear about migrants, we participate directly or indirectly in migration processes. There are people with migration experiences among our family members and neighbours. Perhaps we are contemporary migrants ourselves or actively participate in activities for people affected by migration, perhaps we research with children as migrants and their surroundings. Mass migration is currently also a subject of a heated political debate within the parliaments of particular EU countries and in the European media. It might seem that in the barrage of information incoming from the media, NGO reports and academic research, there are no new topics in this area that would not reproduce what has already been said, studied and published.

And yet we still have blank spots, crises and understatements. Children's migration as a process that marks the lives of both adults and children demands constant reflection and a new, reliable interpretation of the reality in which children as migrants and societies called hosts function. Migration, and especially refugeeism, is usually triggered by situations that are more difficult to face than those encountered by adults and children at the next stage of their journey – in refugee camps and refugee accommodation centres in their new countries of residence. Migration usually stigmatises and forces one into submission. It leaves its mark, especially on migrant children from the Global South. It should be stressed that social research has traditionally focused on the stranger, the other, 'the outsider', the disadvantaged and the marginalised. Unsurprisingly, migrant children are often at the centre of attention in research that examines different aspects of refugeeism, migration, or 'otherness' (Halilovich, 2013: 127).

The importance of child migration for the composition and self-understanding (collective identities) of national societies, for international relations and the world order as well as for the conceptualisation and understanding of childhoods has so far been underestimated. Child migration calls for a new 'geopolitical' approach that strives for the positive change potential of child migration as well as the protagonism of migrant children and the young and future generations influenced by migration.

Migrant children from the Global South in Europe are 'children on the move' in the double sense that they are in motion and cause movement. They are not only embedded in global dynamics but actively involved (Amadasi, 2019). Until now, migrant children have been seen primarily from the point of view of their particular vulnerability and the need for care. Help for migrant children remains important but must be provided in a non-paternalistic way, guaranteeing the children's rights and human dignity. According to Jacqueline Bhabha (2014: 7), 'lone' or 'independent' child migrants are not looking to be 'rescued' into state-run facilities, but require non-paternalistic support and advice. They need to be listened to, given a voice, which empowers them to articulate their concerns related to social and economic rights. It must be asked how the presence of migrant children and adolescents changes societies, their intergenerational relationships and the patterns and conceptions of childhoods. In this way, child migration and migrant children contribute to the decolonisation of childhoods on the local and global level.

The Charter on Ethical Research with Children calls for respect for children, their views and cultures, as well as the requirement to treat all children equally and to prevent discrimination. This is intended to counteract the power asymmetries that have developed over centuries in the relationship between adults and children and are associated with an undervaluation of children and their abilities. This is sometimes called adultism today and results in numerous discriminations (see Liebel, 2014), of which we as adults are rarely aware, even when we act as researchers; LeFrançois, 2018. In order to avoid age-specific discrimination, it is necessary not to degrade children to research objects but to respect them as subjects with their own rights and competencies (see e.g. Thomas & O'Kane, 1998). With the development of studies on children and childhoods that are oriented towards children's rights, subjectivity and agency, the conviction has grown that only research *with* children is suitable for understanding the situation of children (Budde & Markowska-Manista, 2020). It is also considered crucial for bringing children's diverse voices to the fore.

Participation in research is considered particularly important but is also particularly difficult to implement in the case of children (such as migrant children) who are very often socially disadvantaged and live in precarious circumstances. It is often limited to 'symbolic participation' such as observations, periodic consultations or fragmentary interviews. Even when this is intended to enable children to be heard and seen, it rarely considers what this means in relation to the contexts and circumstances in which the children live. In such studies, children may be audible or visible (for example, in photographs or videos), but they usually have no real influence on what happens to their voices and images (Markowska-Manista, 2020: 23). Under these conditions, research does not live up to the ethical claim of benefiting children.

This is especially true for research in which children's participation is limited to the role of informants or respondents, a common practice in survey research. In this case, the knowledge provided by the children is treated as a kind of raw material to be processed by adult experts as they see fit. Analogous to extractivist economies that ruthlessly exploit and destroy non-human nature, one could speak of an extractivist way of research here. This can only be countered if the children participate as co-researchers with their own rights and decision-making powers in all phases of the research process and can influence the research process right up to the use of the results (see e.g. Kirby, 1999; Clark, 2004; Alderson, 2008; Fiedler & Posch, 2009).

However, the inclusion of children as co-researchers has brought new ethical dilemmas and challenges in the case of migrant children who are usually perceived as socially disadvantaged and marginalised (Markowska-Manista, 2018: 53). This arises from the fact that adult researchers, especially if they are only 'visiting'[2], as it were, the children's permanent or temporary (migrants) places of residence during their fieldwork, disappear again after the completion of the surveys. They find themselves in a social situation that is completely different from that of the children (Lee-Treweek & Linkogle, 2000). Their perception of the world and the children's lives is shaped by their own experiences and preconceptions. This often means that only knowledge that is considered pleasant and valuable is taken up, while unpleasant knowledge is devalued as irrelevant and invalid and may even not be perceived at all. The knowledge that is unpleasant for the researchers is thus made invisible. We see an ethical challenge in this context in 'not only whose story it has the potential to tell, but also whose it will hide, why, for whom, and with what consequence' (Strega & Brown, 2015: 6; see also Rancew-Sikora & Cymbrowski, 2016: 14).

The Charter on Ethical Research with Children, referring to a guideline from the children's rights organisation *Save the Children* (2002), puts it this way: 'Harm can occur when children's voices are sought only when they match the interests of adult researchers but are overlooked when they do not' (Graham et al., 2013: 32). Or the danger is pointed out that 'researchers from predominantly individualistic cultures interpret research findings within collective cultural contexts in ways that are consistent with their own views, beliefs and experiences, but inappropriate to the context in which the research takes place' (op. cit.: 37; see also Abebe & Bessell, 2014: 130).

While the professional researchers find themselves in comfortable security, the children, even if they are included in the research process, remain subordinate and powerless; in the case of migrant children, their situation remains precarious (Markowska-Manista, 2017; Eckermann & Meier, 2019). The problem can arise that while the children's voices yield valuable insights for us researchers, they remain a trivial episode for the lives of the children themselves and may even have detrimental consequences. This also applies to the interpretation of the data obtained. It is often guided by beliefs or ideologies that we in academia consider normal, but which are not appropriate to the children's actions in their life contexts.

It is also very important to distinguish whether ethical principles are applied in legally regulated testing procedures ('procedural ethics') or whether they relate to practice in the research field and the use of research results ('practical ethics' of 'participatory ethics') (see Abebe & Bessell, 2014). In the first case, they contribute little or can even make it more difficult for ethical sensitivity to develop among researchers.

The importance of the social place and the epistemological environment

In the last two decades, interest in researching the lives and childhoods of migrant children from the Global South has grown at universities in the North. However, the problems posed by the epistemological environment of the researchers are rarely considered. Research relationships do not exist in a vacuum; they are always part of social relationships and embedded in specific cultural and political contexts. Especially in relation to migrant children from the Global South and their childhoods, imaginations, stereotypes and prejudices of researchers, which they themselves are not aware of, can come into play (see Groundwater-Smith, Dockett & Bottrell, 2015). Above all, the unequal power and socio-cultural distance between the researchers and the children must be considered.

Universities are privileged places because, despite the attempts to transform them neoliberally and turn them into production sites of 'human capital', research and reflection can still take place here largely independently. They still provide space for critical thinking, which should not be underestimated, especially in the education of students, if not only applicable but also reflective knowledge is to be acquired. But research conducted from universities also has a downside. Its actors are usually far removed from the reality of migrant children and exposed to the temptation to use their research for their own scientific reputation rather than in the interest of the children whose interests and rights are at stake. Mexican sociologist José Manuel Valenzuela Arce sees the danger of heteronomisation of the social sciences in the 'niches of comfort' from which academic researchers 'exercise their power of knowledge' and affirm the violence of the powerful in social life. This is done by imposing the researchers' rules, agendas and worldviews on the researched and treating them as 'subordinated participants' whose interests are not taken into account (Valenzuela & José, 2020: 14).

Research in the context of civil society organisations (NGOs) committed to children's rights in migration processes is often closer to migrant children, as it is fed by the needs of practice and is intended to contribute to improving this practice. Often, the childhood research conducted here emerges from practice and is in the hands of people who know and are familiar with the situation of migrant children from their daily experiences. But here too, research has a downside. It is rarely independent, happens from one day to the next and is beholden to the specific interests of the organisations on whose behalf and in whose name it is practised. It is also by no means guaranteed that the prior knowledge resulting from social and pedagogical practice, for example, corresponds to the views of the children and their sense of security in the study areas.

Research that wants to explore the lives of migrant children cannot be conducted from a bird's eye view. Its actors must create a safe communication space and participate in the lives of children and allow themselves to be touched by these lives. This is especially true for migrant children whose lives are very different and far removed from the life experiences of the researchers and whose languages of communication are usually foreign to researchers. Therefore, researchers cannot simply involve migrant children as informants or 'give them a voice'. Rather, they must share children's concerns and always contextualise their research as part of children's (possible) agency. In these circumstances, researchers become people who learn from children, and the knowledge they develop together with children can help to facilitate children's actions. In the optimal case, research can become an instrument through which social transformation is achieved while children generate knowledge that they can apply in practice, and so their agency and subjectivity are ensured (Nichel Valenzuela, 2018: 18).

The Charter on Ethical Research with Children postulates that research should not only harm children, but should also bring them the greatest possible benefit, i.e. that their situation should improve. The latter postulate basically requires researchers to take sides and characterises research that is to be understood as committed. The postulate is very important, but also particularly difficult to implement. If we consider not only the possible harm but also the benefit for the children, we must ask ourselves, for example, which children we are referring to the children involved in the research process or to all children for whom the knowledge produced in the research is of relevance. In any case, we follow an ethics that not only demands responsibility for others (such as the feminist-inspired care ethics; see, e.g., Held, 2006) but also respects them as social subjects with their own interests, rights and perspectives and has their emancipation or liberation in mind (but must not impose Eurocentric solutions).

Such an ethic is derived from the socially disadvantaged and politically oppressed people and population groups and their claim to human dignity. It can be found, for example, in the liberation philosophy of Enrique Dussel (1980), who had to flee to Mexico from the Argentinean military dictatorship, where he still lives today. Or it underlies the liberation pedagogy or *Educación Popular* associated with the name of the Brazilian educator Paulo Freire ([1968]2000), or the pedagogy of tenderness elaborated by the Peruvian educator Alejandro Cussiánovich (2007, 2022). Similar notions of ethics have also been present for at least three decades in the movements of indigenous peoples and the descendants of slaves abducted from Africa, who recall colonial genocide and revolt against their centuries of degradation and enslavement. They are expressed, for example, in a performative ethic of reciprocity focused on appreciative intercultural and intergenerational relationships (see Magnat, 2020; Romm, 2020). The performative ethic emphasises reciprocity and not extractivism or colonisation in research relations with children of migrant origins. Moreover, the inclusion of performative ethics provides an opportunity to disenchant what is hidden under the broad, descriptive and sometimes reductive category of "migrant children". Thus, it makes it possible to see the multiplicity of elements that make up the contexts of this category and the contexts of thinking with such categories taking into account the heterogenic ecology of human relations, nature and the spiritual world.

Such ethical concepts also suggest encouraging children to act as researchers themselves and accompanying them in solidarity taking into account the tangible and intangible aspects of the worlds of their daily lives. Research conducted in this participatory and supportive way can create the epistemological environment necessary to make children's *situated knowledge* and potential for action visible and usable for themselves. The concept of situated knowledge refers to the fact that no knowledge is detached from its context or from the subjectivity of the person who expresses it. The social position of the person is taken into account, since viewpoints are never neutral in ethical terms.[3] We will illustrate what situated knowledge means in the case of children with the question of speaking and silence, sometimes associated with double victimisation of a particular group of children (Markowska-Manista, 2019).

Is it ethical 'to give children a voice'?

In social science research on childhood, which has been developing since the 1980s, the question of children's voice and silence occupies a prominent place.

The main issue is how to pay more attention to children's 'voice' (Grover, 2004), but also what can be hidden behind children's silence. These questions are considered important because an essential task of childhood studies is seen in deconstructing the concept of childhood that dominates the modern Western world, which separates children from adults and places them at the bottom of the social power hierarchy. By making children's voices and views visible, possibly hidden behind silence, childhood studies hope to strengthen children's social status as a social group and contribute to their emancipation in relation to adults. This raises the fundamental ethical question of what it means for children to want to *give* them a voice.

For example, the Finnish childhood researcher Sirkka Komulainen (2007: 23) points out that the 'voice' of children is consistently perceived selectively by researching adults and made into an 'object' that 'can be possessed, recovered and verbalised'. Children's utterances are subjected to a cognitive interpretive scheme that not only ignores the social conditionality and ambiguity of communication between children and adults but also only 'hears' children's voices when they are put into words. Komulainen (op. cit.: 25) expresses her criticism in the play on words: 'More listening may not inevitably mean more hearing'. The British social work researcher Alison McLeod (2008: 21), referring to her own study, points out that adults and children often understand listening differently: While listening from the perspective of adults means that they pay attention to what children say, have an open attitude and respect their feelings, children expect listening to be followed by action.

Cypriot childhood researcher Spyros Spyrou (2011, 2018) also emphasises the need to reflect on the power imbalance and ideological contexts that influence children's voices in the research process. One answer to the question of how children's voices, in their complexity and ambiguity, can be brought to bear and understood might be for children to explore their reality themselves. Adults can certainly play a supportive role in this, but they must also reflect on their inevitable influence. This is usually missed in surveys conducted by children's rights organisations, which are well-intentioned to give children a voice. A recent example is a survey based on interviews and group discussions with more than 1,800 working children in 36 countries, mainly in the South (O'Kane, Barros & Meslaoui, 2018).

Without a doubt, it is necessary to pay more attention to the contexts and conditionality of the children's voices captured, especially in participatory research approaches. Although these research approaches are about overcoming the power imbalances between children and researching adults, this is not easily possible. Mary Kellett (2010, pp. 91–92), a protagonist of this approach, herself draws attention to the fact that children are not unaffected by power differences found among different groups of children (e.g. social background, gender, age, language skills, physical performance or popularity), which strongly influence the research encounter. Adults, moreover, can never become 'natives' in children's worlds, not only because of their unequal physical size but also because of the privileged status they always have, even as co-researchers. It is not enough to want to meet children 'at eye level', because this claim cannot override the continuing inequality of power and can easily degenerate into a euphemism.

The barriers to understanding the voices of migrant children from the Global South are rarely reflected in childhood research. Although the Western bourgeois understanding of childhood is no longer used unbroken as a yardstick for childhoods in such contexts, Eurocentric ways of thinking and forms of 'epistemic violence' (Spivak, 1988) influenced by them have not disappeared from childhood research or are rarely self-critically questioned (see Liebel & Budde, 2017). They can be seen, among other things, in the fact that little attention is paid to the forms of action and articulation of migrant children from the South that are not individually verbalised as real 'children's voices', or that they are hastily classified as not child-specific or externally controlled and thus made invisible. If it is even concluded from this that these children must first be given a voice or helped from outside to have more independence and participation, colonial patterns of relationships are reproduced – often unintentionally.

The social and discursive conditionality of children's voices is usually understood as a limitation or their authenticity is questioned. Very rarely is it asked to what extent the children's voices can also express interests that result from their situation in life, their social status or a particular situation. For example, children's voices may be guided and shaped by an interest in asserting themselves in a situation of unequal power – for instance, in relation to a teacher at school – and in tactically undermining or changing this relationship (Mandell, 1988; Atkinson, 2019). Such a voice can also express itself in deliberate silence or by going into exile, as it were, and only making itself known to other children. In such a situation, it can also become a problem of participatory research or research aimed at empowerment to encourage children to speak. Contrary to its own emancipatory intentions, it contributes in this way to depriving children of the secrets on which they, as subjects of power, are absolutely dependent. When voices are interpreted as expressions of interest, it is also important to consider, in addition to individual expressions, correspondences and discrepancies between them and to relate them to the social or generational situation of the speaking or silent children. Consistencies can be found, for example, in collective expressions and actions of children who come together in groups or social movements to influence their environment.

We see an ethical challenge of contemporary childhood research in recognising the preconditions and limits of one's own epistemologies and knowledge practices and in avoiding any kind of closure. The concepts we use in childhood studies – e.g. agency, voice or participation – also emerged in a specific historical and geopolitical context and are associated with meanings and

28 Urszula Markowska-Manista and Manfred Liebel

assumptions that cannot be transferred seamlessly to other contexts. They have to be questioned in the participatory process of research and re-conceptualised together with the children (sometimes also with their groups, communities) involved in the research. This will only ever be possible in approximate terms and requires, especially in the North-South context, that the researchers, who stand in a Western academic tradition, reflect on their entanglement in (post-) colonial patterns of relationships.

Why decolonisation of childhood studies matter?

The Charter on Ethical Research with Children calls for constant reflection on the impact of researchers' own assumptions, values, beliefs and practices on children. With regard to migrant children from the Global South, this means being aware of the fact that childhood sciences have colonial roots and have not completely freed themselves from this legacy until today. The Austrian educationalist Peter Gstettner had already pointed out 40 years ago that 'the scientific conquest of unknown territories precedes the conquest of the child's soul' (Gstettner, 1981: 15). He shows this in particular in the history of the emergence of developmental psychology but also in the conceptualisation of childhood (and adolescence) in the related sciences as a whole. US educationalists Gaile Cannella and Radhika Viruru (2004) have also shown that the dominant pattern of childhood in the West is the contemporaneous product of the same ideologies that served to justify colonial expansion and conquest. This is expressed in particular in the parallel application of the idea of development from lower to higher degrees of perfection. Childhood, like the non-European regions of the world and their inhabitants, is located at the lower end of the scale, which is also reflected in the fact that people subjected to colonisation are equated with children who have yet to develop (see in detail Liebel, 2020: 43–49).

We conclude that childhood studies must decolonise itself if it is to live up to its ethical maxims. By decolonisation, we mean that it counteracts the 'coloniality of power' (Quijano, 2008) in both its material and discursive manifestations. This includes recognising that there are no 'children (including migrant children) without childhood' in the world, but a great diversity of childhoods. By ignoring this diversity or making it invisible through Eurocentric bias, many 'children out of place' are created, with multiple discriminatory consequences (see Invernizzi et al., 2017). In this sense, it is not enough to simply name the cultural diversity or plurality of childhoods, but it is necessary to acknowledge and problematise that these childhoods are affected by postcolonial material and discursive inequality in different ways.

Although the childhoods of migrant children from the Global South are more often the focus of attention, they are still frequently studied and evaluated with theories and concepts that originated in and relate to Western bourgeois societies. It is true that in the meantime new concepts and research approaches have emerged in social science research on childhood that are more open to the experiences and perspectives of children and differ from traditions of liberal-paternalist thinking. But these concepts are still rarely used in a way that contribute to a better understanding of the lifeworlds of migrant children from the Global South and strengthen their social position.

A troubling legacy of colonisation is also the fact that research on children continues to be dominated by researchers in northern universities who absolutise the standards of academic excellence that apply here. These standards claim to be the only access to knowledge about reality and truth, and therefore exclude many other ways of thinking and knowing, especially those outside academia and in non-Western cultures. The dissemination of research results also depends heavily on publishers and journals based in the North. They are usually only noticed internationally if they are published in one of the former colonial languages, particularly in English.

The fact that interest in the lifeworld's and lifestyles of migrant children from the Global South has increased in recent years in childhood studies can contribute to their decolonisation. However, it is also necessary that it opens up to ways of thinking and knowing from non-Western cultures and cooperates with researchers who are rooted in these cultures and that these researchers are provided with scientific spaces in which their work and research methods are disseminated and taken seriously. This includes questioning the dominance and essentialisation of the research paradigms and methods we are accustomed to, as well as searching for new methodologies and knowledge that introduce balance between the Global North and Global South.

Compared to childhood studies, this process is already further advanced in feminist-oriented research (especially in Latin America and Africa), for example through the critical examination of the colonial implications of the category of the powerful and empowering (white and male) subject and by taking up so-called indigenous or horizontal epistemologies and research methodologies. They are based on the idea that the separation between researcher and researched is abolished and new knowledge is produced jointly (see, e.g., Rivera Cusicanqui, 1987, 2010; Ball, 2005; Kovach, 2010; Corona & Kaltmeier, 2012; Tuhiwai Smith, 2012; Segato, 2013; Santos, 2016; Rodríguez & da Costa, 2019; Cornejo & Rufer, 2020; Kleibl et al., 2020). This idea, which corresponds to the principle of ethical symmetry, is still largely uncharted territory in childhood studies. In order to decolonise knowledge and ways of knowing, the relations between knowledge and power must also be envisaged as the colonial structure frames these relations producing as a result knowledge and research that is neither 'neutral' nor 'pure'. The solution is to integrate political, economic and social aspects at all stages of research (Kaltmeier, 2012: 44).

Such critical self-reflections are also immensely important for childhood studies, as they can play an important role in the recognition of non-Western childhoods and the self-empowerment of migrant children from the Global

South. This is important not least because children experience violence, humiliation and discrimination in their various and interrelated forms first-hand.

Conclusion

The article is an attempt at decolonising migration childhood studies via paradigm change, focusing in research on child perspective, participation and protection of migrant children's rights.

We wish to sensitise researchers to the asymmetries of methodological approaches, the failure to incorporate the specifics of migrant children's living environments, different, non-western methodologies and migrant children's rights. We draw attention to the failure to take responsibility for conducting this type of research and its consequences for migrant children and their communities. Moreover, we advocate the need to adopt a non-Euro-centric approach, indicating that this research rarely incorporated the non-western epistemologies, decolonial approaches and migrant children's participation in childhood studies (which has to be also understood from below). Further, we should consider the possibility of applying ethical symmetry in research with and about migrant children, searching for the topography of ethics that would be proper in this type of research.

The ethical dilemmas of participatory research with migrant children from the Global South cannot be overcome by establishing ethical principles alone. They demand from researchers critical self-reflection on the persisting inequality of power in the globalised postcolonial world and between adults and children. This requires that childhood studies not only expand knowledge about children but also contribute to policy interventions that lead to greater equality and social justice. We see a fundamental condition for this in strengthening the social position of children and giving more attention and support to the ways of thinking, seeing and acting of migrant children from the Global South (in a changing environment of global migration processes).

The decolonisation of thinking about children and their childhoods in the situation of migration as well as the implementation of participatory approaches towards research and practices with children from their perspective, and with their perspective on migration taken into consideration, is of great importance to all of us. Using a great variety of methodologies, approaches and resources- children and communities oriented, we can gain a deeper understanding of the diversity of migrant childhoods and children's situations in the local context. These are crucial dimensions for participatory policies that consider children's perspectives, and so their experiences, views, priorities and expectations and their roles as active agents in their own migration in the new places and spaces of functioning during migration. The incorporation of participation of migrant children in research and practices that concern them on the local level will allow us (as J. Bhabha indicated in 2019) to acknowledge their human rights.

Notes

1 Childhood researchers from different parts of the world were involved in drafting the Charter. It is continuously discussed on a separate website (https://childethics.com/).
2 Visiting refers to research sites/places of temporary residence of migrant children which are by definition culturally/economically different from researchers' living environments.
3 The concept was first formulated by Simone de Beauvoir ([1949]1997) in relation to women's knowledge and related to the knowledge of all subaltern groups by Donna Haraway (1988).

References

Abebe, T & Bessell, S (2014). 'Advancing ethical research with children: Critical reflections on ethical guidelines.' *Children Geographies*, 12(1): 126–133.

Alderson, P (2008). 'Children as researchers: The effects of participation rights on research methodology.' In P Christensen & A James (Eds.). *Research with Children: Perspectives and Practices*. London: Routledge, pp. 241–257.

Amadasi, S (2019). 'Transnational mobility and education continuity in Italian compulsory schools teachers' narratives on children's transnational experiences.' In *Die Vielfalt der Kindheit (en) und die Rechte der Kinder in der Gegenwart*. Wiesbaden: Springer VS, pp. 65–78.

Atkinson, C (2019). 'Ethical complexities in participatory childhood research: Rethinking the "least adult role".' *Childhood*, 26(2): 186–201.

Ball, J (2005). 'Restorative research partnerships in Indigenous communities.' In A Farrell (Ed.). *Ethical Research with Children*. Maidenhead: Open University Press, pp. 81–96.

Bhabha, J (2014). Child migration and human rights in a global age. *Child migration and human rights in a global age*. Princeton: Princeton University Press.

Bhabha, J (2019). 'Governing adolescent mobility: The elusive role of children's rights principles in contemporary migration practice.' *Childhood*, 26(3): 369–385.

Budde, R & Markowska-Manista, U (Eds.). (2020). *Childhood and Children's Rights between Research and Activism: Honouring the Work of Manfred Liebel*. Wiesbaden: Springer Nature.

Cannella, GS & Viruru, R (2004). *Childhood and Postcolonization: Power Education, and Contemporary Practice*. New York & London: Routledge-Falmer.

Christensen, P & Prout, A (2002). 'Working with ethical symmetry in social research with children.' *Childhood*, 9(4): 477–497.

Clark, J (2004). 'Participatory research with children and young people: Philosophy, possibilities and perils.' *Action Research Expeditions*, 4(11): 1–18.

Cornejo, I & Rufer, M (Eds.) (2020). *Horizontalidad. Hacia una crítica de la metodología*. Buenos Aires: CLACSO & Guadalajara, Mexiko: CALAS.

Corona, S & Kaltmeier, O (Eds.) (2012). *Methoden dekolonialisieren. Eine Werkzeugkiste zur Demokratisierung der Sozial- und Kulturwissenschaften*. Münster: Westfälisches Dampfboot.

Cussiánovich, A (2007). *Aprender la condición humana. Ensayo sobre Pedagogía de la ternura*. Lima: Ifejant.

32 Urszula Markowska-Manista and Manfred Liebel

Cussiánovich, A (2022). *Pedagogía de la Ternura – componente del Paradigma del Protagonismo*. Lima: Ifejant.

De Beauvoir, S ([1949]1997) *The Second Sex*. London: Vintage.

Dussel, E (1980). *Philosophy of Liberation*. London: Wipf & Stock Publishers.

Dwyer, SC & Buckle JL (2009). 'The space between: On being an insider-outsider in qualitative research.' *International Journal of Qualitative Methods*, 8(1): 54–63.

Eckermann, T & Meier, M (2019). 'Grenzen der Grenzüberschreitung. Zur Lebenswelt von Kindern und Jugendlichen – oder dem Anspruch ethnographischer Forschung, diese zu erfassen.' In F Hartnack (Ed.). *Qualitative Forschung mit Kindern. Herausforderungen, Methoden und Konzepte*. Wiesbaden: Springer VS, pp. 108–137.

Fiedler, J & Posch, C (2009). *Yes, they Can! Children Researching their Lives*. Baltmannsweiler: Schneider Verlag Hohengehren.

Freire, P ([1968]2000). *Pedagogy of the Oppressed*, New York: The Continuum International Publishing Group.

Graham, A, Powell, M, Taylor, N, Anderson, D & Fitzgerald, R (2013). *Ethical Research Involving Children*. Florence: UNICEF Innocenti Office of Research.

Groundwater-Smith, S, Dockett, S & Bottrell, D (2015). 'Ethical questions in relation to participatory research with children and young people. In S Groundwater, S Dockett & D Bottrell (Eds.). *Participatory Research with Children and Young People*. Los Angeles, CA: SAGE, pp. 37–54.

Grover, S (2004). Why won't they listen to us? On giving power and voice to children participating in social research. *Childhood*, 11(1): 81–93.

Gstettner, P (1981). *Die Eroberung des Kindes durch die Wissenschaft. Aus der Geschichte der Disziplinierung*. Reinbek b. Hamburg: Rowohlt.

Halilovich, H (2013). 'Ethical approaches in research with refugees and asylum seekers using participatory action research.' In K Block, E Riggs, N Haslam (Eds.). *Values and Vulnerabilities. The Ethics of Research with Refugees and Asylum Seekers* Australia: Australian Academic Press, pp. 127–150.

Haraway, DJ (1988). 'Situated knowledges: The science question in feminism and the privilege of partial perspective.' *Feminist Studies*, 14(3): 575–599.

Held, V (2006). *The Ethics of Care: Personal, Political, and Global*. Oxford: Oxford University Press.

Invernizzi, A, Liebel, M, Milne, B & Budde, R (Eds.) (2017). 'Children out of place' and human rights. In *Memory of Judith Ennew*. Cham: Springer International Switzerland, pp. 233–254.

Kaltmeier, O (2012). 'Methoden dekolonialisieren: Reziprozität und Dialog in der herrschenden Geopolitik des Wissens.' In S Corona & O Kaltmeier (Eds.). *Methoden dekolonialisieren. Eine Werkzeugkiste zur Demokratisierung der Sozial- und Kulturwissenschaften*. Münster: Westfälisches Dampfboot, pp. 18–44.

Kellett, M (2010). *Rethinking Children and Research: Attitudes in Contemporary Society*. London: Continuum.

Kirby, P (1999). *Involving Young Researchers*. York: York Publishing Services.

Kleibl, T, Lutz, R, Noyoo, N, Bunk, B, Dittmann, A & Seepamore, B (Eds.) (2020). *The Routledge Handbook of Postcolonial Social Work*. London/New York: Routledge.

Komulainen, S (2007). 'The ambiguity of the child's "voice" in social research.' *Childhood*, 14(1): 11-28.

Kovach, M (2010). *Indigenous Methodologies: Characteristics, Conversations and Contexts.* Toronto: Toronto University Press.

Lee-Treweek, G & Linkogle, S (Eds.) (2000) *Danger in the Field. Risk and Ethics in Social Research.* London & New York: Routledge.

LeFrançois, BA (2018). 'Adultism'. In T Teo (Ed.). Encyclopedia of Critical Psychology. New York: Springer, pp. 47–49.

Liebel, M (2014). 'Adultism and age-based discrimination against children.' In D Kutsar and H Warming (Eds.). *Children and Non-Discrimination. Interdisciplinary Textbook,* Tartu: University Press of Estonia, pp. 119–143.

Liebel, M (2020). *Decolonizing Childhoods: From Exclusion to Dignity.* Bristol & Chicago: Policy Press.

Liebel, M & Budde, R (2017). 'Other children, other youth: Against eurocentrism in childhood and youth research.' In A Invernizzi, M Liebel, B Milne & R Budde (Eds.). *'Children Out of Place' and Human Rights. In Memory of Judith Ennew.* Cham: Springer International Switzerland, pp. 119–136.

Liebel, M & Markowska-Manista, U (2022). 'Ethische Dilemmata partizipativer Forschung mit Kindern des Globalen Südens. Ein Plädoyer für die Dekolonisierung der Kindheitsforschung.' In M Joos & L Alberth (Eds.). *Forschungsethik in der Kindheitsforschung.* Weinheim/Basel: Beltz Juventa, pp. 120–137.

Magnat, V (2020). 'Towards a performative ethics of reciprocity.' In NK Denzin & MD Giardina (Eds.). *Qualitative Inquiry and the Politics of Resistance.* New York & London: Routledge, pp. 115–129.

Mandell, N (1988). 'The least-adult role in studying children.' *Journal of Contemporary Ethnography,* 16(4): 433–468.

Markowska-Manista, U (2017). 'The dilemmas and passions in intercultural field research – a female pedagogue's ethnographic notes.' In U Markowska-Manista & J Pilarska (Eds.). *An Introspective Approach to Women's Intercultural Fieldwork.* Warschau: Wyd. Akademii Pedagogiki Specjalnej, pp. 126–147.

Markowska-Manista, U (2018). 'The ethical dilemmas of research with children from the countries of the Global South. Whose participation?' *Polish Journal of Educational Studies,* 71(1): 51–65.

Markowska-Manista, U (2019). 'Bad Children' – International stigmatisation of children trained to kill during war and armed conflict. In N von Benzon & C Wilkinson (Eds.). *Intersectionality and Difference in Childhood and Youth. Global Perspectives,* 1st ed. London & New York: Routledge the Taylor & Francis Group, pp. 61–75. DOI: 10.4324/9780429466588.

Markowska-Manista, U (2020). 'Clarity about the purpose of research.' In P Alderson & V Morrow (Eds.). *The Ethics of Research with Children and Young People.* Los Angeles: SAGE, pp. 22–23.

McLeod, A (2008). *Listening to Children: A Practitioner's Guide.* London & Philadelphia: Jessica Kingsley.

Nichel Valenzuela, F (2018). 'Experiencia de investigación militante como herramienta de transformación social con niños y niñas organizados de la comuna de Recoleta.' *Trenza. Revista de Educación Popular, Pedagogía Crítica e Investigación Militante,* 1(2): 18–33.

O'Kane, C, Barros, O & Meslaoui, N (2018). *It's Time to Talk! Children's Views on Children's Work.* Duisburg: Kindernothilfe & Osnabrück: terre des

34 Urszula Markowska-Manista and Manfred Liebel

hommes Deutschland. Access: https://www.time-to-talk.info/wp-content/uploads/2018/05/T2T_Report_EN.pdf

Quijano, A (2008). 'Coloniality of power, eurocentrism, and social classification.' In M Moraña, E Dussel & C Jáuregui (Eds.). *Coloniality at Large. Latin America and the Postcolonial Debate.* Durham & London: Duke University Press, pp. 181–224.

Rancew-Sikora, D & Cymbrowski, B (2016). 'Dylematy etyczne i ryzyko w badaniach terenowych.' *Przegląd Socjologii Jakościowej*, 12(3): 6–21.

Rivera Cusicanqui, S (1987). 'El potencial epistemológico y teórico de la historia oral: de la lógica instrumental a la descolonozación de la historia.' *Revista Temas Sociales* (UMSA, La Paz), 11:49–64.

Rivera Cusicanqui, S (2010). *Ch'ixinakax utxiwa. Una reflexión sobre prácticas y discursos descolonizadores.* Buenos Aires: Tinta Limón.

Rodríguez, RP & da Costa, S (2019). 'Descolonizar las Herramientas Metodológicas. Una Experiencia de Investigación Feminista.' *MILLCAYAC - Revista Digital de Ciencias Sociales*, 6(11): 13–30.

Romm, N (2020). 'Reflections on a post-qualitative inquiry with children/young people: Exploring and furthering a performative research ethics'. *Forum Qualitative Sozialforschung/Forum Qualitative Social Research*, 21(1), Art. 6, http://dx.doi.org/10.17169/fqs-21.1.3360

Santos, BS (2016). *Epistemologies of the South: Justice against Epistemicide.* New York & London: Routledge.

Save the Children (2002). *Children and Participation: Research, Monitoring and Evaluation with Children and Young People.* London: Save the Children Alliance.

Segato, RL (2013). *La crítica de la colonialidad en ocho ensayos: Y una antropología por demanda.* Buenos Aires: Prometeo Libros.

Spivak, GS (1988) 'Can the subaltern speak?' In C Nelson & L Grossberg (Eds.). *Marxism and the Interpretation of Culture*, Urbana: University of Illinois Press, pp. 66–111.

Spyrou, S (2011). 'The limits of children's voices: From authenticity to critical reflexive representation.' *Childhood*, 18(2): 151-165.

Spyrou, S (2018). *Disclosing Childhoods: Research and Knowledge Production for a Critical Childhood Studies.* Basingstoke: Palgrave Macmillan.

Strega, S & Brown, L (Eds.) (2015). *Research as Resistance. Revisiting Critical, Indigenous, and Anti-Oppressive Approaches.* 2nd ed. Toronto: Canadian Scholars' Press & Women's Press.

Thomas, N & O'Kane, C (1998). 'The ethics of participatory research with children.' *Children & Society*, 12(5): 336–348.

Tuhiwai Smith, L (2012). *Decolonizing Methodologies: Research and Indigenous Peoples.* 2nd ed. London & New York: Zed Books.

Valenzuela, A & José, M (2020). *Heteronomías en las Ciencias Sociales. Procesos investigativos y violencia simbólica.* Buenos Aires: CLACSO.

Chapter 3

Reflexive Narrative on Identity and Exclusion of the Zimbabwean Child in the Diaspora

'The Odd-Looking Fellow'

Shepherd Mutsvara

Introduction and background

Since early 2000, ever since the radical land reform programme, Zimbabweans have continued to emigrate to neighbouring African countries and international destinations. This has arguably brought dire economic woes and flagrant human rights abuses from early 2000 (Bourne, 2011; Thomas, 2003). The interconnectedness of the political and economic crises made life unbearable resulting in mass exodus to South Africa and international destinations for what De Villiers and Weda aptly call "a transient greener pasture" (de Villiers & Weda, 2017).

For those who arrived in South Africa, many applied for asylum in terms of Section 22 of the Refugees Act No. 30 of 1998. Many of these applications were rejected as manifestly unfounded on the grounds that there was no war in Zimbabwe and the fear of persecution was not supported by objective facts present in the country of origin. This led to many Zimbabweans staying "illegally" in the Republic of South Africa despite facing deportation threats. Arguably, this was premised on the well-founded fear of returning to a country whose government had attracted punitive economic sanctions thus threatening livelihoods and the fundamental rights to life, liberty, and dignity.

The South African government then promulgated Regulation 7 in terms of Act No. 13 of 2002 as a way to "regularize Zimbabweans residing [illegally] in South Africa" and "reduce pressure on the asylum seeker and refugee regime" (Intergate Immigration, 2014). The issuance of the Zimbabwean Special Dispensation Permit (DZP), later to be known as the Zimbabwean Exemption Permit (ZEP), regularized the stay of many Zimbabweans under the following conditions: (1) ZEP permit entitles the holder to conduct work/employment, (2) ZEP permit does not entitle the holder the right to apply for permanent residence irrespective of the period of stay in the Republic of South Africa, (3) ZEP permit will not be renewable/extendable, and (4) ZEP permit holders cannot change conditions of his/her permit in South Africa.

DOI: 10.4324/9781003343141-4

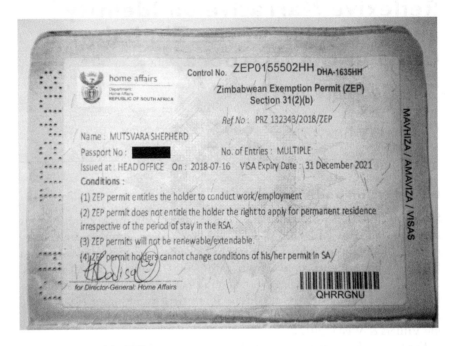

Figure 3.1 Writer's ZEP permit

Writer's ZEP permit

These conditions, as shown in Figure 3.1 above, were welcomed differently by Zimbabweans, non-governmental organizations, humanitarians, lawyers, politicians, and academicians as a compromise in dealing with contemporary forms of persecution and displacement (Moyo, 2018; Thebe, 2017). As shall be discussed in the next sections, the ZEP permit has been slatted as an overt act of exclusion "couched in the language of humanitarianism and African and global solidarity", for it has placed Zimbabweans in a state of liminality (Moyo, 2018). The permits, despite offering a slight ease to the South African Home Affairs Department, carried the stamp of exclusion and constantly reminded Zimbabwean parents and their children of how they have overstayed in South Africa (Matsinhe, 2011).

According to the 2017 Inter-Censal Demographic Survey (ICDS), 19 percent of the enumerated 13,572,560 households had "at least one emigrant", with 87 percent residing in South Africa, while the rest were dotted around other African states and overseas countries (ZimStats, 2017). Media reports further suggest that most Zimbabweans in South Africa and countries like the United Kingdom, New Zealand, Canada, Australia, and the United States of

America are undocumented or have overstayed visas (Newsday, 2020; The Mail & Guardian, 2013).

Caught up in this migration flow is a conservative figure of 132,184 children who were aged between 0 and 19 at the time of departure presumably in the company of their parents or guardians to the new country (ZimStats, 2017, p. 58). Notwithstanding the immigration status of their parents or guardians, these Zimbabwean children have faced a myriad of social and legal challenges in the host countries. While most research has focussed on the "influx of Zimbabweans" in South Africa (Alfaro-Velcamp & Shaw, 2016; Crush et al., 2015; de Jager & Musuva, 2015; Kabonga, 2020; Kufakurinani et al., 2014; Mabera, 2017; Solomon & Haigh, 2009), little attention has been given to the socio-legal impact on children of Zimbabwean descent in the diaspora.

Therefore, the key question for determination in this chapter is whether host countries are providing an inclusive socio-legal policy framework to accommodate the Zimbabwean child in the diaspora. To answer this question, the chapter employs a case study analysis of South Africa and Poland by evaluating the information gathered through an online survey and interviews.

Socio-legal exclusion/inclusion discourse

Socio-legal exclusion/inclusion (SLEI) is a concept mired in blurred lines of demarcation (Cotterrell, 2017; Fitzpatrick, 1995; Schiff, 1976). It raises questions as to whether the exclusion/inclusion of social groups in a community is premised on the law or the dynamics of social integration (Davies, 2005). For what may be defined as unjust or unfair may be seen and defended as a semblance of equity in other social and legal circles. This then creates a continuum of exclusion/inclusion in which social cohesion or lack of it is primarily based on the concepts of belonging, participation, inclusion, recognition, and legitimacy (Jenson, 1998, p. 5).

In the field of migration studies, this gives rise to a binary categorization of migrants as either desirable or undesirable (Jaskulowski & Pawlak, 2020). Using Diego Armus' (2019) differentiation of desired and undesired migrants, the former are perceived to come from economically stable countries and do not intend to permanently stay in the new country, while the latter are viewed as pestilence and an economic burden to the receiving state. Such a categorization fails to keep up with what Davies (2005) calls "theoretical innovation and insistent discourses of human rights and social justice".

To understand this dichotomy, a working definition of SLEI can thus be gleaned from the scholarship on social exclusion and inclusion (Klasen, 2001; Levitas et al., 2007; Popay, 2010). SLEI can be viewed as a multi-dimensional concept in which the law is used to create asymmetrical power dimensions within a society on the basis of one's economic, political, social, and cultural participation (Cotterrell, 2017; Levitas et al., 2007; Schiff, 1976). This leads to unequal access to socio-economic goods and violates rights thereby entrenching inequalities (Curry-Stevens et al., 2011; de La Rosa, 2017; Sullivan & Picarsic, 2012; Vic, 1996).

Borrowing from Duffy's (1995) definition of social exclusion, it can further be added that SLEI is concerned about the ability to effectively participate in mainstream society due to legal impediments attached to one's social hierarchy in a given community. In that regard, the law inadvertently addresses the people through the process of exclusion and inclusion (Davies, 2005; Lægaard, 2010). If we are to discern John Austin's boundaries of *what law is from what it ought to be* (Stumpf, 1960), we are inclined to accept that the socio-legal approach in the field of social justice is:

> ... directly linked to the analysis of the social situation to which the law applies and should be put into the perspective of that situation by seeing the part the law plays in the creation, maintenance and/or change of the situation.
>
> Schiff (1976, p. 287)

Therefore, the law defines social spaces by forming one's identity while at the same time undermining someone's sense of belonging and identity (Davies, 2005). These spaces and boundaries result in systemic communal and institutional violence towards certain social groups within a society leading to "new forms of conflict and prejudice" (Harris, 2003). In the ultimate end, SLEI results in excluding certain groups within the society from enjoying the following:

> A livelihood; secure, permanent employment; earnings; property, credit, or land; housing; minimal or prevailing consumption levels; education, skills, and cultural capital; the welfare state; citizenship and legal equality; democratic participation; public goods; the nation or the dominant race; family and sociability; humane treatment, respect, personal fulfilment and understanding.
>
> Silver (1994, p. 541)

In Durkheim's lexical terms, failure by man to enjoy the above rights and public goods suggests a mismatch between the social structure and the law arising from the constituted legal structures and institutions (Hunt, 1978). The life of a person is carved out from the society they live in. If the society is inclusive, there is a positive move towards social justice, equality, and collectivism as opposed to "differential access to social and economic well-being" (Allman, 2013, p. 2).

Embedded in the SLEI concept, and for the purpose of this chapter, is the exclusion or inclusion of migrant children from participating in the four spaces of interaction within the community. These four spaces (social, political, cultural, and economic) should also be open to children. Studies on child development show that children are socialized to learn about their culture and how the society defines their expected behaviour (Fanti, 2011; Sameroff, 2009). It is also alluded that their exclusion or inclusion from the aforementioned list by Silver (1994, p. 541) may also be hinged on the social hierarchy of human superiority or inferiority.

According to Grosfoguel (2016, p. 10), social exclusion/inclusion is marked by one's colour, ethnicity, language, culture, or religion. These Grosfoguelian markers of exclusion heighten the tension between the excluded and the included social groups and create a social chasm that cuts across class, gender, identity, and sense of belonging (Grosfoguel, 2011, 2016). In a nutshell, the SLEI concept, in the field of migration, has the same connotations of racialization between the desired and the undesirable migrants. In that fold, it is likely that the socio-legal exclusion of such migrants may also be accentuated by the markers of exclusion. In correlation to the theory of racialization, Grosfoguel (2016), as inspired by Fanon (1967) stated that:

[The desired migrants are recognised] ...*socially in their humanity as human beings and, thus, enjoy access to rights (human rights, civil rights, women rights and/or labor rights), material resources, and social recognition to their subjectivities, identities, epistemologies and spiritualities.* [While the undesirable migrants are considered] ...*subhuman or non-human; that is, their humanity is questioned and, as such, negated*

Grosfoguel (2016, p. 10)

In countries like South Africa, the "enemy image of foreigners" is also a source of socio-legal exclusion (Solomon & Kosaka, 2016). The divisive apartheid policy left a legacy of hatred and failure to accept differences. Harris (2002) argues that such socio-legal exclusion can be explained in the form of the following: scapegoating, isolation, and bio-cultural hypotheses.

The scapegoating hypothesis explains the "hostility towards foreigners in relation to limited resources such as employment, housing, healthcare and services coupled with high expectations for social change during a transition" (Harris, 2002, p. 170). In this regard, *undesirable migrants* fleeing economic destitution from their countries are seen as pestilence who have overstayed their welcome in the new country. If the locals face any form of deprivation, they will blame it on the foreigners and thus deepening the social exclusion due to their constrained legal status as undocumented or with limited legal benefits attached to their immigration status.

On the other hand, the isolation hypothesis (Harris, 2002) can be understood in terms of the legacy of the apartheid laws. The theory connects the xenophobic tendencies to be a by-product of South Africa's *exclusion* from the international arena due to apartheid laws. As a result, thereof, "South Africans are unable to tolerate and accommodate difference" (Harris, 2002, p. 172). The structuring of the country into tribal trust lands during apartheid meant that the locals would "alert" the authorities in the event of a "stranger" settling amongst them. In that regard, the law was used as a weapon of social exclusion/inclusion into the society. To that end, the psyche built by such structural exclusion has resulted in isolating African immigrants as *makwerek-were* (loosely translated as lice) (Matsinhe, 2011).

The bio-cultural theorem explains the exclusion of certain social groups on the grounds of "physical biological factors and cultural differences" (Harris, 2002, p. 173). Social groups with an immigrant background are excluded from the society on the account of their accent, manner of walking or talking, physical structure, and colour of skin (Balogun, 2020). These physical markers, just as the Grosfoguelian markers of exclusion, are used at both the communal and institutional levels to exclude or include certain groups from the social benefits, rights, and public goods.

Therefore, the application of the SLEI framework to children requires an understanding of (1) their status as minors and (2) children as "adults". Article 2 of the universally ratified Convention on the Rights of the Child further exhorts all States Parties to respect and ensure that:

> ...each child within their jurisdiction [enjoys the rights set in the treaty] without discrimination of any kind, irrespective of the child's of his or her parent's or legal guardian's race, colour, sex, language, religion, political or other opinion, national, ethnic or social origin, birth, property, disability, or other status.

This acknowledges the fact that children can also make their own decisions and choices. If the spaces and boundaries for economic, educational, and psychological development are constricted for them, this then "crucially affect their positions as adults" in their future life (Klasen, 2001, p. 418). For example, if children of immigrants are excluded socially or legally in a new country, this will compromise their access to resources that are critical for their attainment of socio-economic rights as adults (Raabe, 2019). Furthermore, when child development is examined from an African cultural lens, there is a need to magnify an understanding of the socio-cultural context from which the child comes (Mucherah & Mbogori, 2019). The scholars argue that subtle forms of exclusion begin to manifest themselves if there is no motivation to answer the following questions: How do African children define themselves? And what forms of exclusion can lead to their self-understanding? (Mucherah & Mbogori, 2019).

Cavicchiolo et al. (2020) posit that the starting point towards an inclusive framework for children with an immigrant background should be phased in three phases. First, there is a need for peer acceptance as this helps in building a strong sense of esteem. Second, the community and the institutions should embrace the family and individual characteristics of the children. Understanding the socio-cultural background of the child will be a step towards inclusivity as it widens the meaningful participation of the

Identity and Exclusion of the Zimbabwean Child   41

child in the new society. Third is the gradual adoption of the host language. Proficiency in a national language will move the scales of exclusion towards inclusivity as the children will be able to express themselves, and this initiates the process of peer acceptance and a better understanding of the *odd-looking* fellow.

Methods

The chapter analyses data gathered through an anonymous online survey (n=77) and interviews. The web-based survey ran from 22 May to 15 July 2020. Informed consent was sought from parents or guardians of Zimbabwean descent or citizenship living with their children in the diaspora. The first three days were left open to pre-test the online survey so as evaluate the validity of the questionnaire and fill in the gaps in the tool (Gupta, 2017; Harlow, 2010). During this time the researcher established contact for separate semi-structured interviews with 10 respondents purposively chosen from the following countries: South Africa, Ghana, Poland, the United Kingdom, the United States of America, and Austria. Initially, two respondents in South Africa were known by the researcher, and then, a snowballing method was adopted to reach out to Zimbabweans in other countries. In migration studies, the snowballing technique is helpful in such situations when reaching out to respondents from a specific origin (Beauchemin & González-Ferrer, 2011, p. 105). These respondents were asked five predetermined open-ended questions from the Google form and notes were taken. South Africa and Poland were chosen as case studies as the researcher has lived in South Africa from 2007 to 2019 on several ZEP temporary resident permits, and holds a Polish temporary residence card (*Karta Pobytu).*

Limitations

The online survey was piloted at the height of the severe acute respiratory syndrome coronavirus 2 (SARS-CoV-2) pandemic, herein referred to as COVID-19. During this time, there was a heightened global fear of the pandemic, and people were more focussed on health concerns and general safety (Clay, 2020; Lobe et al., 2020). The COVID-19 challenge was augmented by undertaking telephone/online semi-structured interviews with purposively selected participants in South Africa and Poland. The interviews were recorded, and notes were taken where consent to record was not given. The second limitation is with regard to the definition of the term "child". The research was specifically targeting children aged between 0 and 18 years old. This standard definition was not well received by some potential respondents during the pre-test period. One of the potential respondents said:

> I just felt, you know, the questions were very limited in terms of exploring people's experiences. Because, you know, people are different. So,

mine came here [United Kingdom] as a baby, so I had another one here. So, the experience is different compared to people who came in with their children who were 10 or 15. Those are completely different experiences. So maybe we need to share this with people who've got children who are now probably in their late 20s or 30s.

– Anonymous Respondent

To avoid ambiguity, the survey was not amended during the pre-test period to include the views of "children beyond the age of 18" as this would scatter the focus of the study. It is herein acknowledged that the concerns raised by the respondent are valid and give rise to an opportunity to explore the gap in the literature on the socio-legal exclusion of the Zimbabwean child.

Findings and discussion

The prime case studies for the chapter are South Africa and Poland. The "other" countries were included in the study to measure the level of dispersion of Zimbabweans in the diaspora. These other countries include Botswana, Ghana, Germany, the United Kingdom, Australia, and the United States of America. The study reveals that Zimbabwean children who migrate with their parents or guardians within Africa face a myriad of social and legal challenges in the new country. The migration status of their parents or guardians significantly determines their economic, social, and cultural rights. On the other hand, as Zimbabweans migrate out of Africa, the challenge faced by accompanying children is more social than legal as it is steeped towards social and cultural issues that heavily impact their self-esteem and identity.

The exodus of Zimbabweans within the African continent and abroad aligns with the demographic features of the study. As shown in Table 3.1 below, nearly 60 percent of the respondents live in South Africa, and a combined 87 percent of the sample population in all settings are in their prime age of between 18 and 45 years old. The age profile of the Zimbabweans in the diaspora is significant. This is the age when most young adults begin to establish careers and start a family hence their mobility to countries with a better economy. From the demographic Table 3.1 below, it can be assumed that migrating out of Africa is arguably difficult due to restrictive visa regulations for Europe and other developed countries. The fact that less than 10 percent of the respondents are in Poland further confirms the Haas paradox that migration is selective as people move further out of their country (Haas, 2019). The sample population in Poland is all aged between 18 and 45 years old. For the purpose of this study, they are living with their children in a new cultural environment that requires adaptation to the culture, language, and lifestyle.

Studies on migration trends in Zimbabwe show that the interconnectedness of the push and pull factors led to the massive exodus out of the southern African country (Moyo, 2018; Thebe, 2017). This displacement has led to an

Table 3.1 Demographic features of the survey (n=77)

	Age				Country		
	18–25	30–45	45–60	60+	South Africa	Poland	Other
n	77	6	61	10	0	45	6	26
%	100	7.8	79.2	13	0	58.4	7.8	33.8

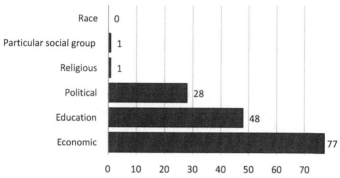

Figure 3.2 Reasons for migration (n=77)

"archetypal form of 'mixed migration' in which refugees and migrants are indistinguishable from one another". (Crush et al., 2015, p. 363).

Reasons for migration (n=77)

It is thus clear from Figure 3.2 above that Zimbabweans continue to emigrate for economic reasons. An unstable economic environment hampers the self-actualization of a young generation hoping to build a career and a family (Juselius & Takáts, 2018). The urge to escape the economic malaise and move to affluent countries is also attached to the level of education. In most cases, those who have left the country for educational purposes have then established new careers and families in the hosting country and have had to deal with raising their children in a new environment.

The study, as indicated in Figure 3.3 below, shows that over 60 percent of the children were born in the new country. This affirms the fact that most young parents would want to raise a family in a stable economic environment so that their children have a better future. Respondents in Poland pointed out that their children have legal resident permits. However, these children face social exclusion on the grounds of their race, colour, and social standing. The literature on children of African descent in Poland further shows that the everyday Polish parlance excludes the African child from being actively engaged in the four spaces of social cohesion. Phrases like *Sto lat za murzynami* (100 years behind the blacks) and *Drzwi się zamyka, to nie Afryka* (Close the door, it is not Africa) are steeped in stereotypes that typify black Africans as a different race (Ohia, 2016; Ohia-Nowak, 2020). This perpetuates "rejection, dislike, curiosity, sympathy or even primitive egocentrism towards blackness" (Balogun, 2020).

As for those children in South Africa, they have faced both legal and social exclusion based on their parents' immigration status. The following respondents alluded to the dynamic nature of this challenge:

> It is difficult for our children to be enrolled or get admissions in South Africa Public schools.
>
> RP74

> [The immigration status of parents] affects the child lot mostly because as parents not having decent jobs, working on contracts, always moving between jobs, cities, towns or province make it difficult to keep on adapting to different environment
>
> RP74

> The fact that [my son's] study permit would have to be processed in Zimbabwe. It's such an inconvenience to go back home to do this.
>
> RP62

> I cannot enrol [my children] in the best schools and [my immigration status] has restricted movement to home country in the waiting period of visas.
>
> RP02

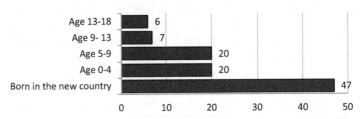

Figure 3.3 The age of the accompanying child in the country of arrival (n=100)

This has affected the assimilation process of their children in the new environment as the requirement for study permits is strenuous and exclusionary. Legal uncertainty in this regard thus creates opportunities for social exclusion as public institutions will be requiring "legal status" before they afford the child fundamental rights like education and health. Such a situation is frustrating for parents as they live in a continuum of exclusion/inclusion and would arguably settle for less to protect themselves.

The age of the accompanying child in the country of arrival (n=100)

As shown in Figure 3.3 above, 42 percent accompanied their parents to the new country while aged between 0 and 9. At this age, children need an environment that can nurture their social and emotional competencies (Mucherah & Mbogori, 2019). While those between 9 and the borderline age of 18 constitute about 17 percent, the study reveals that these children had difficulties in adjusting to the new environment. Some parents have noted, with concern, the psychological change in their children's behaviour upon moving to a new country. Between the ages of 5 and 13, most children would have attained unique personality traits that define them. Settling in a new environment may therefore be disruptive and this is tied to the influence of new peers, lifestyle, language, and the new culture. In Poland, respondents alluded to the fact that learning Polish is demanding and is made more difficult by a diminished circle of peers. One parent poignantly noted the challenges faced in Poland:

> Not having friends because of language and also racism some don't want to touch hands with the black child.
>
> RP38

This is not a conducive environment for children with an immigrant background and African descent as it affects their self-esteem. This increases the chances of institutional exclusion as children might find it difficult to attend school due to anxieties around their level of proficiency of the Polish language or even out of deep-seated fear of humiliation. This is inimical to child development as it curtails meaningful participation in the core activities that bind the society (economic, social, political, and cultural).

Children by nature learn by imitation and assimilation (Yenika-Agbaw, 2009). The results of the study allude to the fact that culture and peer interaction in the new hosting country plays a major role in the social inclusion or exclusion of the child. To that end, they may entirely adopt a new culture at the exclusion of their own in order to fit in and be accepted by peers resulting in conflict with parents when they are at home. These dynamic variables are also illustrated in Figure 3.4 below and are important in understanding how

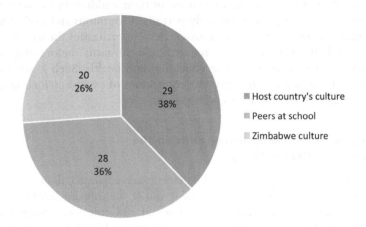

Figure 3.4 The effect of culture and peer interaction on social inclusion

Zimbabwean children in the diaspora may be embraced on both social and legal bases.

One of the cogs towards social inclusion and adaptation is the mastery of the host's language. Children naturally adopt new language skills faster, and this is enhanced by their daily interaction with peers at school and other informal settings. The respondents in South Africa noted that while adopting a new culture has been a challenge, they realized that a large number of Zimbabweans in the country have meant that they maintain much of their Zimbabwean culture. This is so because most Zimbabweans in South Africa tend to live in the same suburbs, and their children attend the same schools. As such, the interaction is not diluted by "other" cultures as children learn both the Zimbabwean culture and language when at home and school.

However, there is an overwhelming concurrence in all settings that the host culture and peer interaction is consequential in understanding social and legal exclusion of the Zimbabwean child in the diaspora. The intersection of these two variables and the challenges that arise thereabout is expressed in the following statements from the respondents:

> They managed to learn the new language quicker. They are becoming more fluent in English and local language, and accustomed to Polish way of living.
>
> RP65

> [My children] are trying to be South African and not proud to be Zimbabwean. 1 had to make them understand be proud Zimbabweans.
>
> RP15

I realized she became very timid, and her self-esteem was lowered. She became confused, not knowing who she really was. She had to be African at home and try to be American in order to fit in.

RP73

Adapting to a new lifestyle [was a challenge]. In Zimbabwe we had house help which we could not afford here, so kids had to learn to cook and doing other house chores at a young age. Finding new friends and adapting to a whole new environment was a challenge.

RP49

It can thus be deduced that those children who adapted quicker to the new environment were influenced by peer interactions and the need to be accepted. This can be achieved if the environment is conducive to such interaction. In the case where children had confusion over their cultural affiliation, it would be a question of them being lost as to their identity in the new environment (Kufakurinani et al., 2014). It is thus concluded: culture and peer interaction in the new society has consequential effects on children. There is a need for the parents and the local public institutions to support children in a manner that is beneficial to their self-development.

At the core of the socio-legal exclusion of Zimbabwean children is the immigration status of their parents. As mentioned earlier, most Zimbabwean parents in the diaspora have limited immigration status. This then extends to their children. And in the process, families are caught up in a continuum of exclusion/inclusion.

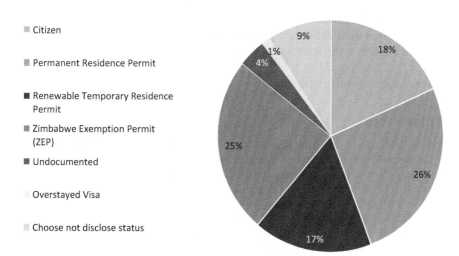

Figure 3.5 Migration status in the country of arrival [South Africa]

As illustrated in Figure 3.5 above, Zimbabweans in South Africa who participated in the study have various immigration statuses. Only 26 percent have permanent residency status. Apart from the 18 percent with citizenship status, it is worth noting that a combined 55 percent of Zimbabweans have a temporary immigration status which invariably puts their lives in abeyance. This immigration status has however been detrimental to the socio-legal inclusion of children who accompanied their parents or were born to Zimbabwean parents, especially in South Africa. Children have had school disruptions and are constantly reminded that their parents have overstayed their welcome and by analogy them too (Ribstein, 2015). The immigration status of the parents is thus reflected on them and allows state institutions to enforce subtle exclusion and discrimination which is inimical to the best interests of the child.

Conclusion

Socio-legal exclusion/inclusion (SLEI) affects social cohesion, assimilation, and a sense of belonging. To children, this may have a negative influence as to how they will grow and perceive society in general. This is because in trying to achieve inclusivity, the community and the institutions may exclude certain groups in society on the basis of their legal status (legitimacy) and level of assimilation (belonging). This then borders on racialisation and may question the "morality" of laws legitimately constituted but bordering on exclusion. In the field of migration, this creates a binary categorization that pits desirable migrants against undesirable migrants. Children are then caught up in this socio-legal chasm, and their development is strictly curtailed, thus affecting realistic chances for them to attain full self-actualization. While States have a sovereign right to choose who should come and reside in their territories, there is a need for a deliberate push towards amenable laws and policies that do not castigate a certain social group as undesirable and odd. This leads to stereotypes and prejudice which is inimical to child development and can lead to family disintegration.

References

Alfaro-Velcamp, T., & Shaw, M. (2016). 'Please GO HOME and BUILD Africa': Criminalising Immigrants in South Africa. *Journal of Southern African Studies*, *42*(5), 983–998. https://doi.org/10.1080/03057070.2016.1211805

Allman, D. (2013). The Sociology of Social Inclusion. *SAGE Open*, *3*(1), 2158244012471957. https://doi.org/10.1177/2158244012471957

Armus, D. (2019). Desirable and Undesirable Migrants. Disease, Eugenics, and Discourses in Modern Buenos Aires. *Journal of Iberian and Latin American Studies*, *25*(1), 57–79. https://doi.org/10.1080/14701847.2019.1579492

Balogun, B. (2020). Race and Racism in Poland: Theorising and contextualising 'Polish-Centrism'. *The Sociological Review*, *68*(6), 1196–1211. https://doi.org/10.1177/0038026120928883

Identity and Exclusion of the Zimbabwean Child   49

Beauchemin, C., & González-Ferrer, A. (2011). Sampling International Migrants with Origin-based Snowballing Method: New Evidence on Biases and Limitations. *Demographic Research, 25*(3), 103–134. https://doi.org/10.4054/DemRes.2011.25.3

Bourne, R. (2011). *Catastrophe: What Went Wrong in Zimbabwe?* (1st ed.). London: Zed Books. http://gen.lib.rus.ec/book/index.php?md5=b516e5d90aaf185742e6ffbe16cbc15e

Cavicchiolo, E., Manganelli, S., Bianchi, D., Biasi, V., Lucidi, F., Girelli, L., Cozzolino, M., & Alivernini, F. (2020). Social Inclusion of Immigrant Children at School: The Impact of Group, Family and Individual Characteristics, and the Role of Proficiency in the National Language. *International Journal of Inclusive Education, 0*(0), 1–21. https://doi.org/10.1080/13603116.2020.1831628

Clay, R. A. (2020, March 19). *Conducting Research during the COVID-19 Pandemic.* https://Www.Apa.Org. https://www.apa.org/news/apa/2020/03/conducting-research-covid-19

Cotterrell, R. (2017). Theory and Values in Socio-legal Studies. *Journal of Law and Society, 44*(S1), S19–S36. https://doi.org/10.1111/jols.12047

Crush, J., Chikanda, A., & Tawodzera, G. (2015). The Third Wave: Mixed Migration from Zimbabwe to South Africa. *Canadian Journal of African Studies/ Revue Canadienne Des Études Africaines, 49*(2), 363–382. https://doi.org/10.1080/0 0083968.2015.1057856

Curry-Stevens, A., Cross-Hemmer, A., Maher, N., & Meier, J. (2011). The Politics of Data: Uncovering Whiteness in Conventional Social Policy and Social Work Research. *Sociology Mind, 01*(04), 183–191. https://doi.org/10.4236/sm.2011.14024

Davies, M. (2005). Exclusion and the Identity of Law. *Macquarie Law Journal.* http://classic.austlii.edu.au/au/journals/MqLawJl/2005/2.html

de La Rosa, G. V. (2017). Inclusion-Exclusion Policy Latin American Democracies and Distributive Policies. *Open Journal of Political Science, 07*(01), 40–54. https://doi.org/10.4236/ojps.2017.71004

de Villiers, R., & Weda, Z. (2017). Zimbabwean Teachers in South Africa: A Transient Greener Pasture. *South African Journal of Education, 37*(3), 1–9. https://doi.org/10.15700/saje.v37n3a1410

Duffy, K. (1995). *Social Exclusion and Human Dignity in Europe: Background Report for the Proposed Initiative by the Council of Europe.* Strasbourg: Council of Europe. https://www.worldcat.org/title/social-exclusion-and-human-dignity-in-europe-background-report-for-the-proposed-inititati

Fanon, F. (1967). *Black Skin, White Masks* (M. Markmann, Trans.; New ed 2008). Pluto-Press. London: Paladin.http://abahlali.org/files/__Black_Skin__White_Masks__Pluto_Classics_.pdf

Fanti, K. A. (2011). Transactional Models. In R. J. R. Levesque (Ed.), *Encyclopedia of Adolescence* (pp. 3003–3013). New York: Springer. https://doi.org/10.1007/978-1-4419-1695-2_7

Fitzpatrick, P. (1995). Being Social in Socio-Legal Studies. *Journal of Law and Society, 22*(1), 105–112. https://doi.org/10.2307/1410707

Grosfoguel, R. (2011). Decolonizing Post-Colonial Studies and Paradigms of Political-Economy: Transmodernity, Decolonial Thinking, and Global Coloniality. *Journal Issue: TRANSMODERNITY: Journal of Peripheral Cultural Production of the Luso-Hispanic World, 1*(1), 38.

Grosfoguel, R. (2016). What is Racism? *Journal of World-Systems Research, 22*(1), 9–15. https://doi.org/10.5195/jwsr.2016.609

Gupta, S. (2017). Ethical Issues in Designing Internet-Based Research: Recommendations for Good Practice. *Journal of Research Practice, 13*(2, Article D1), 1–14.

Haas, H. de. (2019). Paradoxes of Migration and Development. *IMI Working Paper Series, 157*, 1–22.

Harlow, A. (2010). Online Surveys—Possibilities, Pitfalls and Practicalities: The Experience of the TELA Evaluation. *Waikato Journal of Education, 15*(2), 95–107. https://doi.org/10.15663/wje.v15i2.116

Harris, B. (2002). Xenophobia: A New Pathology for a New South Africa? In D. Hook & G. Eagle (Eds.), *Psychopathology and Social Prejudice* (pp. 169–184). Cape Town: University of Cape Town Press.

Harris, B. (2003). Spaces of Violence, Places of Fear. *Conflicts and Urban Violence Panel, Foro Social Mundial Tematico, Cartagena, Colombia*, 15. https://citeseerx.ist. psu.edu/viewdoc/download?doi=10.1.1.523.2544&rep=rep1&type=pdf

Hunt, A. (1978). Emile Durkheim-Towards A Sociology of Law. In A. Hunt (Ed.), *The Sociological Movement in Law* (pp. 60–92). London: Palgrave Macmillan UK. https://doi.org/10.1007/978-1-349-15918-5_4

Intergate Immigration. (2014, August 12). New Zimbabwean Special Dispensation Permit announced. *Immigration South Africa Blog.* https://www.intergate-immigration. com/blog/new-zimbabwean-special-dispensation-permit-announced/

de Jager, N., & Musuva, C. (2015). The Influx of Zimbabweans into South Africa: A Crisis of Governance that Spills Over. *Africa Review.* https://www.tandfonline. com/doi/abs/10.1080/09744053.2015.1089013

Jaskulowski, K., & Pawlak, M. (2020). Middling Migrants, Neoliberalism and Racism. *Journal of Ethnic and Migration Studies, 0*(0), 1–17. https://doi.org/10.1080/ 1369183X.2020.1806046

Jenson, J. (1998). *Mapping Social Cohesion: The State of Canadian Research.* Ottawa: Canadian Policy Research Networks.

Juselius, M., & Takáts, E. (2018). *The Enduring Link between Demography and Inflation* (BIS Working Papers No 722; p. 34). Bank for International Settlements. https:// www.bis.org/publ/work722.pdf

Kabonga, I. (2020). Reflections on the 'Zimbabwean Crisis 2000–2008' and the Survival Strategies: The Sustainable Livelihoods Framework (SLF) Analysis. *Africa Review, 12*(2), 192–212. https://doi.org/10.1080/09744053.2020.1755093

Klasen, S. (2001). Social Exclusion, Children and Education. Implications of a Rights-based Approach. *European Societies, 3*(4), 413–445. https://doi. org/10.1080/14616690120112208

Kufakurinani, U., Pasura, D., & McGregor, J. (2014). Transnational Parenting and the Emergence of 'Diaspora Orphans' in Zimbabwe. *African Diaspora, 7*(1), 114–138. https://doi.org/10.1163/18725465-00701006

Lægaard, S. (2010). What is the Right to Exclude Immigrants? *Res Publica, 16*, 245–262. https://doi.org/10.1007/s11158-010-9122-2

Levitas, R., Pantazis, C., Fahmy, E., Gordon, D., Lloyd-Reichling, E., & Patsios, D. (2007). *The Multi-dimensional Analysis of Social Exclusion.* Project Report. Bristol: University of Bristol Available at: https://repository.uel.ac.uk/download/469129f-180d3060ed6707d32474ae3d29ac0b9635ca19758f989a09936a3a319/1819926/ multidimensional.pdf

Lobe, B., Morgan, D., & Hoffman, K. A. (2020). Qualitative Data Collection in an Era of Social Distancing. *International Journal of Qualitative Methods, 19*, 1609406920937875. https://doi.org/10.1177/1609406920937875

Mabera, F. (2017). The Impact of Xenophobia and Xenophobic Violence on South Africa's Developmental Partnership Agenda. *Africa Review, 9*(1), 28–42. https://doi.org/10.1080/09744053.2016.1239711

Matsinhe, D. M. (2011). Africa's Fear of Itself: The ideology of Makwerekwere in South Africa. *Third World Quarterly, 32*(2), 295–313. https://doi.org/10.1080/014 36597.2011.560470

Moyo, I. (2018). Zimbabwean Dispensation, Special and Exemption Permits in South Africa: On Humanitarian Logic, Depoliticisation and Invisibilisation of Migrants. *Journal of Asian and African Studies, 53*(8), 1141–1157. https://doi.org/10.1177/0021909618776413

Mucherah, W., & Mbogori, T. (2019). Examining Child Development from an African Cultural Context. *Global Journal of Transformative Education, 1*(1), 11–17. https://doi.org/10.14434/gjte.v1i1.26140

Newsday. (2020, July 12). Old and Homeless Abroad. *NewsDay Zimbabwe.* https://www.newsday.co.zw/2020/07/old-and-homeless-abroad/

Ohia, M. A. (2016). Racism in Public Discourse in Poland. A Preliminary Analysis. *Edutainment, 1*, 147–161. https://doi.org/: 10.15503/edut.2016.1.147.161

Ohia-Nowak, M. (2020). Słowo "Murzyn" jako perlokucyjny akt mowy. *Przegląd Kulturoznawczy, 2020*(Numer 3 (45)), 195–212. https://doi.org/10.4467/2084386 0PK.20.023.12583

Popay, J. (2010). Understanding and Tackling Social Exclusion. *Journal of Research in Nursing, 15*(4), 295–297. https://doi.org/10.1177/1744987110370529

Raabe, I. J. (2019). Social Exclusion and School Achievement: Children of Immigrants and Children of Natives in Three European Countries. *Child Indicators Research, 12*(3), 1003–1022. https://doi.org/10.1007/s12187-018-9565-0

Ribstein, S. (2015, April 23). Children's Views on Xenophobia in Africa. *BBC News.* https://www.bbc.com/news/av/world-africa-32432157

Sameroff, A. (2009). The Transactional Model. In *The Transactional Model of Development: How Children and Contexts Shape Each Other* (pp. 3–21). Washington: American Psychological Association. https://doi.org/10.1037/11877-001

Schiff, D. N. (1976). Socio-Legal Theory: Social Structure and Law. *The Modern Law Review, 39*(3), 287–310. https://doi.org/10.1111/j.1468-2230.1976.tb01458.x

Silver, H. (1994). Social Exclusion and Social Solidarity: Three Paradigms. *International Labour Review, 133*(5–6), 531–578.

Solomon, H., & Haigh, L. (2009). Xenophobia in South Africa: Origins, Trajectory and Recommendations. *Africa Review, 1*(2), 111–131. https://doi.org/10.1080/097 44053.2009.10597284

Solomon, H., & Kosaka, H. (2016). Xenophobia in South Africa: Reflections, Narratives and Recommendations. *Southern African Peace and Security Studies, 2*(2), 1–30.

Stumpf, S. E. (1960). Austin's Theory of the Separation of Law and Morals. *Vanderbilt Law Review, 14*(1, Article 6), 117–149.

Sullivan, D. M., & Picarsic, J. (2012). The Subtleties of Social Exclusion: Race, Social Class, and the Exclusion of Blacks in a Racially Mixed Neighborhood. *Sociology Mind, 02*(02), 153–157. https://doi.org/10.4236/sm.2012.22020

The Mail & Guardian. (2013, April 19). Rough Estimates: Millions of Zimbabweans Abroad. *The Mail & Guardian.* https://mg.co.za/article/2013-04-19-millions-of-zimbabweans-abroad/

Thebe, V. (2017). "Two Steps Forward, One Step Back": Zimbabwean Migration and South Africa's Regularising Programme (the ZDP). *Journal of International Migration and Integration, 18*(2), 613–622. https://doi.org/10.1007/s12134-016-0495-8

Thomas, N. H. (2003). Land Reform in Zimbabwe. *Third World Quarterly, 24*(4), 691–712. https://doi.org/10.1080/0143659032000105821

Vic, G. (1996). Graham Room (ed.). Beyond the Threshold: The Measurement and Analysis of Social Exclusion. *Journal of Social Policy, 25*(3), 429–430. https://doi.org/10.1017/S0047279400023710

Yenika-Agbaw, V. (2009). *African Child Rearing in the Diaspora: A Mother's Perspective.* 14.

ZimStats. (2017). *Inter-Censal Demographic Survey 2017.* http://www.zimstat.co.zw/population-census-vital

Chapter 4

Critical Decolonial Interculturality as a Tool to Analyse Best Practices of Inclusion Centred on Migrant Children in a Multi-ethnic Territory of São Paulo City during the COVID-19 Pandemic

Lucas Rech da Silva

Introduction

Unlike Europe or the United States of America, studies in the intersection of the fields of education and migratory studies have been built in Brazil mainly in the last decade (Silva, 2018). This has happened especially after 2010, a period in which the country became a destination for different migratory flows, as it was experiencing a period of political and economic stability. The studies have used different theoretical and methodological perspectives and opened countless possibilities for unfolding the theme (Silva, 2018). The ethnography presented here is based on a critical and decolonial perspective of interculturality (Candau, 2008; Walsh, Oliveira and Candau, 2018), looking at interculturality as a seed and a tool for social transformation in territories historically marked by cultural diversity, structural inequalities and socioeconomic vulnerability.

São Paulo, the largest metropolis in the territory of Abya Yala,[1] has more than 11 million people (Brasil, 2015). The city was built by consecutive colonizing movements and migratory flows. This urban conglomerate built from the destruction of the Atlantic Forest[2] and marked by the enslavement of African and native peoples is characterized today by extreme social inequalities. In the context of the COVID-19 pandemic, inequalities increased and spread together with the virus, thus affecting the work of schools and the education of children. In this sense, this work focuses on the problematization of the possibilities of action, reception, inclusion and resistance of a *sui generis* school community, the Municipal Elementary School (EMEF) "Espaço de Bitita".

Bitita is the childhood nickname of Brazilian writer Carolina Maria de Jesus, who had her diaries edited and published in the 1960s in the book *Quarto de Despejo*, then translated into 14 languages. Bitita, a black woman, granddaughter of enslaved humans, and migrant from the interior of the State of Minas Gerais to São Paulo, had only literacy as a school experience. In her book, she recounts the daily life of her struggles as a paper collector in the city; thus, she supported her three children in the territory of the shantytown,

DOI: 10.4324/9781003343141-5

54 Lucas Rech da Silva

Canindé. It is in this territory described by Carolina as the city's dump that *Espaço de Bitita*[3] is located. The school has 750 students and offers elementary education, in the morning shift for the final years (6th to 9th grade), in the afternoon for the early years (1st to 5th grade) and at night education for youth and adults (EJA). Since 2014, the school has received several municipal and national awards for its work focused on the inclusion of migrant children living in the territory. After receiving the "Educador Grade 10"[4] award for a project that sought to raise awareness among migrant children about the work analogous to slavery that afflicts the Bolivian community, the school was invited by the UNESCO to join its network of Associated Schools.

Due to the school's popularity, it was chosen to carry out this ethnography there—to know what aspects enabled the Espaço de Bitita to be recognized as an example of good practices from a child-centred perspective. The intention is to understand, using the assumptions of critical decolonial interculturality (ICD), how immigrant-inclusive practices were put into action in the midst of the pandemic and what were the main challenges. Therefore, the objective of this essay is to analyse the challenges of a public elementary education that has interculturality as a paradigm. It is important to note that any question asked about the education of migrant children is not only about migrant children, but about how the country and community that receive migrants deal with its social hierarchies and dynamics.

Theoretical dialogues

Ethnography was chosen, above all, because of the complex multiple possibilities it offers. Here, ethnography is not taken only as a method, but as a theoretical and empirical perspective that is articulated with various research techniques (Rockwell and Ezpeleta, 1989, p. 32). Ethnographic work is construction, understanding and interpretation, which are possible through an intersubjective process between the agents involved in the research: researcher and researched subjects (Dauster, 2011; Oliveira, 2013; Tosta, 2014).

Also, this ethnography follows the decolonial perspective. In the late 1990s, intellectuals from several Latin American countries formed the study group called Modernity/Coloniality (MC), creating a critical epistemological movement that radicalized postcolonial concepts. Following the development of postcolonial studies in the 1960s–1970s by the French triad Albert Memmi, Aimé Cèsaire and Frantz Fanon, the Latin American intellectuals of the MC found their own decolonial turn (Ballestrin, 2013).

Liberation theology from the 1960s and the 1970s; the debates in Latin American philosophy and social science on notions such as the philosophy of liberation and an autonomous social science (e.g. Enrique Dussel, Rodolfo Kusch, Orlando Fals Borda, Pablo González Casanova, Darcy Ribeiro); dependency theory; the debates in Latin America about modernity and postmodernity in the 1980s, followed by discussions on hybridity in anthropology,

Towards Decolonial Interculturality in Migrant Education   55

communication and cultural studies in the 1990s; and, in the United States, the Latin American group of subaltern studies – the Modernity/Coloniality group has found inspiration from a wide range of sources, from European and North American critical theories of modernity, to the South Asian subaltern studies group, Chicana feminist theory, postcolonial theory and African philosophy; even so, many of its members have operated from a modified world-systems perspective. Its main guiding force, however, is an ongoing reflection on the cultural and political reality of Latin America, including the subordinate knowledge of exploited and oppressed groups (Escobar, 2003, p. 53).

The MC proposes to reflect ethically and critically on the structural socioeconomic inequalities that keep millions of people around the world living below the poverty line, especially in Africa, Asia and Latin America, which, not coincidentally, were colonies for centuries. Because of this ethical-political concern in thinking about the problems of these realities, starting from their origin, ICD, the pedagogical branch of the decolonial movement in Latin America, is fundamental for the dialogues established here.

Candau (2008), a reference on the subject in Brazil, points out that the debate around the concept of interculturality arises in the context of indigenous school education when the field of popular education movements sought to find viable ways to offer basic education to traditional populations and native peoples without disregarding their ancestral knowledge, without proposing an ethno/eurocentric education, respecting cultural diversity and without imposing the modern western episteme as the only lens to understand the world. In this sense, such socio-pedagogical action is politically positioned as part of the solution to the problems faced by these populations. However, critical interculturality does not only place itself in the context of indigenous education, it goes beyond its gaze to spaces where otherness is a *sine qua non* of people's lives. Today, ICD is conceived within the scope of the curriculum and the construction of pedagogical projects at all levels (Candau, 2008; Gundara, 2015; Walsh, 2007) inside and outside the school and classroom, in territories where these vulnerable populations are fighting for their survival. The coloniality of power (Quijano, 2005) was responsible for the colonization of bodies, subjectivities, knowledge, cultures, languages, spirituality, nature and territories, so in order to rethink an inclusive society, it is imperative to think about how to transform the historical roots of violence and iniquity that constitute these societies.

The existence of disputes and power mechanisms that permeate and constitute the relationships between different cultures are the result of the history of oppression between peoples and cultures; therefore, they also arise from the conflicts and disparities of power that shaped the world we live in. They are marked by hierarchy, prejudice and discrimination by different groups throughout history. Slavery; the ethnocide of traditional and indigenous populations in Abya Yala; the poor in all ages; the ethnic, religious, sexual and gender minorities that are constantly attacked; the "unwanted" migrant – all these are examples of conflicts that arise from the attempt to homogenize culture. Catherine Walsh characterizes interculturality as:

> [...] a dynamic and permanent process of relationship, communication and learning between cultures under conditions of respect, mutual legitimacy, symmetry and equality. An exchange that is built between people, awareness, knowledge and culturally different practices, seeking to develop a new sense between them in their differences. A space for negotiation and translation in which social, economic and political inequalities, and society's power, relations and conflicts are not kept hidden but recognized and confronted. A social and political task that challenges society as a whole, which is part of concrete and conscious social practices and actions and tries to create ways of responsibility and solidarity. A goal to reach.
>
> Walsh (2007, p. 10)

In other words, it does not only mean absorbing the subordinate popular layers, in this case migrants, in the classrooms, but also enabling them to participate in decision-making, in thinking about the actions that are taken and that affect everyone. In this sense, the ICD is built and established as an analysis tool to understand the construction of a society that seeks to transform the structural, cultural, psychological and physical violence that marks the history of modernity/coloniality. In the Brazilian context, we can mention the ethnocide of the original peoples who continue to resist a war that takes them away from their lands, their languages and their cosmologies. Also, the slavery regime never had a historic repair, which means that the upper class that still enjoys the privileges of these periods, including exalting torturers and slavers, is striving to destroy what is left of what the young and fragile democracy managed to build during its few years of progressive governments.

Ethnography: Methodological description and critical interpretative analysis

Here, some considerations and aspects from the ethnography carried out from November 2019 to September 2021 at Espaço de Bitita are pointed out. The critical (Tosta, 2014) interpretive ethnographic analysis (Geertz, 1978) addresses the categories that emerge from this case of best practices of migrant inclusion: lifelong learning *in locu* (JEIF), territoriality, active pedagogies through learning guides (LGs) and projects focused on the inclusion of cultural diversity that build a *sui generis* school culture.

Over the 22 months of fieldwork, the database was built using participant observation, field diary and interviews with teachers, managers and former students. Meetings were initially face to face and then online. The database also included information from the teachers' speeches and reports about the students' daily lives or from some students' reports shared with teachers in pedagogical group meetings. There were 50 meetings of the Special Integral Training Day (JEIF, in Portuguese), four in-person and 46 online, 10 school board meetings (all online), 17 meetings with students' families in live format on Facebook and one in person before the school closed on 15 March 2020. It was also possible to participate in dozens of online meetings between teachers and students where, unfortunately, there was low attendance by students during the pandemic period. The main cause of absence is the lack of access to the resources and materials needed to participate in online meetings. During the isolation/distancing period (March 2020 to June 2021), the JEIF's meetings took place once a week in three shifts (morning, afternoon and evening), and meetings with teacher tutors and students also took place once a week.

Thus, it is necessary to understand São Paulo as a city where, since its creation, countless flows of people converge: a metropolis with more than one million students in public schools. It cannot be said that the career of education professionals in the city is the best in the country, nor that the structural situation of the system does justice to the wealth of the city, which is considered the economic heart of Brazil. However, only São Paulo had the privilege of having Paulo Freire as the Secretary of Education in the city in the 1990s, and this feat still preserves transformations that guarantee the career of education professionals some benefits. It is also his actions in the government that allowed some advances within the city's educational system. One of the particularities is called JEIF. It is a specific workload for lifelong learning for teachers *in locu*, designed by peers and based on the themes that emerge in the school and in the territory. All participants in these formation sessions are paid for this workload (4 hours per week) and progress in their careers with the training time also in these spaces. It is from these weekly training meetings that action projects centred on migrants and vulnerable children are designed and developed.

After the hybrid[5] return in June 2021, JEIF meetings remained online once a week. During the 50 training meetings, according to the field diary, throughout 2020 and 2021, it can be concluded that this is also where the process of innovating and transforming pedagogical tools occurred. It has to also emphasize that the territory, in the context of migrations, needs to be thought of as multi-territoriality (Haesbaert, 2007); knowing the communities where migrants live is fundamental to be able to understand their specific needs. Without recognizing the otherness that makes up the multicultural territories of cities, it is impossible to build a public education that is connected to the challenges that students experience in their daily lives.

Territoriality [...] is not just "something abstract", in a sense that is often reduced to the character of analytical, epistemological abstraction. It is also an immaterial dimension, in the ontological sense that, as an "image" or symbol of a territory, it exists and can be effectively inserted as a political-cultural strategy, even if the territory to which it refers is not concretely manifested – as in the well-known example of the "Promised Land" of the Jews, territoriality that accompanied and boosted them through the ages, even though there was no concrete territorial construction (Haesbaert, 2007, p. 25).

Migrant people carry cultures, knowledge and references with them from their homelands and do not arrive as blank sheets in their places of destination. Therefore, human mobility needs to be understood as a total social fact (Sayad, 1998) that provides cultural, political, economic, pedagogical and also psychological changes for those who migrate and for those who receive the migrants.

> [...] immigration is, first of all, a displacement of people in space, and above all in physical space; in this, it is primarily related to the sciences that seek to know the population and the space [...] But the space of displacement is not just the physical space, it is also a qualified space in many senses, socially, economically, culturally, politically [...].
>
> Sayad (1998, p. 15)

Bitita, as mentioned, is not the official name of the school, but its name by claim. Claim for the name has to be in accordance with the territoriality that constitutes it. Transforming Carolina de Jesus'[6] life and work in the name of the school in the territory where she lived and wrote a large part of her work is to try to make the school and the author part of the school. When the school tries to unlink its official name from a white aristocratic Portuguese man (Infante Dom Henrique, who lived in the fifteenth–sixteenth century) who was responsible for the beginning of the trade of enslaved people to honour a black woman writer descendant of enslaved people that recounted the life in the favela means to say that it is necessary to listen to the voice and respect the representation of those who have been subordinated.

In addition to claiming the name of the school and the JEIF, it is important to mention the LGs: a pedagogical didactic resource designed by the teachers, which is used by students as a script of activities for the autonomous development of learning in the final cycle (6th, 7th, 8th and 9th year, also referred to as authorial cycle) of the elementary education. Students are also tutored by a teacher who is responsible for monitoring the development of activities throughout the school year. Each class has approximately 30 students and 2 tutors, 15 students for each teacher, to follow the formative path throughout the learning process, a practice that was still uncommon in the Brazilian public system.

Teachers have the freedom to create activities or use others already available in textbooks, recycling and updating teaching materials so that they are in accordance with the reality of their audience. The theme of cultural diversity, with attention to issues of migration, is included in activities especially because it is a territory where, historically, migrant communities are concentrated. Issues related to work analogous to slavery are also addressed (a practice still common in the textile industry in the territory and which the Bolivian and Bengali communities are more exposed to): activities on gender and violence; on the environment and global climate issues and how they relate to deforestation in the Amazon Forest; mining in indigenous lands; fires in the Cerrado and the Pantanal.[7]

It is important to note that all these topics are approached critically and reflectively throughout the teaching process throughout the academic year and not punctually, according to the calendar of dates. For example, issues related to the structural racism of Brazilian society are addressed daily, not just on November 20, the day of black consciousness in Brazil. Issues about diversity or violence and gender equality are also addressed throughout the course and not just on March 8 or June, the month of LGBTQIA+ pride. The topics related to the environment are also addressed throughout the year and not only on the day of the tree or on the day of the earth or water. It is worth remembering that the coloniality of power (Quijano, 2005) affects all aspects of human life, from spirituality to culture and the human relationship with the environment. Thus, interculturality is placed in a critical way by making it possible for all aspects of life in society (Gundara, 2015; Walsh, 2007; Walsh, Oliveira and Candau, 2018) to be worked on in the educational locus between all the actors involved in the teaching and learning processes. This is because it makes it possible for all aspects of life in society to be worked on in the educational locus among all the actors involved in the teaching and learning processes.

A regional and universal knowledge base, which is recontextualized in Asian societies, presents curriculum planners in education systems with a difficult but essential challenge. A non-centralized curriculum can enable educators and students to develop inclusive and shared value systems important to democratic Asian societies. Special attention needs to be given to teaching history from a non-triumphalist perspective, so that the past is used to develop greater levels of mutuality among the citizens of states [...]. However, these curriculum developments need to be part of mainstream education, but they must be based on basic education and language and literacy acquisition. Some of the initiatives may require the development of school–community linkages and measures to minimize conflict in socially diverse schools and educational strategies to improve the educational performance of children from immigrant families and children, especially from the poorest parts of the majority community. This can be facilitated through the development of bilingual and multilingual strategies as well as innovative curriculum development. Notions of public security and policies to defend human rights and the plural social environment in societies are of fundamental importance for civil status (etat de droit). This can help the development of a civil society with a strong civic culture and encourage active citizenship among all young people. The school as an educational institution has a formative role in the development of a constitutional ethic, oriented towards peace and inclusive among all young people. This can help ensure that all children in a state learn together, play together, grow together and then come together through shared public and social values (Gundara, 2015, p. 62).

Although Gundara is thinking about the Asian context, it is possible to bring his reflection to the Brazilian reality to think about critical interculturality and how it is placed at Espaço de Bitita. The LGs are also oriented by (multi-)territoriality (Santos, 1999); they work with popular knowledge and cultures, bringing these to the academic knowledge that is inscribed in the curriculum of the city,[8] which is, by its nature, a dynamic field in constant dispute (Arroyo, 2013). A new version is currently in force, launched by the political project in force in the city hall, which, in turn, came to replace the previous one, which had as one of its guidelines the decolonization of the curriculum, where the guiding policy sought to bring value to activities of indigenous and Afro-Brazilian, Afro-Latin (González, 1988) and feminine cultures that have always been on the margins of textbooks produced and distributed en masse in the country (Monteiro, 2016). With this type of collaborative pedagogical construction centred on the children's reality, created among the professionals who are at the "school's ground",[9] it becomes possible to innovate and transform teaching practices, also collaborating to improve learning.

> The quality of education is intrinsically aligned with issues related to valuing the individual and collective processes of educators who are currently in the classroom. Even in the existence of numerous structural problems, the quality of human capital, when widely and fully valued, can bypass the purely physical issues of the school environment in a creative and collaborative way.
>
> Guilherme, Antunes and Da Silva (2016, p. 155)

The LGs were responsible for ensuring that migrant and non-migrant children who attended the final years of elementary school, in 2020, could maintain some pedagogical link with the school, as they were already familiar with the autonomous dynamics of the process of learning. Those who had material conditions (access to the Internet and technology devices to be present at the weekly meetings with teachers) advanced in their studies, but a large portion lost the pedagogical link due to the lack of the same material conditions. It is estimated that one-third of the students (from the final cycle) successfully completed the RAs in 2020, having also passed in public technical schools that are present in the territory. One-third managed to maintain some bond, completing and delivering the tasks, but without being present in the virtual meetings with their tutors or without being able to participate in the synchronous activities offered by the school. The remaining one-third almost completely lost the pedagogical link with the school, as there was no material or structural condition for them to be able to be virtually present or just deliver in the activities that were sent by WhatsApp, Facebook and Google Classroom and made available in prints for collection in the school. Among the students who completed elementary education in 2020, there was an increase from 8 (in 2019) to 12 among those who were approved in public technical schools (state and federal) in the territory.[10] Among those approved, it is worth noting that the majority are girls and migrants.

It is important to highlight that, in October and November 2020, there was an election for the mayor of the city and that the mayor who was victorious used the argument that the city's schools would be receiving educational tablets for distribution to students as an electoral propaganda resource; however, it was only in May 2021 that the city's schools began to receive materials to distribute to students, one for each enrolled student. Few cities in the country were able to make this investment in the future of their children and, despite the technical problems in some devices or the bureaucracy that hampered delivery, after students received the material, attendance at synchronous meetings increased significantly, reaching 90 per cent of students of each class.

In addition to the JEIF meetings, during the isolation period, teachers also met once a week to discuss and think about actions to maintain the students' bond, to organize the learning routines (materials sent weekly to students from 1st to 5th year of the initial cycle, working at home with their families), as well as for the actions that were called "Active Search", that is, calling each family's phone to find out how they were going through the period of isolation, how were their studies, if the families were able to remove the printed materials at the school, if the students were able to follow the activities, if the family was experiencing any difficulties. Over the period, several actions of donations of basic food baskets were carried out to help families living in a situation of socioeconomic vulnerability. The 6th- to 9th-grade students continued to work with the LGs and their tutor teachers. The tutor provided a time a week to meet the tutoring group students. However, there were several reports of teachers who were only able to contact students when they could use their parents' phone, for example, Sunday morning or on random days late at night. Mentioned below is a specific case that demonstrates a little about the reality of the families and students that Bitita serves and how the work of welcoming tutors and school management is done in cases of risk or vulnerability of the child or adolescent. The name of the school is disclosed here in respect of the choice of the school community that claims this recognition, but pseudonyms are used for research informants:

> I have good memories of Bitita Space. Something that made the difference for me is that, when the director arrived, he proposed that we should do a study, like a preparation to be able to enter the Technical Schools. There is a Federal Institute of Education (IF) practically behind the school. So he arranged the means so that the students of this IF could

prepare us for the entrance exams. And that was my first contact with the entrance exam. Knowing that I would have the opportunity to attend a technical school, I would have the opportunity to, perhaps, enter a public college. Until then I was unaware of all this, I was still a child. So I took that preparatory course for me to enter the IF. I didn't make it, but I feel very grateful for this opportunity, because that's where I was awakened by this desire to prepare myself to do well and enter into good institutions. After I left school, I did a technical course, yes, a technical course in administration at another public school that is also close to the region. [...] Then I left the technical course school, and this course showed me what I wanted to do, until then I didn't know what I wanted to study. I did the Administration technician and I realized that I don't like accounting, I don't like numbers, I'm well in the Humanities area and there I had contact with Law and it caught my attention. I liked the subjects, so I decided I wanted to study law. I realized that the monthly fees were expensive, but I also remembered the prep course we took, the preparatory course, and I started looking for preparatory courses for the entrance exam. And coincidentally, this public school where I studied also had students from USP, the University of São Paulo, teaching classes on Saturdays, preparing for entrance exams. I did, it was an opportunity to talk to students who were studying at a public college, I got to know USP through them and fell in love with the university city. And well, leaving school I took the national high school exam, I took the entrance exam and I still didn't make it. So I did a private preparatory course for another year because I really wanted to enter a public university and especially a university that had a university city because I wanted that university coexistence, I wanted to walk around the university city and talk to other students from other courses. [...] I graduated in 2014, I tried in 2016 and failed, I tried again in 2017 and got it at the Federal University of Minas Gerais, UFMG, and at the Federal University of Santa Catarina, UFSC. [...] UFMG is better placed than UFSC, but the Law building is outside the university city, so I chose UFSC because the building is inside the university city. So that's how I decided to go to UFSC.

Interview report from former student (August 2021)

The case evidenced above was collected from an interview in the last month's fieldwork. This case is about a migrant former student, and it allows us to reflect on the importance of teaching involvement in working with children and adolescents regardless of their origin, as the same reception occurs with non-migrant students and families. In a conversation with the school director, he reports that in 2014, the school received an award from the city hall for the project developed with migrant children called "Appropriate School".[11] In this project created in 2012, the first project to focus on migrant children, the objective was to promote the integration between Brazilian students and Bolivian students, as it was found that there was a segregation of Brazilians from Bolivians. The project still exists, but its work was affected by the pandemic and only resumed after the return to hybrid classroom teaching. The project's dynamic consists of biweekly meetings with migrant students, where each one invites a Brazilian student to participate in the conversation. The proposal is simple: promote dialogue and knowledge of the other's culture and reality, in order to demystify the prejudices suffered by migrant communities (Escola Apropriada, 2017).[12]

There was an opportunity for a group of students to travel to Bolivia in 2014 with the amount received in one of the awards that the school won for the project, a group of migrants and non-migrants accompanied by teachers. The delegation consisted of eight students, four migrants and four non-migrants. The four migrants were chosen according to the document protocols, while for the non-migrants, there was great difficulty in finding four members who could travel, as the non-migrants did not have the necessary documents or authorizations. In the end, five migrant and three non-migrant students accompanied by four teachers travelled. The purpose of the trip was to enable those who had the opportunity to get to know Bolivia to go back to school and share what they had experienced with other classmates. They visited museums and schools and had contact with the culture of the largest migrant community in the territory. On the way back, each student made a presentation of their travel diary. Through observation experiences and interviews during the 22 months of fieldwork, both in the face-to-face observations and in the observations of meetings between teachers and students, it was possible to perceive that if there was segregation between migrants and non-migrants, now they no longer exist. An example that can be cited is the participation of migrant and non-migrant students in an inter-school poetry slam[13] contest, encouraged by the art teacher. While competing with each other and with students from other schools, they supported them with words of motivation, as some of them were nervous or insecure in front of the screen when reciting their poetry. It was possible to watch student participation in these contests in 2020 and 2021.

There are some migrant students who are shyer and do not interact much with the rest of the class. It is possible to notice that some students, especially Asians, are more reserved or shy, as it can be seen, due to their language difficulties, not because of the silencing of their voices by colleagues or the school. This is because many students will use only the Portuguese language at school, but in their daily lives in the family and community, they mostly use their native languages. An example in which this could be observed occurred in the first days of school in 2020 when two boys from Bangladesh, brothers, talked to a teacher. One of them had already finished elementary school and had changed schools, while the other was starting at Espaço de Bitita. The eldest went along with the younger brother throughout the first week to help him communicate with colleagues and teachers. It was possible to notice that the older one was always comfortable with the environment, while the younger one appeared to be a little intimidated by the amount of information, but he relaxed when in the company of other Bengali students.

Communication with some of the migrant families is still a challenge for the Bitita Space, especially with families from non-Latin-speaking cultures. Although the school has an Assistant Directing Teacher, who lives in the neighbourhood, speaks Arabic and is from the Muslim community, the communication that needs to be done in English (especially the Bengali and Pakistani communities) is a challenge. Even if the school has English teachers and that these teachers always collaborate in communication when requested, other professionals who work at the school in other sectors (secretaries, technical assistants, teaching inspectors who also work directly with families and students) have great difficulty in communication with these families. One way to minimize these communication failures would be to provide these professionals with language courses when they enter the municipal public network. The existence of a teacher who belongs to the Muslim community[14] at the school is essential for the work with a large part of the families that communicate in Arabic to happen. In addition to acting as an intercultural mediator within the school, this teacher knows many of the families and has a trusting relationship with the community that respects her, as she lives in the territory and is part of it. This does not mean that only teachers from the territory should work at the school, but it is true that this direct relationship helps to bring the school and the community closer together.

Everything we can do in order to summon those who live around the school, and within the school, in the sense of participating, of taking the destiny of the school in their own hands is still little, considering the immense work that lies ahead of us, which is to democratically take over this country (Freire, 1997).

In order to improve communication with the community during the period of social isolation, a group of teachers created the Rádio de Bitita, a project developed among teachers to bring information about the pandemic and the work of the school to the community. Audios shared via WhatsApp informed about activities and data from the pandemic, but also about topics relevant to the territory. The audios became podcast episodes with collaborative creation, editing and finishing between teachers, but nowadays also with student participation. By the end of 2020, 40 episodes had been produced, including the participation of migrant and non-migrant students in many of these episodes. Among the topics covered in the episodes included the issue of internal and international migration, Brazilian and international environmental issues, Brazilian popular culture, gender violence and ethnic-racial issues that also guided debates in society throughout 2020. Now, in 2021, with face-to-face feedback, Rádio de Bitita has been transformed into the

Espaço de Bitita Audio-Visual Centre (CAEB), where teachers are using audio and video production techniques for the production of pedagogical content by students and for students.

A YouTube[15] channel was created for the school, where videos are being published with the students' stories, with content produced by teachers and students. For the wounds opened by the pandemic in the school's pedagogical work, Rádio de Bitita was the main dressing to help maintain the link between the school and the children and their families. In 2021, the project was a finalist in two awards in the city of São Paulo, the Paulo Freire Award in the centenary edition of the patron of Brazilian Education, where it received the second place in the category of Youth and Adult Education, and also the Human Rights Education Award, which was awarded in October 2021.

Both awards highlighted the importance of collaborative work between teachers and their peers and how this example helps to promote creativity and collaboration also among children who are now beginning to take ownership of projects that were born during social isolation and that will remain over the years, bringing important changes to the work developed at the school. Despite the countless losses, anguish and suffering caused by the pandemic that, in Brazil, has already killed more than 607 thousand people, the innovations that the inventiveness of remote work produced in this school are powerful, as the collaborative work inspired other teachers to also start work together and create solutions to everyday problems in the middle of chaos.

Final considerations

Here, only some of the good practices focused on children, migrants and non-migrants were mentioned, from Espaço de Bitita that, during the year 2020/2021, were implemented to maintain the link between school and students. As stated in the introduction to this chapter with some notes of a school ethnography, questions to be asked about the education of migrant children are not only about migrant children, but also about how the country and community that receive immigrants work with their hierarchies and social dynamics, as it is on these dynamics and hierarchies that children will be educated. Therefore, in order to think about the quality of education offered to migrant children, it is important to think about how their own society is educated. The migrant child already experiences otherness through their own existence, but the local child does need to be educated to understand and respect otherness. However, as pointed out by Walsh (2020) at a conference during the pandemic, from the cracks (grietas in Spanish) and wounds of our history can be born flowers of hope and transformation, but for this, critical interculturality and decolonial thinking need to reach and be taken to all instances of decision-making and participation so that the coloniality of power and knowledge (Quijano, 2005) can be transformed into a real liberation of colonized peoples.

In addition to the actions mentioned here, countless partnerships made between the school and other institutions made it possible to keep alive, amidst the political and sanitary chaos of 2020/2021, the hope for transformative pedagogical work. The school, which is recognized by the UNESCO as an example of good practices centred on migrant children, went through numerous difficulties, grief[16] and attacks by the media and governments that forced them to return in person when there was no sanitary condition for it. In February 2021, when the country recorded a daily average of deaths >1,000 and with the government's intention to return to face-to-face work, municipal public school teachers enacted the "Strike for Life" that lasted more than 100 days.

The strike resulted in the inclusion of teachers in the priority list for vaccination and made it possible to prevent the transmission of the virus among education professionals and among children and adolescents. During the strike period, teachers organized weekly meetings with students and strike actions to raise awareness in the school community on the importance of social distancing and to pressure governments for vaccination which, at this time, was taking slow steps in the country as a result of corrupted attempts in the purchase of vaccines by the federal government. Salinas and Reyes (2004) point out in their studies on the school success of migrant children on the Texas-Mexico border that the role of the defender teacher, one who is engaged in social issues and in the defence of human rights, is fundamental for good performance and integration of migrant students in host societies. In addition to the figure of the teacher, it is important that the school management and the pedagogical project of the school are also in line with the engaged work of the teacher who is concerned with the rights of migrant children as citizens of a globalized world: a world with a globalized economy, but which still imposes and builds walls, barriers and borders for the movement of human beings who seek better living conditions or flee from the conflicts created by the geopolitics of economic power.

Bitita does not present us with a complete or perfect path, nor a manual on how to include migrant students, but a path marked by critical resistance, by social engagement for the public it serves and for the inclusion of all, migrants or nationals, boys or girls, cisgender or transgender. It is in educating ourselves for otherness and solidarity that Bitita shows us how to be broadly inclusive, both for the migrant and for the homeless, sheltered family, to educate boys and girls for a society with less gender inequality. Kohatsu (2019, p. 71) points out that "xenophobia as an aversion to what is foreign, as well as other forms of discrimination, reveals the difficulty in recognizing the humanity of the other who shows himself to be different". By celebrating all its diversities, common to any territory, Bitita teaches us that education is the same for everyone. What differs is the look at everyone through the lens of care, reception, human rights and their singularities that, as a whole, transform everyone into equals in difference.

Bitita is not a conflict-free space; there are aspects where further progress is needed. However, many of these contradictions do not necessarily come from the school, but from problems that are external to it. Bitita does not have a special teaching plan for migrant students, but it puts into practice actions that make it possible for these students to be able to build their paths according to their needs through the autonomy provided by the LGs. In this sense, tutors and regular teachers are able to establish a bond and a unique follow-up for each student, bringing the curricular contents to their reality.

And, in case it hasn't been made explicit, Bitita puts into practice a critical and also decolonial intercultural education by questioning the societal paradigms that structure the inequalities of Brazilian society and also of the school. Not accepting the coloniality of power as it is structurally instilled in minds and bodies, resisting since the attempt to change the name of EMEF so that it is in accordance with the territoriality that constitutes it and even making gender intersectionalities, pedagogical agenda, race, class and place of origin that cross it community, Bitita presents us with the results of the transforming power of critical interculturality when applied to the reality of the school.

Notes

1 Origin name Kuna, original people that inhabit the central region of the continent that came to be baptized, in a Christian and Catholic perspective, of America after the European invasion.
2 Biome of great biodiversity that was almost extinct during the process of occupation and exploration of the territory.
3 The official name is suppressed here as an ethical and political position that respects the community that has been trying to change the name of the school so that it is connected with the reality and history of its surroundings. The current name of EMEF refers to a Portuguese nobleman who lived in the 15th century and was responsible for the beginning of naval activities of Portuguese conquest and exploration, as well as for the beginning of the trade of enslaved peoples.
4 National competition that highlights the best teachers and your best work.
5 Due to distancing protocols and the precarious infrastructure of the school building, each group of students attended the school for a week and, in the following week, attended synchronous meetings with the teachers.
6 One of the main writers of Brazilian literature of the 20th century who lived in the school's territory. Her autobiographical work portraying the life of a poor black woman and single mother has been translated into 16 languages. Bitita is her childhood nickname.
7 Biome of Brazilian biodiversity, which endured the lack of conservation policies.
8 It is possible to access it online through the website of the Municipal Department of Education of São Paulo: < https://curriculo.sme.prefeitura.sp.gov.br/ >
9 Common expression to identify the teachers who are the struggles of public education.
10 These are schools with technical secondary education that have entrance exams and high competition.
11 In Portuguese, the word appropriate has two meanings: (1) appropriate in the sense of appropriation, of appropriating something for oneself. (2) Appropriate in

68 Lucas Rech da Silva

the proper sense, convenient. And the intention of the name of the project is to understand in both senses, the school you want and the school that is yours.
12 It is possible to see a documentary about the project through YouTube.
13 Competition in which poets recite their original poetry.
14 In Brazil, the Muslim community is numerically very smaller compared with several countries in Europe.
15 "Canal de Bitita" YouTube.
16 A math teacher died from complications of COVID-19 in July 2020; numerous family members of students and school professionals also died during 2020/2021. The grief is collective.

References

Arroyo, Miguel G. Reinventar a política: reinventar o sistema de educação. *Educação & Sociedade*, v. 34, n. 124, p. 653–678, 2013.

Ballestrin, Luciana. América latina e o giro decolonial. *Revista Brasileira de Ciência Política*, v. 11, p. 89–117, 2013.

Brasil. Ministério da Justiça. *Migrantes, apátridas e refugiados: subsídios para o aperfeiçoamento de acesso a serviços, direitos e políticas públicas no Brasil*. Ministério da Justiça, Secretaria de Assuntos Legislativos. Brasília, DF: Instituto de Pesquisa Econômica Aplicada, 2015. Disponível em: http://pensando.mj.gov.br/wp-content/uploads/2015/11/PoD_57_web2.pdf. Acesso em: 11 nov. 2019. https://doi.org/10.26668/indexlawjournals/2526-026x/2018.v4i1.4365

Candau, Vera Maria. Direitos humanos, educação e interculturalidade. *Revista Brasileira de Educação*, v. 13 n. 37 jan./abr. 2008. http://www.scielo.br/pdf/rbedu/v13n37/05.pdf

Dauster, Tania. Etnografia, modo de conhecer: entre a Antropologia e a Educação. Educação on-Line. *(PUCRJ)*, v. 9, p. 10–15, 2011.

Escobar, Arthuro. Mundos y conocimientos de otro modo: el programa de investigación modernidad/colonialidad latinoamericano. *Tabula Rasa*, v. 1, p. 58–86, 2003.

Escola Apropriada. *Documentário. Diversitas*. Universidade de São Paulo, 2017. Disponível em: < https://www.youtube.com/watch?v=PfKi69lASR0 >. Último acesso em 12 de Fevereiro de 2020.

Freire, Paulo. *Professora sim, tia não. Cartas a quem ousa ensinar*. São Paulo: Olho D'Água, 1997.

Geertz, Clifford. *A interpretação das culturas*. Rio de Janeiro: Zahar, 1978.

Guilherme, Alexandre Anselmo; Antunes, Denise Dalpiaz; Silva, Lucas Rech. *Educação Continuada na Docência: Concepções, Avanços e Desafios na Perspectiva de Bourdieu e Gur-Ze'ev' in*: ANPED SUL, Brasil, 2016. Acessível em: http://hdl.handle.net/10923/15920.

Gundara, Jagdish. *The case for intercultural education in a multicultural world*. Oakville, ON: Mosaic Press. 201.

González, Lélia. Por um Feminismo Afro-latino-americano. *Revista Isis Internacional*, vol. IX, p. 133–141, 1988.

Haesbaert, Rogério. *Território e Multiterritorialidade: um debate*. In: Revista GEOgraphia (Universidade Federal Fluminense). Ano IX, n. 17, 2007. Disponível em: https://periodicos.uff.br/geographia/article/view/13531/0

Towards Decolonial Interculturality in Migrant Education 69

Kohatsu, Lineu Norio Imigração, assimilação e xenofobia: algumas notas. In: *Dossiê Migrações. Cadernos CERU*, vol. 30 n. 1, p. 50–75, 2019. Recuperado de: http:// www.periodicos.usp.br/ceru/article/view/158699

Monteiro, Paolla Ungaretti. *(In)visibilidade das mulheres brasileiras nos livros didáticos de história do Ensino Médio (PNLD, 2015)*. Dissertação de Mestrado, Pontifícia Universidade Católica do Rio grande do Sul, Porto Alegre, 2016.

Oliveira, Amurabi. Por que etnografia no sentido estrito e não estudos do tipo etnográfico em educação? *Revista da FAEEBA – Educação e Contemporaneidade, Salvador*, v. 22, n. 40, p. 69–81, jul./dez. 2013.

Quijano, Aníbal. *Colonialidad del poder, eurocentrismo y América Latina*. In: E. Lander (Org). A colonialidade do saber: Eurocentrismo e ciências sociais. Perspectivas latino-americanas (pp. 71–103). Buenos Aires, CLACSO, 2005.

Rockwell, Elsie; Ezpeleta, Justa. *A pesquisa participante*. São Paulo: Cortez, Autores Associados, 1989.

Sayad, Abdelmalek. *Imigração ou os paradoxos da alteridade*. São Paulo: Edusp, 1998.

Salinas, Cinthia; Reyes, Reynaldo. Creating successful academic programs for Chicana/o high school migrant students: The role of advocate educators. *The High School Journal*, v. 87, no. 4, p. 54–65, 2004. doi:10.1353/hsj.2004.0015.

Santos, Milton. *Território e Dinheiro*. In: Território e Territórios. Niterói: Programa de Pós Graduação em Geografia – PPGEO-UFF/AGB, 1999, p.08. Disponível em: https://periodicos.uff.br/geographia/article/view/13360/8560.

Silva, Lucas Rech. *A inclusão de imigrantes haitianos no Ensino Médio em Caxias do Sul: um estudo de caso na perspectiva das violências de Galtung e Fanon*. Dissertação de Mestrado, Programa de Pós-graduação em Educação PUCRS, 2018.

Tosta, Sandra Pereira. *Uma Etnografia para a Escola na América latina*. Trabalho apresentado na 29ª Reunião Brasileira de Antropologia, realizada em Natal, Rio Grande do Norte, 2014.

Walsh, Catherine. *Interculturalidade e Decolonialidade do Poder: um pensamento posicionamento "Outro" a partir da diferença colonial*. In: CASTROGÓMEZ, Santiago; GROSFOGUEL, Ramón (Comp.). *El giro decolonial: reflexiones para una diversidad epistémica más allá del capitalismo global*. Bogotá: Siglo del Hombre Editores et al., 2007. 308p. (p. 47–62). Disponível em: https://periodicos.ufpel.edu.br/ojs2/index. php/revistadireito/article/download/15002/10532

Walsh, C.; De Oliveira, L. F.; Candau, V. M. F.; Colonialidade e Pedagogia Decolonial: Para Pensar uma Educação Outra. *Education Policy Analysis Archives*. v. 26, n. 83, Julho 2018.

Walsh, Catherine. *Insurgencias desde las Grietas*. Seminario de formación permanente en Pensamiento Crítico. CEIP Histórica de Argentina, Centro de Investigación RÍUS de Clacso-México y Otras Voces en Educación, 2020. Disponível em: https://www.youtube.com/watch?v=SuMPMn4sOuc

Part II

Intersectional Inequalities, Racism, Stereotypes, and Discrimination of Migrant Pupils

Chapter 5

'Othering' and Integration of Migrant Children and Young People of Albanian Ethnic Origin

Evidence from Slovenian Schools

Mateja Sedmak, Zorana Medarić, and Lucija Dežan

Introduction

In this article, we discuss the issue of the integration of migrant children and young people into the Slovenian society in educational settings (primary and secondary schools). The point of interest lies in the integration process (challenges and constraints) of a specific group of migrant children, namely children of the Albanian ethnic group, mainly from Kosovo and North Macedonia and rarely from Albania. The reason for focusing on this particular group of children/youth is not accidental, as children of Albanian ethnic background are perceived as 'more difficult to integrate' and are subject to greater prejudice from educational staff as well as from other children and youth (Dežan & Sedmak, 2021; Sedmak et al., 2018, 2020). In order to better understand the integration process of children and youth of Albanian ethnic background, the concept of othering as an analytical starting point will be used. Othering is the process and discourse when the members of the other ethnic communities/immigrants are perceived as completely different and opposite to us, to 'our' culture and 'our' ethnicity. Othering is always constructed on a binary division of 'us' and 'them', 'civilised' vs. 'uncivilised', 'developed' vs. 'underdeveloped', etc. (Jensen, 2011).

Our starting points for analysis are as follows. First, in relation to the Albanian ethnic community and in relation to children of Albanian ethnic background, the process of othering can be observed; second, othering has a negative influence on the integration process; and third, de-othering policies and practices would positively influence the integration of migrant children and youth with an Albanian ethnic background. When discussing the influence of the process of othering on the integration of migrant children into the host society in education, the impact of at least three separate but interrelated levels should be considered, namely, othering at the macro level (reflected in official policies and media discourse), at the mezzo level (othering in relation to the ethnic group/community), and the process of othering at the individual level (discrimination and stigmatisation in everyday school life by teachers, peers, and classmates).

DOI: 10.4324/9781003343141-7

Our discussion draws on the findings of field research conducted as part of the Horizon 2020 MiCREATE project Migrant Children and Communities in a Transforming Europe.[1] The field research was conducted among members of the educational institutions (headteachers, teachers, counsellors, and migrant and local children) between June 2019 and June 2021. Various methodological approaches were used (participant observation, interviews, collection of autobiographical stories, and focus groups) during the fieldwork.

The following sections present (1) the theoretical background of the concept of othering, (2) the methodological protocol and methodology used during data collection, (3) the analysis of the main findings of the study, and finally, (4) a critical discussion of the findings from the othering perspective.

The others and the process of othering

In relation to ethnicity, the discourse about 'others' who are distinctively different from 'us' and 'our' culture originates from the authors of postcolonial theory (Frantz Fanon, Edward Said, Gayatri Spivak, etc.). One of the first references to the process of othering was made by Edward E. Said (1978) in his writing on imagined geography, which constructs the Orient as 'the other'. The Europocentric perceptions of the Orient, he noted, are extremely reductionist and contain elements of pathologisation and exoticisation. The Orient is portrayed from a Europocentric perspective and to Europeans as alien, diverse, and as the ultimate other. This is also reflected in the commonly used term *orientalism*, which exposes the exaggeration of differences, Western superiority, and clichéd analytical models for perceiving the 'Oriental world'. Gayatri Chakravorty Spivak (1985), in her essay 'The Rani of Sirmur: An Essay in Reading the Archives', was the first to approach the concept of othering more systematically by analysing three dimensions of British colonial power in India. Firstly, the othering process is about power. The subordinate group must be aware of who holds the power, and at the same time, the holders of the power produce the other as a subordinate. Secondly, the other is constructed as pathological and morally inferior, and thirdly, the othering process implies that knowledge and technology are the property of the powerful. Caught in the personal experience between her husband's patriarchy and British imperialism, Spivak perceives and analyses the process of othering as multidimensional and intersectional. The process of othering, she argues, is classed, raced, and gendered, and othering is also a way of expressing racism and sexism.

As Sune Qvotrup Jensen (2011) highlights in the overview of the 'othering' literature, the concept has been used by different scholars pointing out different emphases.

However, all underline the processes of subordination, differentiation, and demarcation that draw the line between 'us' and 'them' and between more and less powerful while exposing social and cultural distance, stereotypes, reduction, and essentialism. All characteristics ultimately lead to the dehumanisation of the other. Jensen himself defines othering as:

A discursive process by which powerful groups, who may or may not make up a numerical majority, define subordinate groups into existence in a reductionist way which ascribe problematic and/or inferior characteristics to these subordinate groups. Such discursive processes affirm the legitimacy and superiority of the powerful and condition identity formation among the subordinate.

Jensen (2011, p. 65)

Ukrainian authors Kutsenko et al. (2020), analysing the othering process, highlight three structural features essential to the process of othering, namely, first, the existence of a binary opposition of in-group and out-group, built on the principles of subordination/dominance and hierarchy; second, the exclusion and segregation of out-groups, use of social distancing from them, which entails stigmatisation, symbolic degradation, and stereotyping; and third, the discursive violence against the out-group as a weak and voiceless social actor deprived of social status, symbols, and prestige.

Shifting back to Spivak, and as all presented reflections on othering point out, *power* is at the centre, because the other is described as the one with less power, as inferior, and not fascinating (Spivak, 1985).

The process of othering takes place and is reproduced at the micro, mezzo, and macro levels of social life, at the level of everyday life (small talk, stereotyping, stigmatisation, discrimination, etc.), and in the media and political (mainly right-wing populist) discourses. Fielder and Catalano (2017) analyse the process of othering of 'new' migrants from Eastern and Southern Europe in the UK through the media and right-wing populist discourse. They find that othering discourses move along a continuum ranging from voicing intergroup bias, through prejudiced statements about ethnicity and nationality, to explicitly racist comments. What is particularly illustrative of how the othering process can operate in the case of migrants is the perverted and twisted portrayal of the dominant group as the victims of Bulgarian and Romanian migrants who burden social services. Similar conclusions were reached by Andreja Vezovnik (2017), who examined otherness and victimhood in a discursive analysis of the most widely read daily newspaper in Slovenia. In the newspaper, migrants are portrayed as dirty and cunning. Finally, media depicts Slovenians as victims of migrants who pose a cultural and security threat, and as victims of 'false'/economic migrants (who are not 'proper' refugees and only 'false' victims) (ibid.). The mass-media effect on the perception of migrants and refugees by young people in Slovenia can also be seen in the research Youth 2020: The Position of Young People in Slovenia. The results of the study show that even long after the peak of the migration wave in 2016, young people's perceptions of how migrants contribute to society were still unfavourable, while media reports reinforced their xenophobic attitudes; these effects were also visible in 2020 (Lavrič & Rutar, 2021).

The process of othering is closely related to the process of acceptance and integration of migrants. As othering increases intergroup social distance and general mistrust, it negatively impacts the process of integration of migrants into the host society. In their work *De-othering politics and practices of forced migrants in modern society*, Kutsenko et al. (2020) address this perspective, the influence of othering on the social life, integration, and radicalisation of migrants.

They also introduce the opposite process, namely 'de-othering', as a policy and practice with a positive impact on the social integration of migrants. The politics of othering, the authors claim, can be explicit (lack of state support for migrants, media/everyday discourses on migrants as 'a threat', 'a burden', etc.) or more latent (hidden behind official rhetoric of tolerance and understanding of forced migrants). Nevertheless, the process of othering supports the social inequality that generates the desire of forced migrants to resist discriminatory practices and overcome the subordinate format of interaction with representatives of the host society (ibid.). On the other hand, the concept of 'de-othering' (originally introduced by Jonathan O. Chimakonam (ibid.)) tends to eliminate the differences between the in-group and the out-group, between 'us' and 'them', the host population and the migrants. De-othering practices are associated with the process of social adaptation to the new social and cultural context, active engagement in social life, and integration. With the words of Jensen (2011), the de-othering process also includes 'the refusal of the status of the other'. The de-othering process means attempts of a subordinate group (in our case migrants) to change their status, accumulate social, cultural, symbolic, and economic capital of/in the host society, and integrate (Kutsenko et al., 2020).

Following this, the de-othering politics and practice mean:

1 the deconstruction of the binary opposition between in-group/out-group; the rejection of the elevation of any group at the expense of another one; and the elimination of the principles of subordination and hierarchy;
2 the inclusion/involvement of the out-group of forced migrants in the social life of the host society; the abandonment of practices of their social distancing and stigmatization;
3 the criticism of the discourse of indulgence towards forced migrants and the use of the discourse of involvement of migrants in the host society (Ibid.: 64).

In accordance with the paper's main objective, the discussion of the influence of the othering process on the migrant children's integration into the host society in the educational settings, the three levels of othering were also considered. Namely, othering at the macro level (reflected in official politics and media discourse), at the mezzo level (othering in relation to ethnic group/community), and, most importantly, the process of othering at the individual level (discrimination and stigmatisation in everyday school life by school professionals, peers, and classmates).

As Piekut et al. (2021) highlights, the treatment of migrant children's families and community members by school staff and local authorities has a crucial impact on the integration process of migrant children. Non-acceptance, mistrust, suspicion, and disrespectful treatment of the migrant child's family negatively affect the child's well-being and willingness to adapt and integrate into the host society.

In the collective imaginary the Slovenes, the Albanian community represents the ultimate other. The othering process and its consequences are, therefore, focused on members of the Albanian community, which abundantly affects children as well. The increasing intolerance towards members of the Albanian community has also been observed by other researchers. For example, Marijanca Ajša Vižintin (2018) points out intolerance and prejudice against Albanian-speaking children and their parents, who migrated to Slovenia in the 21st century mainly from Kosovo, North Macedonia, occasionally Montenegro, and to a very small extent from Albania. She presumes that the intolerance is a consequence of the increasing number of Albanian-speaking children enrolling in Slovenian schools, unfamiliarity with the Albanian language, and feeling of powerlessness due to insufficient professional knowledge about the inclusion of migrant children (2018, p. 94). The observed intolerance towards children of this ethnic group is also due to the perception of the majority group of the Albanian migrant community living in Slovenia as 'closed', 'self-sufficient', 'culturally completely different', also 'underdeveloped', 'traditional', 'not willing to learn the Slovenian language or/and adapt' etc., thus focusing and revealing the cultural distance and strong/closed ethnic boundaries of the Albanian community (Klopčič et al., 2003, Sedmak et al., 2018, Sedmak & Medarić, 2020). The increasingly negative perception of the Albanian community is also due to the increasing immigration of Albanians in the last two decades, due to their low socioeconomic status and low level of education. Albanians are predominantly economic migrants. As a rule, it is the men who migrate to Slovenia, sometimes followed by their wives and children. A strong influence of intersectionality can also be observed. In addition to cultural differences, the generally very low level of education of Albanian migrants from Kosovo and North Macedonia (but not from Albania) has a major impact on the process of othering (SURS, 2018). The place of emigration is very important, as Albanian men and women who come from the rural areas of these countries have often attended only primary school or less; men are usually low-paid workers and unskilled employees in construction sites or bakeries. A plethora of wives is predominantly unemployed and not looking for work, according to official statistics, mostly with primary school qualifications or less, sometimes illiterate (SURS, 2018). Intra-group marriage patterns and a 'centralised' organisation of family life still prevail in the Albanian community, with the eldest man deciding on important family and financial decisions. Moreover, arranged marriages still exist and family honour is closely tied to the 'appropriate' behaviour of sisters, daughters, and wives. In contrast to Bosnian Muslim women, Albanian women are often veiled, which further reinforces anti-Albanian sentiment (Blasutig et al., 2020; Klopčič et al., 2003; Lenarčič & Sedmak, 2019; Mandelc & Gajić 2022, Sedmak et al., 2018, followed by Sedmak, 2020, Sedmak & Medarić, 2020, Žišt, 2008).

Discussion of the methodological approach

Our discussion on othering and the integration of migrant children and youth is based on data from the research among the educational staff and migrant learners that was conducted in primary and secondary schools in the period from June 2019 to June 2021. Our research included primary and secondary schools from the western, eastern, and central parts of Slovenia. The selection criteria were to include schools from urban areas with a high migrant population and the resulting cultural and ethnic diversity and to reach the most diverse sample possible in terms of migrant children's experiences. In the first phase, a research study was conducted among members of the educational community (June–December 2019). We conducted individual interviews with educational staff (teachers, teachers of additional Slovenian language courses as well as teachers responsible for integration, principals, school psychologists, and counsellors). This phase was followed by focus groups. Initially, 16 schools were involved; 38 interviews and 14 focus groups were conducted. In the following phase, seven primary and secondary schools were selected, in which the observation participatory phase for a minimum of 15 days per school was initially organised. Participatory observation days were conducted as the 'field entry' phase. A combination of passive and moderate participation approaches (Fine & Sandstrom, 1999) was used. In the former, we participated as uninvolved observers in daily school activities to gather information about the general climate, daily routines, interactions, class and peer relationships, and general social dynamics in schools. Later, a moderate observation approach was used to develop a rapport and establish a level of familiarity and trust which helped us to conduct the collection of autobiographical life stories with children and young people.

A total of 60 autobiographical life stories were collected. All interviews were recorded, transcribed verbatim, and analysed following the rules of qualitative data analysis (Denzin & Lincoln, 2011) using the NVivo software. The children and young people involved in the study were between 10 and 19 years old, of both genders, of different socioeconomic status, cultural and ethnic backgrounds, and with different academic achievements and personal interests – this also allowed observing intersectionality (Cakir et al., 2020). What followed was the application of focus groups with three to six children/young people where participants discussed selected topics more thoroughly, e.g., migration, multi-culturalism and cultural diversity in school, discrimination, racism, and similar. Altogether, 14 focus groups were conducted with either the same or different children that already participated in the individual interviews.[2]

Othering and migrant children of the Albanian ethnic background

What follows is the analysis of various characteristics of othering practices in the everyday school life of migrant children of the Albanian ethnic back-ground. Our aim was to examine how these practices affect their integration. Although these factors are interrelated, they are presented separately for the purpose of analysis. To contextualise the analysis of othering that follows, it needs to be explained that we refer to the majority of migrants of the Albanian ethnic background in Slovenia, who come mainly from Kosovo and North Macedonia, and to a lesser extent from Albania.[3] They are affili-ated with the Muslim religion (rather than, for example, Orthodox, Catholic, or secular Albanians), are traditional, organised in tribal communities, and have achieved, according to the official statistics, predominantly low levels of education. The latter is particularly common for women. According to the Statistical Office of the Republic of Slovenia, the majority of migrant women with an Albanian ethnic background have completed primary-level educa-tion or less (SURS, 2018). All these characteristics influence the othering perceptions and practices. The children and adolescents from our analysis are thus subject to intersectional othering related to ethnicity, family socioeco-nomic position, religion, and gender.

'Us' and 'them': The existence of binary opposition of in-group and out-group dynamics

The process of othering inherently involves the construction of in-group and out-group dynamics and a hierarchical differentiation between 'us' and 'them'. Compared to other migrant groups in Slovenia, the Albanian ethnic group represents the group that is perceived as the most different and very 'closed', with strong ethnic boundaries (Barth, 1970), as one secondary school student described:

> Albanians, they are very different. I am not saying it just like that, I also have friends who are Albanians and we understand each other very well. But they stick to theirs mostly, they are with their own, everyone sticks to their own.
>
> (Girl, 17, born in Slovenia)

This is also evident from the narratives of school staff, who often emphasise the difference between children of the Albanian ethnic background and other migrant children from the former Yugoslavia. The former are perceived as the most culturally diverse, partly because they speak a language of non-Slavic origin. The primary school headteacher highlights the closed boundaries of children of the Albanian ethnic background and the cultural differences in comparison to other migrant ethnic groups, emphasising that consequently language acquisition and integration are the most difficult challenges for them:

> Those who come from the Albanian-speaking area are particularly held back. The cultural difference is so much greater there. When we talk to children from Serbia or Croatia, we see that our cultural differences aren't so large, we live a similar life, we have a similar culture, we don't have very different religious habits. The language barrier is the most difficult for them to overcome. For others, it's very fast, they overcome these barriers quickly.
>
> (headteacher in a primary school)

However, the language, religion, and other cultural differences are not barriers *per se* but are perceived as problematic especially in relation to this group. The latter is presumably because of their strong in-group orientation and the general perception that they 'do not want to adapt'. This is evident from the next sentence of the headteacher, who states that even children who come from Syria and China, i.e. from a completely different cultural environment:

> [They] overcome the language barrier faster than children who come from Albanian-speaking areas. For Albanian-speaking children it's difficult to integrate because their language is completely different, they have no parallels to draw. So, yes, Albanian speaking children have most difficulties integrating in all aspects, from social to linguistic.
>
> (Headteacher in a secondary school)

Additionally, their communication in the Albanian language was frequently problematised in schools. When asked if there are differences between the various ethnic groups in the use of their own language in school, children of Albanian ethnic background were most often portrayed as those who communicate in their own language and are socialised within a closed group:

> I think it's more the Albanians. They also socialise more with each other. Bosnians also socialise with others. Albanians hang out only with their own.
>
> (Counsellor in a secondary school)

This is perceived as problematic by both school staff and children, as the interview with two Slovenian girls shows:

B: In classroom, I never heard them speak Slovene. Never. And that bothers me.
I: Why?
B: Because … if you came to Slovenia … then you could at least try. Because you can't be in Slovenia and speak only your language. It's a sort of responsibility.
A: Yes, and it gets on my nerves when, for example, the Albanians are sitting in front of us [in class] and they are non-stop shouting in that language.

(Girls, 17, born in Slovenia)

On the other hand, following the children's perception, it seems that those of Albanian ethnic origin not only face the challenge of being accepted by their Slovene peers but are also challenged by migrant peers:

These others that come, for example Bosnians, they are not nice to Albanians. I don't know why.

(Girl, 16, born in Kosovo)

Othering was articulated also by highlighting the differences in educational systems and the distinction between 'our' and 'their' educational system, the latter being perceived as less 'advanced', less proper, and inferior:

…let's say they didn't have P.E., everything was so informal that sometimes I can't believe that this was a proper school. For example, when they give me a school report, but I see that the certificate is from Kosovo, there's no signature, no signature of the headteacher. In Slovenia, this is done completely differently.

(Counsellor in a primary school)

Exclusion and social distancing

In relation to the Albanian migrant community and migrant children, various practices of exclusion and social distancing could be observed. These are often based on stereotypical characteristics ascribed to this group. As stated by a secondary school counsellor, the negative attitude of teachers sometimes leads to exclusion and discriminatory behaviour towards learners of the Albanian ethnic background. In her view, due to their attitudes and perceptions, teachers do not make an effort to include migrant learners and leave them unnoticed during the classes as long as they do not disrupt the learning process. Consequently, teachers exclude them from the school activities. However, it is interesting to observe that the discourse used by teachers simultaneously reproduces stereotypes about these learners behaving inappropriately and disrespectfully.

> I think there could be a more individual approach to teaching. I hope my colleagues don't hear me criticising them, but it seems to me that we still have quite a few teachers who have a negative attitude towards them and don't even bother. If it means that they can't be graded, if they just sleep and sit in class, let them be. However, if something is wrong, of course, if they behave inappropriately and so on, they report them quickly... Because sometimes they do, they are not exactly respectful to teachers. I don't want to make any differences, etc., but these Albanians just can't behave like that.
>
> (Counsellor in a secondary school)

Such exclusionary practices negatively affect the integration of migrant children and reveal the underlying general negative attitudes and stereotypes towards children and youth of Albanian ethnic background, from which educators are not exempt. Our interviews highlighted existing negative perceptions about language learning and motivation, even though teachers' experiences were sometimes different:

> As far as I have heard, it's known that children from Albania are not good at learning the Slovenian language, have no motivation and so on. But I had the first group, three children from Albania, and I must say they were excellent.
>
> (Teacher in a primary school)

One of the teachers problematised the perceived general negative attitude and intolerance of local children towards children of Albanian ethnic background and stressed the importance of changing the discourse at the macro level.

> I see the problem more in local children, since I notice a great deal of intolerance towards everything different. Not just to their Albanian classmates. Maybe we could start doing more about this, but it is a wider problem of our society, politics and so on.
>
> (Teacher in a secondary school)

Friendships present one of the most important elements of integration and a significant foothold in the new society (Grzymała-Kazłowska, 2016). They play a crucial role in adapting to the new environment, overcoming the initial difficulties, helping to learn the language, etc. While the narratives of children and youth report strong in-group ties among children and youth of Albanian ethnic background, they also reveal experiences of exclusion:

> Whenever I try to cooperate, the other children say: No, go baaack, you don't know anything!
>
> (Boy, 10, born in Kosovo)

Similarly, a 13-year-old girl from Kosovo reported that:

> I was always standing outside alone during the breaks. Nobody came to talk to me. I felt very, I don't know, bad. Always, always there were teachers asking me why do I not hang out with somebody? I wanted to, but nobody said anything to me, they didn't talk with me.
>
> (Girl, 13, born in Kosovo)

The exclusion and existing stigma, as well as discrimination, affect their well-being and sense of belonging (Sedmak & Medarić, 2022 *in press*). A teenager of Albanian ethnic background reflects on her negative experiences in school:

> In 6th grade, it was enough for me to be excluded, I was alone. When they said something and laughed, I didn't understand a thing, I always thought it was about me. I remember feeling bad, I cried every night because I didn't want to go to school anymore.
>
> (Girl, 17, born in Albania)

As research shows, it is particularly important for successful integration not only to establish friendships but also to have friends among local children (Piekut et al., 2021). In order to avoid exclusion, to be accepted by schoolmates who are not of Albanian ethnic background, in order to integrate, young people also reported that they want to differentiate themselves from their ethnic group, thus 'rejecting the category of the other' and 'claiming normality' (Jensen, 2011, p. 73).

> I have classmates who are Albanians and these girls said at the beginning what they are and they talked with eachother. At the beginning, I didn't want to hang out with them at all, because I thought that everyone would see it and say 'Oh, look, she's hanging out with her own' and they would have something against it.
>
> (Girl, 17, born in Albania)

The account above reflects the existing stigma and stereotypes among her peers. However, children of Albanian ethnic background sometimes

84   Mateja Sedmak et al.

say that they tend to socialise within their ethnic group because they share the same cultural values and family traditions, and are subject to similar expectations. All these circumstances make it difficult to find sympathy and understanding among local peers.

> Albanians get along more with Albanians than with Slovenes, especially girls. Girls understand better our relationships with family and relatives. They know better what's going on in our world because they are in the same situation. It's easier to share your private matters with someone who belongs to your nation. Slovenes can understand this to some extent, but family matters differ a great deal in Slovenia and Albania. They wouldn't understand what we're going through.
>
> (Girl, 18, born in Kosovo)

In some cases, migrant children and youth of Albanian origin work additionally hard, as a 'survival tactic', to refuse negative perceptions about themselves:

> [classmates] often think that we can't speak Slovenian, but we proved that we can. In fact, in our class, we, foreigners are more successful than Slovenes. Of course, we have more successful Slovenes, but if you look at the majority and consider that we are from abroad, we are very successful and we strive to get good grades.
>
> (Girl, 18, born in Kosovo)

Discursive violence

The narratives of teachers and children also reveal the existence of discursive violence and even second-generation children of Albanian ethnic background report experiences of generally negative behaviour and also slurs derived from ethnic affiliation. Sometimes, these are based on visual differences, such as wearing the headscarf:

> On the street, it often happens to me when I'm with my mom, because my mom wears a scarf. Sometimes, people watch a lot…Many times, when I talk to someone in Albanian, people also shout 'What's wrong with you, Shiptars?!'.[4] I also hear that word at school because they use it as an insult, as a joke. But it's not very nice to say that.
>
> (Girl, 17, parents were born in North Macedonia, she was born in Slovenia)

A primary school counsellor also reports about ethnic-based violence in their school:

> They insult each other with slurs: Bosnian, Albanian, Shiptar.

Othering & Integration: Children and Youth of Albanian Origin   85

Even if these are simple ethnic denominations, they are used in a pejorative way with the aim of insulting and are understood in an extremely negative way.

Religion is often the element of discursive violence, used with the aim of exclusion:

> In elementary school, the problems began. I didn't have a good relationship with boys, not with all boys, but with the leaders. They didn't like me, they didn't want me in the class, but I didn't understand it. I didn't know they didn't want me there. And then they started insulting me because of my religion and all that.
>
> (Girl, 18, born in Kosovo)

The same girl experienced a hostile behaviour from a teacher who took the Charlie Hebdo shooting to accuse her of belonging to 'a religion of terrorism'.

> It was the time of a terrorist attack in France and one teacher attacked me, saying that I was one of them and that I belong to a family of terrorists since we're Muslims.
>
> (Girl, 18, born in Kosovo)

Some children expressed negative and hostile attitudes towards the Albanian community in the interviews, addressing various aspects of hostility:

> I mean they are all so poorly educated. Why do they even come here? Let them stay in Albania and work there.
>
> (Boy, 14, born in Slovenia)

Various stereotypes, such as the perception of the Albanian community as an economic burden on the one hand, and the often-repeated story that migrants steal jobs from the locals on the other, are frequently echoed in the narratives of children. An Albanian girl, upset by this, critically points out the paradoxical views:

> We never talked about it at home, and here, in secondary school, it was the first time that I heard that Roma and Albanians live on welfare. And it's wrong to live on social welfare but at the same time it's wrong to take away jobs from Slovenians. Excuse me, but what is this?!
>
> (Girl, 17, born in Albania)

Like similar othering characteristics, discursive violence in general has a negative impact on the well-being and integration of migrant children and youth of Albanian ethnic background. A plethora of examples when children adopted the strategy to suffer in silence was observed.

> I learnt to live with it. I was always silent when they were mocking me, always. Of course, I was sad but also angry.
>
> (Girl, 17, born in Albania)

The next example shows to what extent children are willing to go in order to become part of the group:

> Once, I was so crazy, I wished to be one of them. One boy pushed me, and I hit the edge of the table. He said that if I won't tell the teacher, they will hang out with me. And I believed him! I didn't tell, although I should have.
>
> (Girl, 17, parents born in North Macedonia, she was born in Slovenia)

On the other hand, it became clear from the interviews that the general situation for many children of Albanian ethnic background would be even worse if it were not for the teacher's advocacy.

> Unless teachers ask them [classmates] to help me, they don't. They never help me.
>
> (Boy, 10, born in Kosovo)

This example illustrates the teacher's role regarding migrant children's well-being and general integration process. However, as illustrated above, teachers are not always helpful, fond, and fair figures.

Conclusion

This article examines the othering discourse and practices toward children and youth of Albanian ethnic background focusing on the three characteristics of othering identified by Kutsenko et al. (2020), i.e. the hierarchically characterised in-group and out-group binary opposition, the exclusion and segregation practices and social distancing (see also López, 2021) based on stigmatisation, symbolic degradation, and stereotyping, as well as the existence of discursive violence. All these could be identified in the discourses and practices of teachers and children in Slovenian educational institutions, but also observed at the macro level through their reports. The perception of Albanian ethnic community as the definitive other is reflected in the observation of a girl who moved to Slovenia from Kosovo:

> Slovenians are open to foreigners, but not to Albanians.

Perceiving this group as subordinate, the existing exclusionary practices and discursive violence significantly affect the integration of migrant children and youth with Albanian ethnic background. For children, integration means, above all, being accepted by their friends and teachers and being part of their class and school (Dežan & Sedmak, 2021; Sedmak, 2021; Sedmak et al., 2020). The narratives presented show that this is often not the case. As it has been demonstrated, the way mass media report about migrants significantly contributes to the process of othering. Although school professionals are able to challenge and refute such effects, observations indicate that more often teachers act in a way that additionally forges migrant children with Albanian ethnic background to their 'outside' position. Instead of providing an equal ground for all learners, the schools in our sample were more often unsuccessful in tackling specific problems migrant children with Albanian ethnic backgrounds have. Consequently, several dimensions of successful integration were compromised, for example, their language acquisition, their well-being, peer relations, academic achievement, and general life satisfaction. It needs to be emphasised that in this article, observations are limited to the educational context, and the outlined experiences describe the specific characteristics of othering. Yet, it is important to highlight that also the coexistence of de-othering discourse and practices could be observed simultaneously. As with the process of othering, members of the educational community have a vital role also in the processes of de-othering. Several interviews highlighted that migrant children with Albanian ethnic background thrive when they are supported by teachers who encourage them to fulfil their potential and present their culture. These teachers overcame the initial concerns and barriers that often appear when one is introduced to Albanian-speaking migrants and arise mostly from language and cultural differences. The practices of de-othering and a more active approach towards the demystification of the others could be used in the future along with addressing existing gaps between integration policies and practices (Dežan & Sedmak, 2020; Medarić et al., 2021) to address the integration of migrant children and youth with Albanian ethnic origin more successfully.

Notes

1 The authors acknowledge the financial support from the part of the *MiCREATE project – Migrant Children and Communities in a Transforming Europe* that has received funding from the European Union's Horizon 2020 research and innovation programme under grant agreement N°822664) and the Slovenian Research Agency (research core funding No. P6–0279).
2 For more information about methodology and results of study among children and young people see Dežan, L. & Sedmak, M. (2021). *National report on qualitative research among newly arrived migrant children, long-term migrant children and local Children: Slovenia.* (Report). Science and Research Centre Koper.
3 There are no official data on the number of Albanian children enrolled in Slovenian schools or on the educational attainment of learners of Albanian origin, as no data is collected regarding the ethnicity of enrolled children. Since 2001, this data has been treated as private and as data that should not be collected.
4 A word 'Shiptar' is used as a negative naming, a slur for Albanians.

References

Barth, F. (1970). *Ethnic Groups and Boundaries: The Social Organization of Culture Difference.* Bergen, Oslo: George Allen & Unwin.

Blasutig, G., Lenarčič, B., Medarić, Z., Sedmak, M., & Zago, M. (2020). Le donne straniere al confine orientale: un'analisi statistica delle principali caratteristiche socio-demografiche. In: D.G. Zotti and O. Urpis (Eds.). *La salute sessuale e riproduttiva delle donne migranti: una prospettiva transfrontaliera.* Milano, Laboratorio Sociologico: Ricerca empirica ed intervento sociale.

Cakir, A., Wolter, S., Liepold, M., & Sauer, B. (2020). Intersectional contestations – the meanings of integration of 'migrant' pupils in Austrian schools. *Annales-Series Historia et Sociologia, 30(4)*, 587–600.

Denzin, N. K. & Lincoln, Y. S. (2011). *The Sage Handbook of Qualitative Research.* London: Sage Publication.

Dežan, L. & Sedmak, M. (2020). Policy and practice: The integration of (newly arrived) migrant children in Slovenian schools. *Annales-Series Historia et Sociologia, 30(4)*, 559–574.

Dežan, L. & Sedmak, M. (2021). *National Report on Qualitative Research among Newly Arrived Migrant Children, Long-term Migrant Children and Local Children: Slovenia.* (Report). Science and Research Centre Koper.

Fielder, G. E. & Catalano, T. (2017). Othering others: Right-wing populism in UK media discourse on "new" immigration. *Faculty Publications: Department of Teaching, Learning and Teacher Education, 255*, 207–234. Retrieved from: http://digitalcommons.unl.edu/teachlearnfacpub/255

Fine, G. A. & Sandstrom, K. L. (1999). *Knowing Children: Participant Observation with Minors.* Newbury Park, CA: SAGE.

Grzymała-Kazłowska, A. (2016). Social anchoring: Immigrant identity, adaptation and integration reconnected? *Sociology, 50(6)*, 1123–1139.

Jensen, S. Q. (2011). Othering, identity formation and agency. *Qualitative Studies, 2(2)*, 63–78.

Klopčič, V., Komac, M., & Kržišnik-Bukić, V. (2003). *Albanci, Bošnjaki, Črnogorci, Hrvati, Makedonci in Srbi v Republiki Sloveniji: ABČHMS v RS: Položaj in status pripadnikov narodov nekdanje Jugoslavije v Republiki Sloveniji.* Ljubljana: Inštitut za narodnostna vprašanja.

Kutsenko, O., Bataeva, E., & Babenko, S. (2020). De-Othering politics and practices of forced migrants in modern society. *Ideology and Politics Journal, 2(26)*, 62–82.

Lavrič, M. & Rutar, T. (2021). General trends in young people's values and attitudes. In: T. Deželan (Ed.), et al. Youth 2020: The position of young people in Slovenia (1st ed., pp. 37–77). Maribor: University of Maribor Press & University of Ljubljana Press.

Lenarčič, B. & Sedmak, M. (2019). Reproductive health of migrant women in Slovenia: State of the art. In: S. Ličen, I. Karnjuš & M. Prosen (Eds.). *Women, Migrations and Health: Ensuring Transcultural Healthcare* (pp. 35–57). Koper: Univerza na Primorskem.

López, D. G. (2021). A phenomenological approach to the study of social distance. *Human Studies, 44*, 171–200.

Mandelc, D. & Gajič, V. (2022). Odnos večinskega prebivalstva mesta Celje do priseljencev albanske narodnosti. *Teorija in praksa, 59(1)*, 115–137.

Medarić, Z., Sedmak, M., Dežan, L., & Gornik, B. (2021). Integration of migrant children in Slovenian schools. *Culture and Education, 33(4),* 758–785.

Piekut, A., Hellesdatter Jacobsen, G., Hobel, P. Sindberg S., & Høegh, T. (2021). *National Report on Qualitative Research Among Newly Arrived Migrant Children, Long-term Migrant Children and Local Children: Denmark.* (Report). University of Southern Denmark.

Said, E. (1978). *Orientalism.* London: Penguin Books.

Sedmak, M. (2020). Requestioning identity: Female descendants of immigrants from former Yugoslavia in Slovenia. In: R. Mirsa (Ed.). *Migration, Trafficking and Gender Construction: Women in Transition.* New Delhi: SAGE.

Sedmak, M., Gornik, B., Medarić, Z., Zadel, M., & Dežan, L. (2020). *Educational Community and School System: Slovenia. Migrant Children and Communities in a Transforming Europe.* (Report). Science and Research Centre Koper. Retrieved from: http://www.micreate.eu/wp-content/uploads/2020/09/D4.1-National-Report-on-Educational-Community_Final_ZRS111.pdf

Sedmak, M., Lenarčič, B, Medarić, Z., & Gornik, B. (2018). *Spolno in reproduktivno zdravje migrantk v Sloveniji: Študija primera treh obalnih občin.* (Report). Science and Research Centre Koper.

Sedmak, M. & Medarić, Z. (2020). La discriminazione istituzionale e la salute sessuale e riproduttiva delle donne migranti. In: G. Delli Zotti & O. Urpis (Eds.). *La salute sessuale e riproduttiva delle donne migranti:una prospettiva transfrontaliera* (pp. 74–93). Milano, Laboratorio Sociologico: Ricerca empirica ed intervento sociale.

Sedmak, M., & Medarić, Z. (2022). Anchoring, feelings of belonging, and the complex identities of migrant teenagers in Slovenia. *Studies in Ethnicity and Nationalism, 22(2),* 99–116.

Spivak, G. C. (1985). The Rani of Sirmur: An essay in reading the archives. *History and Theory, 24(3),* 247–272.

Statistical office of the Republic of Slovenia (SURS). (2018). Retrieved from: https://www.stat.si/statweb/Field/Index/17/104

Vezovnik, A. (2017). Otherness and victimhood in the tabloid press: The case of the "refugee crisis" in Slovenske Novice. *Dve domovini/Two Homelands, 4(5),* 121–135.

Vižintin, M. A. (2018). Developing intercultural education. *Dve domovini/Two Homelands 47,* 89–106.

Žišt, P. (2008). Ekonomski migranti albanske narodnosti v Slovenski Bistrici. [Unpublished seminar paper]. Faculty of Arts, University of Ljubljana.

Chapter 6

Online Learning during a Pandemic and its Impact on Migrant Children in Manchester, UK

"When the School Closed...and being Isolated at Home I Feel Like My Heart is Closed"

Hadjer Taibi, Shoba Arun, Farwa Batool, Aleksandra Szymczyk, and Bogdan Negru

Introduction

According to UNESCO (2020), the COVID-19 pandemic since its beginning in January 2020, has impacted the life and education of an estimated 1.6 billion children in more than 190 countries, thereby making it one of the biggest interruptions to education systems in history. This disruption has particularly had its toll on vulnerable children, increasing the inequalities within education that have already existed prior to the global pandemic. Remote education requires access to technological equipment and a good internet connection (Morgan, 2020), which is not available to all children. Research has shown that in Europe, 6.9 per cent of students do not have access to the internet in their homes (Van Lancker and Parolin, 2020). Disadvantaged groups such as low-income families and migrants are more prone to such inequalities with the social, educational, and economic gap widening during COVID-19. In the UK, Blundell et al. (2021) published a report about the ways in which the pandemic is aggravating inequalities in education and skills as well as socio-economic status and health. Results from the report show that the rates of unemployment drastically increased during the pandemic, raising the number of poorer households. Socio-economic status has always played a role in children's educational achievement as children from low-income households have a lesser chance of achieving higher scores and accessing higher education (Hansen and Hawkes, 2009). This in turn hinders social mobility and widens the gap between poorer and richer individuals.

In times of crisis and during the global pandemic, the impact of the differences in socio-economic status on children's schooling was evident. Andrew et al. (2020) noticed that during the first lockdown in the spring of 2020, children from higher-income families were much more likely to report that their schools provide online classes and access to videoconferencing with teachers. These children also reported that they are more likely to have access

DOI: 10.4324/9781003343141-8

to resources such as online classes, text chatting, and study spaces. In addition to resources like computers and tutors (Benzeval et al., 2020), which prompt them to spend way more time on home learning than children from lower-income households. Migrants and displaced populations, particularly, individuals who already faced pre-existing, socio-economic, health, and educational inequalities and vulnerabilities have been significantly affected by the global pandemic (Jourdain et al., 2021). In the UK, research has shown that migrant children and families face many challenges at schools (Manzoni and Rolfe, 2019), including a lack of familiarity with the UK education system such as expectations around the level of parental engagement, feelings of isolation because of cultural differences, and language barriers. With the outbreak of coronavirus and the school closures, the challenges become heightened. The safety restrictions and social distancing measures forced children to be separated from their peers who found themselves not only having to deal with the new threat of the virus but also having to adapt to different learning environments. Children, families, and teachers alike were put under the enormous pressure of having to switch to online platforms in a very short time and without any prior planning. In the following section, light will be shed on some of the key challenges that teachers and students faced upon the transition to online learning.

Online learning during COVID-19

By the end of March 2020 and as a response to the pandemic face-to-face classrooms were replaced by online platforms. Online learning was the government's attempt to avoid learning loss, that is the loss of knowledge and skills due to a discontinuity in students' education (Atteberry and McEachin, 2021), and to ensure continued effective learning. In an era of rapid technological developments and digitalisation, considerable research into the challenges and opportunities offered by the online in educational contexts was conducted (McFarlane, 2019). As Redmond (2015) and Reid (2012) noticed, online learning has been transforming traditional face-to-face learning, shifting students' and teachers' roles (teachers becoming learning facilitators and students taking more control over the learning process), and enhancing teachers' digital competence. On the other hand, online learning was also found to incur feelings of anxiety, lack of motivation, frustration, and raise feelings of emotional resistance (Palloff and Pratt, 2013). This is mainly due to the lack of physical interaction and lack of familiarity with the online settings. Online learning also requires advanced and thorough planning which was not possible during the unprecedented COVID-19 crisis (Barbour et al., 2020). Considering the short notice that was given to teachers and schools and the short time in which the move online was expected to happen, online learning proved to be challenging. Many teachers reported their low confidence, autonomy, and need for more support to teach online (Yan and Wang, 2022) as well as an increasing level of stress (MacIntyre et al., 2020), daunting amounts of workload (Darmody et al., 2020: 34), and lower levels of well-being (Burke and Dempsey, 2020). Students, on the other hand, besides challenges with a potential complex home environment, mental health problems, and lack of motivation (Liang et al., 2020), were also left susceptible to many equity issues as a result of the shift to online learning.

Increasingly, research is showing that children and young people are facing high levels of vulnerabilities and inequalities due to school closures and the shift to online learning (Darmody et al., 2020). This is mainly because of the uneven access to resources such as computers and the internet, with children from disadvantaged socio-economic backgrounds exhibiting significant inequalities (Coleman, 2021: 3). The digital divide, that is access, or lack thereof, to digital technologies (Coleman, 2021: 9), was not only pointed out within individual children and families but also between schools. Schools in urban areas, for instance, had better accessibility to high-speed broadband, they also varied in their accessibility to digital devices, and the level of their support to pupils (Darmody et al., 2020: 34). Montacute and Cullinane (2021) found out that almost half the number of state schools in England were only able to provide computers to half or fewer pupils within the school. Moreover, in the UK, in their study, Major et al. (2020) reported that during the first lockdown of March 2020, 74 per cent of pupils in private schools were benefitting from daily, full-day, online school days compared to only 38 per cent of pupils from state schools. Within state schools, there was also a clear divide between children from higher-income households whose parents reported they are much more likely to receive help from their schools as opposed to children from lower-income households (Andrew et al., 2020).

Research has also shown that children from disadvantaged backgrounds received little to no support from their parents to help them with the new learning technologies because the parents themselves lacked the necessary skills (Coleman, 2021: 25). Evidently, the shift to online learning has exposed and deepened some of the already existing inequalities. Children from disadvantaged backgrounds, in particular, were the most affected with potentially long-standing consequences (Andrew et al., 2020; Eyles et al., 2020). Although there is a significant body of literature on the impact of COVID-19 on children's education, research addressing the impact of the emerging inequalities on disadvantaged groups, particularly migrant children, is scarce. In the following, special attention to the impact of the pandemic on children and migrant children will be given.

Migrant children in times of crisis

The COVID-19 pandemic affected the lives of millions of children and adolescents around the world. This unprecedented public health emergency disrupted every aspect of children's day-to-day lives including their educational and social lives. As a result of school closures, separation from peers, limited social interactions, and reduced physical activities, many children and young people were at risk of increased feelings of loneliness, isolation, stress and anxiety about their education, besides mental and psychological challenges (UNICEF, 2021). To cope with the changes and the challenges, children and young people were spending larger amounts of time online (Ofcom, 2020). The American Academy of Child and Adolescent Psychiatry (2020) noted that on-screen time among children increased by 6 hours above the recommended hours. This meant further risks to children's physical and mental health can emerge such as sleep problems, myopia, and difficulties in concentration (Pandya and Lodha, 2021; Singh and Balhara, 2021). The lack of structure resulting from the pandemic also had an impact on the time that children spent on their learning. In a study of Children's Media Lives during the lockdown, 14 children across the UK were interviewed by the Office of Communications [Ofcom] (2020) to unravel their online and digital activities during the period of quarantine. Findings showed that children spent less time on schoolwork when compared to the time they would spend in regular term-time. Parents of these children also were struggling to balance between supporting their children with their online learning and their remote work. That besides the lack of extra-curricular activities resulted in children spending more time on their electronic devices and more time isolated in their rooms (Ofcom, 2020).

Although COVID-19 impacted the lives of all children around the world, it has had particularly devastating effects on vulnerable and disadvantaged children and young people. The pandemic put extra burdens on families that already struggled financially. School closures meant increased costs of living as children would, for instance, no longer receive the free school meals. This also meant that children were at higher risks of harm, neglect, abuse, and exploitation, especially with limited access to support services which switched to working remotely (Barnardo's, 2020). Children from low-income families with limited access to laptops, phones, and the internet were also at risk of stigma and shame (The Children's Society, 2020). Inequalities exacerbated by the pandemic were also evident in how children from Black, Asian and ethnic minority backgrounds were more likely to experience feelings of anxiety and stress. and seek help for suicidal thoughts (Barnardo's, 2020). One particular group that was at higher risks of financial struggles, discrimination, stigmatisation, social isolation, and mental health challenges is migrant children and refugees. Refugees and migrants would usually rely on specialist services in order to access their rights and entitlements, however, as a result of the immense pressure put on these services because of COVID-19, accessibility was restricted. Incidents of increased poverty, issues of housing, linguistic barriers, and lack of familiarity with the education and health systems of the host country would put refugees and migrants at increased levels of vulnerability and make migrant children among the most disadvantaged groups during a global health crisis (The Children's Society, 2020).

The pandemic has complicated matters for children from migrant backgrounds in many aspects of their lives including their learning. Prior to the COVID-19 crisis, migrant children already faced many challenges in education; this included language barriers, lack of qualified teachers who speak their mother tongue, and teachers who are trained in intercultural competence (Child-Up, 2020). Migrant children also struggled with the negative stereotyping of their teachers, their parents not being familiar with the schools' systems which meant less support, and not being able to benefit from kindergarten and pre-school classes (Child UP, 2020). These factors greatly affected migrant children's achievement outcomes together with the differences in the socio-economic and educational backgrounds of their families. During the lockdown, these inequalities were made even worse as schools for migrant children do not only represent a space for learning but also a space for socialisation and integration. School closures interrupted this process of integration by separating migrant children from the mainstream population. This ultimately would have a negative effect on their mental health and school performance (Child UP, 2020). Additionally, after school closures, migrant children's English language skills were also affected. Teachers of English as an additional language (EAL) reported a decrease in the language skills for children acquiring English (Demie et al., 2020). Furthermore, because access to additional support and quality online learning was determined by the technical equipment and resources, migrant children's educational experiences were further affected. As such and taking into consideration the unprecedented challenges and exacerbated inequalities that migrant children faced during the COVID-19 crisis, a focus on these issues to find new ways of reducing the inequalities becomes a pressing need. The aim of this chapter is to prioritise the unheard voices of a disadvantaged group and stimulate their sustainable integration.

Approaches for the integration of migrant children

In the state of the highly diverse, mobile, and modern societies, talks about 'integration' have been long echoing. With the growing trends of global migration, the concept of integration has attracted much scholarly attention (Grzymala-Kazlowska and Phillimore, 2018). In the field of migration studies, there is no agreed-upon definition of integration, however, many scholars draw attention to the necessity of making the distinction between integration and assimilation (e.g. Phillimore, 2012). As opposed to assimilation, which is a process of fully absorbing the dominant culture and risking the abandonment of the heritage culture and identity (Smith et al., 2019), the EU foregrounds an understanding of integration as 'a dynamic, two-way process of mutual accommodation by all immigrants and residents' (European Commission, 2004). A process that aims at the inclusion of migrant groups in the host societies to create social cohesion and promote equality (Rutter, 2015). Many scholars have argued that the goal of integration can only be attained through equal access to quality education and life-long learning for migrant children (AbuJarour, 2020). Therefore, the successful integration of migrant children at schools is vital for their successful integration in the host societies.

Nevertheless, this process of integration is not hassle-free (Koehler and Schneider, 2019). At schools, besides issues of language barriers, cultural differences, socio-economic factors, and parental influence, migrant children's integration can also be hindered by the dominant approaches to integration and the adult-centred discourse around it.

Sime (2017) argues that current approaches to integration focus on concepts of community, locality, migrants' identity, and participation in the host society and holds migrants accountable for the process of their own integration and withholds any responsibility from receiving societies (Spencer, 2011). Although these approaches acknowledge the challenges that migrant children face, for instance, hostility and segregation at school (Devine, 2009) poorer educational attainment, and lower school performance (OECD, 2012), they are adult focused. They put adults in a position of power and decision-making which results in children's voices being marginalised (Sime, 2017: 5). Adult-centred approaches to integration had often stripped away migrant children's agency and depicted them as victims of migration, powerless, and passive. This led to calls for changing the discourse into one that empowers them and stimulates their agency. A child-centred approach aims at understanding children's individual experiences of migration from their perspectives and prioritises their needs and voices (Sancho-Gil et al., 2021). To date, very little attention has been given to the study of migrant children's experiences (Sime, 2017). As such, in this chapter, instead of looking at migrant children as 'trapped in a miserable structural conflict of living between two cultures' (Mannitz, 2005: 23), the aim is to focus on children's voices, agency, and resilience in issues that matters to them such as their inclusion in their schools and in the societies they inhabit. To meet this aim, this chapter addresses the following research questions: (1) How did the COVID-19 pandemic and the switch to online learning affect migrant children's integration into schools? And (2) how can the employment of a child-centred approach to study the learning experiences of children during the pandemic inform and contribute to our understanding of migrant children's integration?

The study

The data presented in this chapter is part of the Migrant Children and Communities in a Transforming Europe (MiCREATE) project, which was funded by the European Union through its Horizon 2020 research programme. The MiCREATE researchers from 12 European countries, including researchers from Manchester in the United Kingdom, have conducted research activities with more than 3,000 migrant children in order to understand the contemporary experiences and challenges they face and how they can be best supported within the community and their educational environment. The project aims to promote the inclusion of migrant children by adopting a child-centred approach to migrant children's integration on educational and policy levels as well as in research. That is, to develop a policy framework that has the child's well-being and active participation at its heart and educational practices that stimulate migrant children's agency for their integration, research should be conducted through methods that recognise children as the most relevant source of information (Gornik and Sedmak, 2021). To do so, different methods were deployed including participant observation, art-based methods, and narrative interviews. The focus was on methods that keep children in the central position of the data collection and analysis processes.

During the COVID-19 pandemic, however, one of the main points of interest that emerged from the situation was how online learning and school closures affected the integration of school children with migrant backgrounds. Therefore, MiCREATE researchers in Manchester conducted a sub-study between November and December 2021, with 13 children aged 14–15 from a public secondary school in Manchester (see Table 6.1). The aim of the sub-study was to explore the impact of school closures and distance learning on children's learning processes, integration, inclusion, well-being, and mental health. Data were elicited from the children through semi-structured interviews which were conducted by a member of staff at the school.

The inclusion criteria for recruiting participants for this study was newly arrived migrant children, that is children who arrived in the UK within the past five years, who are still in the process of getting acquainted with the schools' environment as well the host society. The disruption and interruption caused by COVID-19, therefore, could have a greater impact on the education and integration of this particular group of migrants, hence they can be more prone to social inequalities. We aimed at understanding their needs and struggles from their perspective and acknowledging the best ways to supporting them as they themselves see the best fit for that purpose. With the help of school, children who met the criteria were recruited and written consent was obtained from them and their guardians to participate in the study after explaining to them the purpose and the objectives of the project. Data were elicited from the children through semi-structured interviews which were audio recorded and then transcribed. All personal data were removed and completely anonymised, and participants' names were replaced by pseudonyms. Data were coded and analysed using a thematic analysis framework (Braun and Clarke, 2006).

In terms of methodological ways of engaging critically and reflexively with a child-centred approach, we move away from a binary researcher–participant process. We give attention to the complexities of educational researcher positionality through both practice and identity. Moving away from the notion that researcher is often seen as homogenous, we focus on critical self-analysis in two ways. First, with all members of the research process being of migrant backgrounds, and non-foreign UK born, we bring in a diverse outlook on migration through intersectional identities, theoretical knowledge and linguistic orientation that act as reflexive and reflective tools to explore how migration affects and shapes children both as migrants and pupils. For this, we draw on Roger et al. (2018)'s finding that researcher identities are determiners of positive and negative emotions of belonging and self-confidence. Following Dennis (2018), rather than just 'asking' pre-prepared fixed questions, we strive to base the research process on participation and co-creation of dialogue to establish trust, truth-telling and interaction (See Yoon and Uliassi, 2022).

So, in the current study, the decision to recruit a teacher as a researcher was a strategic one, based on the premise that as a staff member with deep connections with students, the teacher would have high levels of rapport with the young people. Also, given the troubling times during which these interviews were conducted, it was felt that researchers asking such personal questions may pose additional distress to the young people. There are pitfalls of using a teacher as a researcher, namely that the young people may feel compelled to participate and therefore less able to access their rights to consent and withdraw. To overcome this issue, we ensured that young people received information about the study from the research team. For example, a week prior to

Table 6.1 Participants' Socio-demographic Information

No.	Participant	Age	Gender	Country of Origin	Time in the UK
1	C1	15	Male	Kuwait	4 years
2	C2	15	Male	Pakistan	6/7 months
3	C3	14	Male	Kuwait	2/3 years
4	C4	15	Female	Pakistan	1 year
5	C5	14	Male	Pakistan	5 years ago
6	C6	14	Female	Spain	3 years
7	C7	14	Male	Kuwait	2 years
8	C8	15	Female	Pakistan	2/3 years
9	C9	15	Female	Norway	2/3 years
10	C10	15	Male	Kuwait	2/3 years
11	C11	14	Male	Iraq	1/2 years
12	C12	15	Male	Kurdistan/Norway	7/8 months
13	C13	15	Female	Syria	4/5 years

the interviews, the teacher informed young people about the study using a script the researchers had prepared. Before the interview, the teacher played the young people a video of the researchers once again explaining the study, its purpose, their rights to consent and withdraw at any time they wish, and information related to what will happen with their data. In this interview, the researchers emphasised that the interviews are designed to elicit their views and opinions and that there are no right or wrong answers. The young people were also given this information in the form of an information sheet. It is anticipated that this will have helped to mitigate the power dynamics that naturally exist in the teacher and pupil relationship.

Findings

Interviews with migrant children during the COVID-19 pandemic and schools' closure highlighted the role of schools not only for learning but as places for socialisation and integration. Findings show that school closures during the pandemic and the switch to online learning had an impact on both children's learning as well as their well-being. The findings presented in this section will first shed light on the struggles of migrant children during the pandemic, which ultimately affected their integration. After that, we will also present some of the children's suggested solutions on how to tackle and overcome the issues emerging as a result of the global pandemic.

Grappling with forced social isolation

The pandemic affected the livelihood of millions of people around the globe causing disruptions and changes to social activities and everyday life practices. As a result of the safety and social distancing measures, many children and young people gave up outdoor activities and meeting with their friends and sometimes had to find solace in online:

> I just play outside, but like, when pandemic came, I can't go outside with my friends, and I can't play with them.
>
> (C8, Female, Pakistan, 15yrs)

> If you're going to stay like in one room you feel like you're in a prison
>
> (C1, Male, Kuwait, 15yrs)

> I used to go and play a lot with my friends but now I spent the whole day playing video games and stuff like that.
>
> (C2, Male, Pakistan, 15yrs)

During the lockdown, schools were closed, and many forms of social gatherings were prohibited. People were not allowed to leave their homes except

Online Learning during a Pandemic and its Impact   99

for very limited purposes such as shopping for essentials and physical exercise once a day. The impact of this kind of forced social isolation had a significant impact on children's mental health and well-being:

> When the school closed it and being isolated at home, I feel like my heart is closed. You can't breathe and you feel like you're being a little bit Crazy, because like, at home, you don't have nothing do. Finish online lesson, like sometimes your friend is not going outside. Like going to other countries, you stay at home alone. Sometimes your family are not at home. Your brother has like school and your mom, and your dad are not at home. Like, you feel like Lonely.
>
> (C11, Male, Iraq, 14yrs)

Feelings of loneliness and isolation were recurrent themes in many of the interviews. The loss of in-person and physical contact with friends, peers, and close family, disturbed children's social lives. Some children felt they lost their confidence, especially because the online space was not a space where they could get the support they needed:

> I can't tell my friends or someone else and online telling people stuff, it's weird and it's strange, I don't know.
>
> (C1, Male, Kuwait, 15yrs)

Feelings of dread and what seemed like a never-ending and continuous social isolation cycle left many young people frustrated and immensely affected their social lives, especially for those for whom the school was the only place for socialisation. This at times was aggravated by the lack of access to digital means or lack of support from family, who in turn struggled with their own digital literacy skills:

> I was feeling like… I didn't know isolation was like that. I thought it was just one week or two weeks and then it was more and more and more. The learning, the teachers didn't do online because it was like… I didn't have Teams. My sister did not know about it. My sister used to teach me at home the subjects, most of the subjects.
>
> (C9, Female, Norway, 15yrs)

It seems that overall young people's experiences were marked with negativity as is demonstrated by the word cloud in Figure 6.1.

The challenges of online learning

During the interviews, children emphasised that they preferred being at school for learning and reported that their experience with online learning

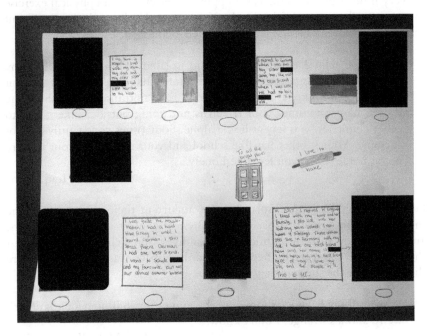

Figure 6.1 Is a collection of words young people used in their interviews to describe their feelings during the pandemic

was unpleasant. All children stated that it was more difficult to learn online and that they felt their educational attainment was affected by the switch:

> In the school, you learn like more than you learn at home.
> (C1, Male, Kuwait, 15yrs)

> Because we can't learn in school, it's more hard to learn at home… Because in school its better, I can get help from teachers.
> (C13, Male, Syria, 15yrs)

> So basically, I forget what I learnt in Year 9.
> (C4, Female, Pakistan, 15yrs)

> Because when I was at home, in lockdown, I didn't learn anything.
> (C12, Male, Kurdistan/Norway, 15yrs)

> I think it affected, not only me but a lot of people and we lost a lot of time, we wasted so much time that we are bad at our level now…I think if you want to learn better, you have to be at school.
> (C2, Male, Pakistan, 15yrs)

For newly arrived migrant children, as is the case in this study, the struggles and difficulties are exacerbated, especially because they are still in the process of becoming familiar with the educational system in their schools.These newcomers were burdened with the extra issue of language barriers. Many of the children interviewed reported on how schools' closure impacted their learning because they struggled with their language skills and in some cases, it affected their English language learning itself:

> Because I was new here and it was lockdown, and I don't speak English.
> (C4, Female, Pakistan, 15yrs)

> It's the chance to and first time to like, to understand from the online and the, you know, when your English is not every well. So, that's the challenge. It was challenging, sir.
> (C10, Male, Kuwait, 15yrs)

> Yeah. I'm not learning English more, yeah
> (C7, Male, Kuwait, 14yrs)

This same issue of language barrier might have prevented some parents from adequately supporting their children with their homework as in the case of the below child:

> Because like my father and my mother is old and them can't speak English, and I have a brother, some brother like that work, they have job.
> (C7, Male, Kuwait, 14yrs)

Language was not the only challenge to online learning that migrant children experienced. In one case, it was also reported that technical problems might have an effect on the quality of online learning such as unreliable internet:

> Mostly, because like sometimes I have a problem with the internet.
> (C11, Male, Iraq, 14yrs)

Another child stated that even if they struggled with understanding the material, they might feel reluctant to ask the teacher for help online. This is because the child felt more self-aware of how this would make the teacher feel:

> Some of the pupils maybe are struggling to study at home because of the online learning, but to learn in school it will make it easier to learn. I feel like to learn at school it's easier than at home because online if you ask the teacher every time, she will stop and explain and it will be boring for her. But here, she can ask me every time.
> (C9, Female, Norway, 15yrs)

Online learning can also lead to reducing children's ability to focus. The physical absence of teachers might result in children's loss of interest as well as lack of structure:

> Because like learning at home, you can't learn when there are like screens or something, because the teacher is not like in front of you and then just telling you what you have to do... Like you don't learn too much. You know like sometimes, when you're at home and reading you do ... sometimes, you don't focus on the teacher, because you know what? You know what you do? You're at home. Like some kids playing with the phone and doing their lessons...Yeah, because you've got your mind is going to go to other things you have to do because you stay at home, and he's not seeing me, he's not listening to me...Yeah it's harder to concentrate, yeah, but at school, you don't have nothing to play with there, you have to concentrate on the teacher.
>
> (C11, Male, Iraq, 14yrs)

Tackling the pandemic's challenges: Children's perspectives

Having presented some of the challenges that were shared during the interviews by participants, in this section, we focus on what children think about how these challenges can be tackled. To help with pupils' well-being, C2 below suggests raising awareness among children and young people at schools by creating an inclusive, shared, and safe space for all children where they can learn about mental health issues:

> Okay, so we can't help everyone, but we have to try to help people that have problems because some are good for life, because of COVID, there were a lot of suicides and I don't know, maybe they could have made it a special lesson, where we have to talk about how do we feel, an extra lesson for our online classes, where everyone could join.
>
> (C2, Male, Pakistan, 15yrs)

Besides designing lessons that would help children understand the intricacies of well-being and creating a space where they can share their experiences and struggles, professional help should also be made available to children and be easily accessible at schools as well as at home as one child suggested:

> My opinion is they need a psychologist in school or at home so they can help the kid.
>
> (C6, Female, Spain, 14yrs)

For children who struggle with the English language, more time can be allocated to their learning of the language. Issues related to linguistic discrimination as well as bullying and cyberbullying should also be high-lighted and given more attention:

> So, in school, we need to give one day, for that person who doesn't speak English and we need to teach them, and we need to check if they are being bullied or not about their speech and online, we need to give more time to that one.
>
> (C4, Female, Pakistan, 15yrs)

These suggested solutions can still be relevant to the aftermath of the pandemic even with the gradual back-to-normal of everyday life in schools. This is because some of the effects can be long-lasting and require to be addressed and talked about even if we are now approaching a post-pandemic era. Furthermore, they can serve as a lesson for schools and societies in the case of similar events in future.

Discussion and conclusion

Schools' closure and the shift to online learning reshaped the practices of everyday life, education, and social life. Findings presented in this chapter shed light on migrant children's struggles both in their education and their social life during the pandemic and they accentuated the role of schools in children's socialisation and integration processes for newly arrived children particularly. During the lockdown, the day-to-day practices of migrant children and young people changed and many of them experienced feelings of isolation and lack of support with this change. Such social isolation has an impact on how migrants form meaningful, nurturing social bridges and bonds in the host country (Barker, 2021: 37). According to Barker (2021), successful social integration for newcomers requires the fostering of meaningful social bonds (ties to co-ethnic, co-religious, and co-national communities), social bridges (ties to the different, diverse groups in the community), and social links (links to the structures of the state). The formation of such social connections is essential for migrants in order to build trust and shared values in the host society to function effectively. For newly arrived children and young people who are yet to form such social connections, schools are an important resource and space where social bridges, bonds, and links can be built and maintained. Thus, schools' closure and the forced social isolation may leave a severe and long-lasting impact on their social integration.

The damaging psychosocial impact of COVID-19 on newly arrived children that was evident in Section 6.1 of the findings was also extended to children's learning. Children in this study reported many challenges to their online learning that often confirmed challenges reported in previous studies; namely learning loss (Atteberry and McEachin, 2021), lack of motivation and feelings of boredom (Liang et al., 2020), lack of access to quality internet (Morgan, 2020). Because of the lack of familiarity with the new learning setting and the absence of face-to-face interaction, pupils might also be more self-aware and reserved to ask for support and help from their teachers. These challenges were amplified in the case of migrant children as findings suggest. Online learning increased children's struggles, especially regarding their English language learning which is essential for their integration. Language is a cognitive as well as a social phenomenon and with schools' closure, children missed out on the opportunity of learning English collectively in the classroom. Language classrooms are important sites for fostering social inclusion and active participation and citizenship as well as sites where pupils can learn about the host country and build connections beyond the classroom (Bednarz, 2017: 80; Barker, 2021: 37). This coupled with having much less exposure to English at home would put EAL pupils at a disadvantaged position (Sutton, 2020) and may result in increased existing inequalities in educational attainment in the long-term.

Methodologically, we focus on the principle of researcher as instrument (following Creswell, 2009; Yoon and Uliassi, 2022) for enriching educational practice, and instrumentalising researcher positionality more reflexively (Soh et al., 2020). With the strategic use of research positionality and identity within a child-centred approach in this study, we were able to foreground children's understandings of, and reflections on, the impact of COVID-19 on their learning and well-being. This is particularly important because children are more likely to experience the impact of the pandemic for years to come. The inequalities and gaps created and aggravated by this health crisis are to be traced in their educational and career prospects in future. Echoing the voices of children and young people and including it in the pandemic discourse was also through listening to their suggestions for improvement and addressing the issues. Pupils stressed their need for an inclusive and safe space to address their particular struggles and challenges with access to specialised and professional help with their well-being and mental health as well as their struggles with language skills. These findings might help teachers, policymakers, and practitioners in understanding the educational and social struggles and needs of migrant children. Although such challenges emerged and were highlighted by the pandemic, it is important to address them during and post the pandemic, especially because their imprint on migrant children's lives is lasting and would have an impact on their integration and inclusion and equal opportunities to active participation in the society.

References

AbuJarour, S. A. (2020) 'Social inclusion of refugees through digital learning: Means, needs, and goals.' In *Proceedings of the Pacific Asia Conference on Information Systems* (PACIS), Dubai, UAE (pp. 20–24).

American Academy of Child and Adolescent Psychiatry (2020) '*Media Habits During COVID-19: Children & Teens on Screens in Quarantine.*' [Accessed on 24/03/2022] https://www.aacap.org/App_Themes/AACAP/Docs/resource_libraries/covid-19/Screen-Time-During-COVID.pdf

Andrew, A., Cattan, S., Costa-Dias, M., Farquharson, C., Kraftman, L., Krutikova, S., Phimister, A. and Sevilla, A. (2020) 'Learning during the lockdown: real-time data on children's experiences during home learning.' Briefing Note. Available online at: https://www.ifs.org.uk/publications/14848

Atteberry, A. and McEachin, A. (2021) 'School's out: The role of summers in understanding achievement disparities.' *American Educational Research Journal*, 58(2), 239–282.

Barbour, M., LaBonte, R., Kelly, K., Hodges, C., Moore, S., Lockee, B., Trust, T. and Bond, M. (2020) 'Understanding pandemic pedagogy: Differences between emergency remote, remote, and pnline teaching.' *Canadian eLearning Network*. https://k12sotn.ca/wp-content/uploads/2020/12/understanding-pandemic-pedagogy.pdf

Barker, M., (2021) 'Social integration in social isolation: Newcomers' integration during the COVID-19 pandemic.' *New Horizons in Adult Education and Human Resource Development*, 33(2), 34–45.

Barnardo's. (2020) 'Supporting the hidden victims of COVID-19: Lessons from the first wave.' https://www.barnardos.org.uk/research/supporting-hidden-victims-covid-19-lessons-first-wave

Bednarz, F. (2017) 'Professional and social integration of migrants and language learning: convergences and challenges at the European level'. *The Linguistic Integration of Adult Migrants/L'intégration linguistique des migrants adultes: Some lessons from research/Les enseignements de la recherche*, edited by Jean-Claude Beacco, Hans-Jürgen Krumm, David Little and Philia Thalgott, Berlin, Boston: De Gruyter Mouton, pp. 75–82. https://doi.org/10.1515/9783110477498-010

Benzeval, M., Borkowska, M., Burton, J., Crossley, T. F., Fumagalli, L., Rabe, B. and Read, B. (2020) 'Briefing note COVID-19 *survey: Home schooling.* Understanding Society at the Institute for Social and Economic Research.' Briefing Note. Available online at: https://ideas.repec.org/p/ese/ukhlsp/2020-12.html

Blundell, R., Cribb, J., McNally, S., Warwick, R. and Xu, X. (2021) 'Inequalities in education, skills, and incomes in the UK: The implications of the COVID-19 pandemic.' *Institute for Fiscal Studies.* https://ifs.org.uk/inequality/inequalities-in-education-skills-and-incomes-in-the-uktheimplications-of-the-covid-19-pandemic

Braun, V. and Clarke, V. (2006) 'Using thematic analysis in psychology.' *Qualitative Research in Psychology*, 3(2), 77–101.

Burke, J. and Dempsey, M. (2020) 'Covid-19 practice in primary schools in Ireland report.' 10.13140/RG.2.2.14091.03369.

Child-Up (2020) 'The achievment gap: Obstacles and opportunities in the integration of migrant- background children in schools – CHILD UP practice analysis.' https://www.child-up.eu/wp-content/uploads/2022/03/CHILD-UP-MS9.pdf

Coleman, V. (2021) 'Digital divide in UK education during COVID-19 pandemic: Literature review.' Cambridge Assessment Research Report. https://www.cambridgeassessment.org

Creswell, J. (2009). *Research Design: Qualitative, Quantitative, and Mixed Methods Approaches* (3rd ed.). Thousand Oaks, CA: Sage.

Darmody, M., Smyth, E. and Russell, H. (2020) 'The implications of the COVID-19 pandemic for policy in relation to children and young people.' *ESRI Survey and Statistical Report Series*, 94, https://www.esri.ie/system/files/publications/SUSTAT94_3.pdf

Demie, F., Hau, A., Bellsham-Revell, A. and Gay, A. (2020) 'The impact of school closures on pupils with English as an additional language.' https://www.lambeth.gov.uk/rsu/sites/www.lambeth.gov.uk.rsu/files/the_impact_of_school_closures_on_pupils_with_english_as_an_additional_language_2022_0.pdf

Dennis, B. (2018). Validity as research praxis: A study of self-reflection and engagement in qualitative inquiry. *Qualitative Inquiry*, 24(2), 109–118. https://doi.org/10.1177800416686371

Devine, D. (2009) 'Mobilising capitals? Migrant children's negotiation of their everyday lives in school.' *British Journal of Sociology of Education*, 30(5), 521–535.

European Commission. (2004) '*Common Principles of Integration.*' Retrieved from https://www.temaasyl.se/Documents/EUdokument/Kommisionsdokument/De%20europeiska%20grundprinciperna%20f%C3%B6r%20integration.pdf

Eyles, A., Gibbons, S. and Montebruno, P. (2020) 'Covid-19 school shutdowns: What will they do to our children's education?' *A CEP Covid-19 analysis Briefing note No. 001.* 2020. http://eprints.lse.ac.uk/104675/3/Eyles_covid_19_school_shutdowns_published.pdf

Gornik, B. and Sedmak, M. (2021) 'The child-centred approach to the integration of migrant children: The MiCREATE project.' *Migrant Children's Integration and Education in Europe*, 99. https://www.researchgate.net/publication/352019076_The_Child-Centred_Approach_to_the_Integration_of_Migrant_Children_The_MiCREATE_Project

Grzymala-Kazlowska, A. and Phillimore, J. (2018) 'Introduction: Rethinking integration. New perspectives on adaptation and settlement in the era of super-diversity.' *Journal of Ethnic and Migration Studies*, 44(2), 179–196.

Hansen, K. and Hawkes, D. (2009) 'Early childcare and child development.' *Journal of Social Policy*, 38(2), 211–239.

Jourdain, J., Bertini, R., Arnold, D. and Rossi, L. (2021) *Assessing the Socio-economic Impact of COVID-19 on Migrants and Displaced Populations in the Middle East and North Africa.*

Koehler, C. and Schneider, J. (2019) 'Young refugees in education: The particular challenges of school systems in Europe.' *Comparative Migration Studies*, 7(1), 1–20.

Liang, S. W., Chen, R. N., Liu, L. L., Li, X. G., Chen, J. B., Tang, S. Y. and Zhao, J. B. (2020) The psychological impact of the COVID-19 epidemic on guangdong college students: The difference between seeking and not seeking psychological help. *Frontiers in Psychology.* 2020 Sep 4, 11, 2231. doi: 10.3389/fpsyg.2020.02231. PMID: 33013582; PMCID: PMC7499802.

Macintyre, P., Gregersen, T. and Mercer, S. (2020) 'Language teachers' coping strategies during the Covid-19 conversion to online teaching: Correlations with stress, well-being and negative emotions.' *System.* 94, 102352. 10.1016/j.system.2020.102352.

Major, L. E., Eyles, A. and Machin, S. (2020) 'Generation COVID: Emerging work and education inequalities. A CEP COVID-19 analysis. Paper No. 011.' *Centre for Economic Performance.*

Mannitz, S. (2005) *Coming of Age as the Third Generation: Children of Immigrants in Berlin. Children and Migration: From Experience to Agency.* Bielefeld: Transcript Verlag, pp. 23–52.

Manzoni, C. and Rolfe, H. (2019) 'How schools are integrating new migrant pupils and their families.' *National Institute of Economic and Social Research,* https://www.niesr.ac.uk/wp-content/uploads/2021/10/MigrantChildrenIntegrationFinalReport.pdf

McFarlane, A. E. (2019) 'Devices and desires: Competing visions of a good education in the digital age.' *British Journal of Educational Technology,* 50(3), 1125–1136.

Montacute, R. and Cullinane, C. (2021) *Research Brief: January 2021: Learning in Lockdown.* London: Sutton Trust. https://dera.ioe.ac.uk/id/eprint/37194

Morgan, H. (2020) 'Best practices for implementing remote learning during a pandemic.' *The Clearing House: A Journal of Educational Strategies, Issues and Ideas,* 93(05/03), 134–140.

OECD. (2012), *Untapped Skills: Realising the Potential of Immigrant Students,* Paris: PISA, OECD Publishing, https://doi.org/10.1787/9789264172470-en

Ofcom. (2020) 'Ofcom children's media lives: Life in lockdown.' *Ofcom.* https://www.ofcom.org.uk/__data/assets/pdf_file/0024/200976/cml-life-in-lockdown-report.pdf

Palloff, R. M., & Pratt, K. (2013) 'Lessons from the virtual classroom.' *International Journal of Information and Communication Technology Education,* 10(2), 93–96.

Pandya, A. K. and Lodha, P. (2021) 'Social connectedness, excessive screen time during COVID-19 and mental health: A review of current evidence.' *Frontiers in Human Dynamics,* 3, 684137. 10.3389/fhumd.2021.684137

Phillimore, J. (2012) 'Implementing integration in the UK: Lessons for integration theory, policy and practice.' *Policy & Politics,* 40(4), 525–545.

Redmond, P. (2015) 'A pedagogical continuum: The journey from face-to-face to online teaching.' *In* P. Redmond, J. Lock, & P. A. Danaher (Eds.), *Educational Innovations and Contemporary Technologies* (pp. 107–132). London, UK: Palgrave Macmillan.

Reid, S. (2012). 'The changed role of professor in online courses.' *IJOPCD,* 2, 21–36. 10.4018/ijopcd.2012010102

Roger, K., Bone, T. A., Heinonen, T., Schwartz, K., Slater, J. and Thakrar, S. (2018). 'Exploring identity: What we do as qualitative researchers.' *The Qualitative Report,* 23(3), 532–546. https://doi.org/10.46743/2160-3715/2018.2923

Rutter, J. (2015) *Moving Up and Getting on: Migration, Integration and Social Cohesion in the UK.* Bristol: Bristol Policy Press.

Sancho-Gil, J. M., Soler-Campo, S., Domingo-Coscollola, M. and Hernández-Hernández, F. (2021) 'Immigrant students' knowledge and experiences around the school: A relational, child-centred approach (Saberes y experiencias del alumnado inmigrante en torno a la escuela: Aproximación relacional y centrada en la infancia).' *Culture and Education,* 33(4), 677–701.

Sime, D. (2017) 'Challenging barriers to participation: Doing research with migrant children and young people.' 10.1007/978–981-287-020–9_4.

Singh, S. and Balhara, Y. P. S. (2021) '"Screen-time" for children and adolescents in COVID-19 times: Need to have the contextually informed perspective.' *Indian Journal of Psychiatry*, 63(2), 192.

Smith, R., Spaaij, R. and McDonald, B. (2019, August 01) 'Migrant integration and cultural capital in the context of sport and physical activity: A systematic review.' *Journal of International Migration and Integration*, 20(3), 851–868.

Soh, S. L-H., Lane, J. and Tan, C-W. (2020). Researcher as instrument: A critical reflection using nominal group technique for content development of a new patient-reported outcome measure. *International Practice Development Journal*, 10(2), 1–9. https://doi.org/10.19043/ipdj.102.010

Spencer, S. (2011) *The Migration Debate*. Bristol: Policy Press.

Sutton, D. (2020) 'The impact of school closures on the attainment of disadvantged EAL pupils.' [Blog post]. *The Bell Foundation*. Retrieved from https://www.bell-foundation.org.uk/news/blog-the-impact-of-school-closures-on-the-attainment-of-disadvantaged-eal-pupils/

The Children's Society. (2020) *The Impact of COVID-19 on Children and Young People*. Briefing Note. Available online at: https://www.childrenssociety.org.uk/information/professionals/resources/impact-of-covid-19- on-young-people

UNESCO. (2020) *UN Secretary-General Warns of Education Catastrophe, Pointing to UNESCO Estimate of 24 Million Learners at Risk of Dropping Out*. [Online] [Accessed on 24/03/2022] https://en.unesco.org/news/secretary-general-warns-education-catastrophe-pointing-unesco-estimate-24-million-learners-0

UNICEF. (2021) *Impact of COVID-19 on Poor Mental Health in Children and Young People 'Tip of the Iceberg'*. [Online] [Accessed on 24/03/2022] https://www.unicef.org/press-releases/impact-covid-19-poor-mental-health-children-and-young-people-tip-iceberg

Van Lancker W. and Parolin Z. (2020) COVID-19, school closures, and child poverty: A social crisis in the making. *The Lancet Public Health*;5, e243–e244. doi: 10.1016/S2468–2667(20)30084-0

Yan, C. and Wang, L. (2022) 'Experienced EFL teachers switching to online teaching: A case study from China.' *System*, 105(2022), Article 102717, 10.1016/j.system.2021.102717

Yoon, B. and Uliassi, C. (2022). "Researcher-as-instrument" in qualitative research: The complexities of the educational researcher's identities.' *The Qualitative Report*, 27(4), 1088–1102. https://doi.org/10.46743/2160-3715/2022.5074

Chapter 7

Impact of the Pandemic on Refugee Education in Greece

Nektaria Palaiologou and Viktoria Prekate

Introduction

Most of the school year 2020–2021 in Greece was spent in remote learning in all educational contexts. Refugee children, already under-represented in education, were disproportionately affected. Those living in large Refugee Hospitality Centers (RHCs) were even more disadvantaged, as camps were subjected to stricter lockdown rules than the mainstream population. Shortage of digital connection, lack of digital competencies and long-standing malfunctions in the refugee education system contributed to a deterioration of refugee access to education, as it happened for other disadvantaged social groups, like Roma children. Worsening conditions at home, lack of space, increased family violence, and the stress and trauma of the pandemic were in themselves aggravating factors, affecting refugee students' access and involvement in education. A mini-survey was conducted with the help of certain key education factors, such as Refugee Education Coordinators, teachers in mainstream schools with a high proportion of refugees/migrants, and volunteer teachers in refugee camps. The results are compared with the literature findings. The study concludes with a discussion of how online learning could be used to enhance refugee education and bridge the gap left by intermittent schooling and displacement trauma.

Literature review

According to OECD (2015) indexes, Greece has been placed in the last position regarding ICT resources and digital use at schools. Therefore, the extent of digitalization was relatively low even before the pandemic. As Greece's digital competence levels have been receiving low scores internationally, it became a governmental priority to digitize school environments (Ministry of Digital Governance, 2020), and schools were equipped with smartboards and online microcosms to enhance in-person learning. Additionally, there is a Digital Education Action Plan for the years 2021–2027 designed to correct gaps regarding access and opportunities in ICT (European Commission,

DOI: 10.4324/9781003343141-9

2020). Some University-affiliated schools and intercultural schools adopted curricula to enhance digital competence (Office of the Secretary-General of the European Schools, 2021). Curricula and resources had already been digitized and enriched before the pandemic, with complementary material, activities, videos, simulations, virtual visits, online exercises, storylines, quizzes, links to reference material, etc. Several online learning platforms (e-me, e-class, moodle, Webex, sch. gr, etc.) already existed to connect participants in a cost-free, officially approved and digitally safe way. Teachers have been routinely trained on digital equipment tools use, such as smartboards with special subjects during their undergraduate and postgraduate training and numerous continuous professional development courses (Pedagogical Institute, 2008).

However, despite efforts to increase digital learning, access has not been equal among student populations. The digital competence goals have not been fully achieved, neither for native nor for non-native populations, as show through recent research by the Institute of Labor and Human Resources shows (Paidousi, 2020). Vulnerable social groups, such as migrant/refugee children and ROMA children, have systematically had less access to connectivity and digital services. In the last decade, ICT support has been auxiliary to the educational process and, even before the pandemic, many refugee/migrant students relied heavily on ICT for translation, homework assistance, peer communication about homework and socialization through social media. Successive Greek governments have attempted to prevent early school leaving by assisting the educational efforts of refugees/migrants (CEDEFOP, 2020). Implementation of European decisions has been a governmental priority and several initiatives have been launched.

For example, the Greek government recently implemented plans for digital education for refugee children, such as the Erasmus 'Hopeful' program (CESIE, 2021), training secondary school teachers in the teaching of digital skills to refugee and/or migrant children with low local language skills and multiple school gaps. The program also provides secondary diagnostic tools for the assessment of the individualized needs of each student, according to the Greek National Strategy for migrants' inclusion (Ministry for Migration Policy, 2019) and the construction of individualized learning plans in Reception Classes, which aim at helping migrant children with Greek language accelerated lessons (Ministry of Education, Research and Religious Affairs, 2017).

Discussion of methodological approach

A mini-survey was conducted with professionals who had extensive experience in refugee/migrant education. The questionnaire consisted of closed or short open-ended questions and concerned refugee students' participation in online learning during school closures and initiated a discussion about possible obstacles, strengths, challenges and suggestions. As researchers could not access refugee students directly during the pandemic, we conducted our mini-survey with the following eight refugee education professionals: two Refugee Education Coordinators (RECs) at a large RHC, a non-formal education teacher and a non-formal education coordinator at the same RHC, three teachers at mainstream junior high schools with a high percentage of refugee and migrant students, two teachers at Intercultural schools and three non-formal education teachers in other structures for refugees. All of these professionals had direct knowledge of hundreds of refugee/migrant students' attendance of formal education during the pandemic. The questionnaire was additionally sent to four more teachers in mainstream schools with second-generation migrants, or migrants who have been in Greece for some years and spoke basic Greek (non-beginners). The results from the two groups (12 professionals in total) are then compared. The professionals involved each have direct knowledge of the educational attendance of about 200 children (aged 12–18, secondary education), whereas the RECs are involved in the education of several hundreds of refugee children, aged 5–18. The questionnaires were anonymous so that professionals would not feel inhibited, but all professionals were on duty in education during the pandemic period.

The questionnaire consisted of five multiple-choice questions and four short open-ended questions. It was compiled in Google Forms and was sent to the participants by email. Personal communication after the email request followed with a small discussion on clarifications of results. As a mini-survey, the data had some limitations. First, the 12 participants answered quantitative questions from memory and personal knowledge. It was not possible to determine which responses were based on standardized data and which were based on personal estimates and immediate experience. Second, educators can be constrained by personal and political considerations, which may affect their estimates positively or negatively. Third, there was no differentiation in the questionnaire regarding student ethnicity or the influence of other factors, such as prior schooling and length of time in Greece. The influence of these factors on access to education could be investigated in future research.

Findings

In our mini-survey, interviewees generally emphasized that participation of refugee pupils during the online learning period was reduced compared to in-person learning (despite the difficulties in physically accessing schools from remote camps). For the sake of comparison, the answers of eight professionals of refugee newcomer students are shown separately from the answers of the four teachers of second-generation/non-beginner migrants. The answers to the questionnaire are presented in tables titled with each question posed (Tables 7.1–7.9).

112 Nektaria Palaiologou and Viktoria Prekate

Table 7.1 Evaluation of Access of Refugee Children to Online Learning during the Pandemic

	Teachers for Refugee/Migrant Newcomers	Teachers for Second-generation Migrants/Nnon-beginners
Excellent		
Very good		
Good		
Poor	3	1
Inadequate	4	3
No reply	1	
TOTAL	8	4

Table 7.2 Evaluation of Access of Refugee Children to Specific Means of Online Learning

	1 (Poor)	2 (Inadequate)	3(Good)	4 (Very Good)	5 (Excellent)
Access to data connection (Wi-Fi, USB data sticks, landline data, etc.)	5	5	1	1	
Access to digital equipment (laptops, mobile phones, terminals, etc.)	4	5	3		
Access to instructions	3	5	2	2	
Parental supervision-involvement	4	6	2		
Students' digital skills		7	3	2	

Table 7.3 Prioritization of Funding Needs for Future Improvement of Refugee Access to Online Learning

	1 Least Important	2 Not so Important	3 Fairly Important	4 Very Important	5 Most Important	No Reply
Data connection				2	9	1
Digital equipment			1	4	6	1
Interpreters/ mediators hiring	2	1	3		3	3

Note: (1= least important, 5= most important).

Impact of the Pandemic on Refugee Education   113

Table 7.4 Estimates of Refugee Population Percentage Aged 5–15 Participating in Online Education during School Closures in 2020–2021

	0–20 percent	20–40 percent	40–60 percent	60–80 percent	80–100 percent
Teachers of refugee and migrant newcomers	7	1			
Teachers of migrant second-generation/ non-beginners	1		3		

Note: This was a multiple-choice question with one possible answer in the above ranges.

Table 7.5 Estimates of Refugee Population Percentage Aged 5–15 Participating in Online Education during School Re-openings in 2020–2021

	0–20 percent	20–40 percent	40–60 percent	60–80 percent	80–100 percent
Teachers of refugee and migrant newcomers	2		5	1	
Teachers of migrant second-generation/ non-beginners		3	1		

Note: This was a multiple-choice question with one possible answer in the above ranges.

Table 7.6 Comparison of Refugee in-person Attendance after Re-opening of Schools Compared to Prior to the Pandemic

	Zero	Much less	Less	Equal	More	No Reply
Teachers of refugee and migrant newcomers			5	2	1	
Teachers of migrant second-generation/ non-beginners			2	1		1

Note: This was a multiple-choice question with one possible answer in the above ranges.

114 Nektaria Palaiologou and Viktoria Prekate

Table 7.7 Reasons for Differences between in-person Attendance Before School Closures and after School Re-openings

	Answers Given
Teachers of refugee and migrant newcomers	*Insecurity about status, routine disruption.* *Fear of covid* *Fear of the pandemic, cut off from daily school routine* *Pre-existing problems in refugee education* *Lack of information about re-opening covid measures; confusion; disappointment* *Marginalization; ghettoing* Participation increased after re-openings compared to previous years because children missed school
Teachers of migrant second- generation/ non-beginners	*Pre-existing host language difficulties* Already many absences; disappointment

Note: This was an open-ended question and individual answers given by teachers are presented here in concise form.

Table 7.8 Suggestions Regarding the Improvement of Refugees' Access to Online Education

	Answers Given
Refugee and migrant newcomers	*Improvement of data connection in RHCs* *Coordination between formal and non-formal education actors* *Provision of quality internet connection and equipment* *Funding for data, regular communication between parents and school via interpreters* *Education of children in digital literacies* Training of teachers in inclusive education
Migrant second- generation/ non-beginners	*Better equipment, student training in its use* *Strengthen host language skills* *Pilot program of inclusion through intensive language courses in all schools with refugees/migrants* Intensive host language courses, so that refugees/ migrants are not just spectators in class

Note: This was an open-ended question and individual answers given by teachers are presented here in concise form.

Impact of the Pandemic on Refugee Education   115

Table 7.9 Obstacles in Refugee/Migrant Student Inclusion in Class

	Answers given
Refugee and migrant newcomers	Lack of awareness and lack of training of teachers.
	Lack of coordination between state schools and RECs regarding difficulties on children's school inclusion
	Continuous movement of student population and lack of capability/willingness of schools to include refugees in school life
	Language obstacles, lack of individualized support
	Lack of training of staff in intercultural education
	Lack of adequate access of refugees in digital equipment and data
	Lack of interpreters, cultural mediators and psychologists at schools
	Lack of space for online learning (Isobox containers do not provide adequate space)
Migrant second-generation/ non-beginners	Inadequate numbers of staff
	Need for better school unit organization
	Inadequate planning, equipment and materials

Note: This was an open-ended question and individual answers given by teachers are presented here in concise form.

Discussion

In our study, the majority of participants answered that 0–20 per cent of refugees participated in online learning, whereas second-generation migrants had a higher participation percentage (40–60 per cent). The majority of refugee education professionals and teachers claimed that participation was reduced during the pandemic and access to education was poor or inadequate. This is in agreement with other surveys, which find that during the COVID pandemic, there was a significant drop in attendance: Refugee Support Aegean (2021) on refugee student participation in online learning, only 11 per cent of the refugee school-aged population attended online learning when 64 per cent of the same population had attended formal education classes before the COVID-19 lockdowns. Other figures show that enrolment rates in formal education state schools fell from 12.867 in March 2019 to 8.637 in March 2021 (Alfavita education website, 2021). At the Reception and Identification Centers (RICs) in the Aegean islands (mostly overcrowded camp facilities for newly-arrived refugees, with less freedom of movement than RHCs) the situation was even worse. For example, on Lesbos island, with 2.090 school-aged refugee children, only 178 were enrolled in state schools and only seven managed to actually attend school. Another example is the 850 students of Ritsona RHC, who stayed completely out of school for 11 months, as local authorities claimed there were no resources or staff to cater to the needs of these students (Alfavita education website, 2021b). The RHC of Vagiochori near Thessaloniki was put into lockdown since the 23rd of October 2020 (unlike the rest of the city), so the refugee children hosted hardly managed to attend any school at all (Alfavita education website, 2021c).

Regarding the reasons for the limited access to education during the pandemic, participants mentioned the lack of equipment and connections, the fact that closures in refugee camps lasted more than the general public, plus pre-existing, endemic difficulties in refugee education. Our survey finds some differences among newcomers and second-generation migrants: Refugee/ migrant newcomers at camps showed higher rates of return to in-person schooling after re-openings, as children at camps greatly missed socialization, school routines and generally, life outside the camp. During the closures though, students at camps had less participation during online learning than second-generation migrants, probably because the latter had already achieved better fluency in Greek and more solid bonds with their school communities. Differentiation was also noted among refugees in different accommodation structures, such as camps versus unaccompanied minors' hostels:

> Unaccompanied minors in hostels were in a slightly better position than refugee children in camps, as there was digital equipment and guardian supervision to assist them. However, as there were many children in need of digital connection at the same time and digital equipment was not enough for all, in that case, children did not have stable access.

Regarding the role of interpreters, participants place a higher priority on hiring interpreters at mainstream schools than camps, simply because schools don't as yet have any interpreters. Education facilitators at camps often 'borrow' interpreters from NGOs operating on site, or sometimes adult refugee beneficiaries volunteer themselves, so the need for translation is partly covered, but mainstream schools do not have this option. During closures, it was even more difficult for teachers to communicate instruction to migrant students who did not speak Greek. Thus, access to instruction is found to be poorer for migrants in mainstream schools than for newcomers in refugee camps, because of the lack of support available. Homework clubs by NGOs at camps played an important role in keeping the connection between formal education and the refugee camp community. It seems that, during the pandemic, organized structures of accommodation, such as camps, had some advantages (NGO support, interpreters available), but also drawbacks. As one participant noted:

> Refugees in camps get marginalized, through living outside the urban network, with inadequate or no access to basic services. During the pandemic, camps looked more like closed detention centres than hospitality centres, because of the exhaustive controls at entrance gates, very

The four aspects of online education access

It is worth analysing the survey's results in terms of the four different aspects of online education access:

a **Access mindset** means an awareness of the necessity regarding the use of digital tools. It means changing beneficiaries' views about digital tools as not only pastime/socialization accessories, but as equivalent routes to formal learning as live participation in the classroom. During the first part of the pandemic (spring of the school year 2019–2020), online education was not compulsory and hardly any information or instruction was available in most schools. This was an initial experimental stage, where many teachers familiarized themselves with the digital teaching environments. In this survey, teaching instruction received a better rating for refugees at camps (mostly thanks to RECs and non-formal education support) than second-generation migrants in mainstream schools, who had no other sources of support. This finding is in agreement with the Refugee Support Aegean (2021) survey, where lack of information was rated as one of the most important reasons for not participating. It should be noted that the platforms established by the Ministry of Education were set in the Greek language with no adaptation for non-native speakers. It was not easy to communicate instructions to parents, as schools did not hire interpreters for this purpose, and most parents could not monitor their children's online participation and progress.

b **Physical access** includes the use of digital equipment, such as PCs, mobiles, tablets and data connections. According to the mini-survey's participants, physical access was generally seen as not adequate, with data connection in the most urgent need of funding. Usually, it is data that is the most expensive item for refugee children and, even if families can afford it, the quality of mobile phone connectivity is often not workable. Family size also affected the quality of connections, as data has to be shared among many family members, whereas there was no privacy or quietness when many members of the same family were confined to work in the same space simultaneously. The pandemic forced all children into house isolation, and households often had three or four users working remotely on the same line. Many local families immediately upgraded their connection. However, low socio-economic status households (even those who had a landline connection) could not afford the upgrading and therefore students were often offline or with intermittent connection (CEDEFOP, 2020). This is in accordance with other findings, as 82 per cent of the refugee camps in Greece, reported a lack of access to digital equipment and Internet connections (Alfavita education website, 2021d). The Refugee Support Aegean survey (2021) results are slightly different, claiming that the equipment and data for digital learning have been available, but the provision was not always satisfactory and there were considerable differences among different camps.

Regarding physical access to online education, it is important to emphasize the partnership between formal and non-formal education actors: The Greek government did fund free internet connection in RHCs, but the speed of the connection for thousands of children and adults was mostly unworkable, as a huge volume of data was consumed indiscriminately by all beneficiaries. However, data was also provided by NGOs supporting education during the lockdown. For example, NGOs Elix and Danish Refugee Council (DRC) assisted refugee families with the provision of data, through purchased USB sticks, instructions in several languages for online platform use, activation of vouchers for the purchase of digital equipment, translation in several languages regarding the use of COVID-19 self-tests and the process of live schooling restart, mediation with schools regarding homework and helpdesk operation about the pandemic (Elix, 2021). The role of non-formal actors in RHCs was critical in formal education participation, as children enrolled in non-formal education classes within RHCs participated at a much higher rate (72 per cent) in formal online schooling compared with the children that were not enrolled (20 per cent) (CEDEFOP, 2020).

Last, but not least, it was not only lack of physical equipment, but pre-existing, festering **malfunctions** in the refugee education system, that contributed to the lack of access in education, such as delays in teacher staffing, delays in establishing Welcome Classes and afternoon Structures for the Welcoming and Education of Refugees (the Greek acronym being 'DYEP') and high staff turnover (The Press Project, 2020).

c **Digital skills** varied among refugee/migrant students, but, in general, a lack of ICT skills is not seen to prevent refugee students' access to online learning. According to the mini-survey participants, refugees' digital skills were not seen as a major obstacle, in contrast to second-generation migrants. The reason for this differentiation may be that refugee students have received some non-formal digital training at camp and many developed these skills during their journey through frequent online communication with relatives in different countries.

d **Socio-emotional** reasons and parental involvement also seem to play a role in the learning gap between refugee/migrant students and the general student population. Even after school re-openings, participation did not always resume, with 'insecurity', 'fear of covid' and 'disturbance of daily routines' reported as the main contributing emotional factors to absenteeism. Results from other surveys are in accordance, including additional factors, such as lack of motivation and insecurity about refugee status: The Refugee Support Aegean survey (2021) finds lack of motivation in 21 per cent of boys, compared to only 4 per cent of girls and a contributing factor is the state of uncertainty about whether the families would be able to stay in Greece. When Turkey was declared a 'secure third country,' this led to increased dropout for refugee/asylum-seeking students (Efsyn News Agency, 2021). On a more general note, emotional factors that affected not only refugees, but the general population, such as increased family violence during closures, the stress and trauma of the pandemic, economic uncertainty, depression increase among teenagers were in themselves hindering factors for school attendance (Huffington Post, 2020).

One of the most important socio-emotional factors for children's engagement in education is **parental involvement**. It is known that when parents possess digital competence, the learning processes of their children are positively affected, as parents can help their children access and translate materials, supervise and guide them using their own educational capital, help them look into resources, etc. (Marsh et al., 2005). In the mini-survey's participants did not rate parental supervision as adequate. Supervision means monitoring what their children do online, communicating with teachers online, checking homework uploaded/corrected, receiving teachers' feedback, etc. Poor parental digital skills do not contribute positively to online learning supervision. Similar results were found in a research study held by the University of West Macedonia (Nikou, 2014): most of the migrant parents have a low educational and socio-economic status, meaning little involvement with children's education and are not expected to contribute to their children's online education. Interestingly, it is often through peer teaching that children acquire new ICT skills, rather than through their parents.

Finally, fear of online bullying could be considered as another socio-emotional reason for refugees' low participation in online learning. The School Education Gateway (2019) supports that refugee/migrant children are often discriminated against and can be targeted victims of cyberbullying. However, no participant mentioned fear of online bullying among the obstacles for online education access. On the contrary, it was mostly when schools re-opened for in-person schooling that some individuals in local communities expressed concern. The skepticism was about hygiene conditions in RHCs and whether isobox containers could be regarded as separate households, fulfilling social distancing criteria. The suspiciousness was exacerbated as lockdown restrictions were held longer for RHCs than for the general population. On the other hand, refugee families were equally afraid of infection during the re-opening in May 2021, with many not sending their children back to school, so there was apprehension on both sides.

Conclusions and suggestions

COVID-19 introduced new challenges to the digital inclusion of refugee/ migrant children that are likely to remain in future. This study found that online participation of refugee/newcomer migrant students was from inadequate to poor, with the main obstacle being the lack of digital equipment and data. Second-generation migrants or migrants with several years in Greek formal education were reported to score higher rates of online attendance. Participants of the survey rated the provision of adequate equipment and free data for refugees, as a priority for future funding. Governments could also introduce 'zerorating' Internet connections in refugee camps so that the entire population has workable speed data connections. Assistance with instruction and hiring interpreters were also rated as important. The benefits gained from online learning could continue, even upon return to in-person schooling: distance education can be incorporated in a complementary way, especially in the context of Reception Classes and accelerated programs. The online learning environments could be an auxiliary tool for homework support, intensive Greek language classes, programs of accelerated learning and fast-paced programs for parents. The online platforms could also be used to bridge the gaps in schooling, during the time spent by refugee children on waiting lists for school registration.

On a more general note, governments should ensure that all refugee children are enrolled in formal education and actually attend, whether online or in-person (not being 'ghost' students). Universities could run research projects on the efficiency of different digital learning methods, as well as develop digital learning resources. It is also important to have measurements of educational results from the use of these different tools, in order to ensure the effective allocation of funding resources. The pandemic gave an opportunity to reduce the learning divide between refugee and local student populations. Unfortunately, this opportunity was largely missed, but the online tools developed can still be used in future efforts to provide educational continuity for refugees, especially during the multiple transitions they face, such as from camp to camp, from camp to apartment, from one school to another, from one area to the next or, ultimately, from one country to a different one.

References

Alfavita (Education website) (2021, April 30). *Because I wanted to learn and you taught me.* Available at: https://m.tvxs.gr/mo/i/336502/f/news/eyropi-eop/gnorizei-i-komision-pos-i-elliniki-kybernisi-kobei-ta-paidia-ton-prosfygon-apo-sxole. html Date of access: 10/12/2021

Alfavita (Education website) (2021b, January 29). *The Holocaust of education in Ritsona camp.* Available at: https://www.alfavita.gr/ekpaideysi/342625_ritsonaolokaytoma-tis-ekpaideysis Date of access: 10/12/2021

Impact of the Pandemic on Refugee Education   121

Alfavita (Education website) (2020c, December 22). *Teachers: 'No' to the exclusion of refugees and migrants.* Available at: https://www.alfavita.gr/ekpaideysi/342625_ritsonaolokaytoma-tis-ekpaideysis Date of access: 10/12/2021

Alfavita (Education website, 2021d, April 21). *Refugee Education: Only 14,2% attends school.* Available at: https://www.alfavita.gr/ekpaideysi/348125_ekpaideysi-prosfygon-molis-142-foita-sta-sholeia Date of Access: 11/12/21

CEDEFOP (2020). *Digital gap during COVID-19 for VET learners at risk in Europe.* CEDEFOP Report on June 3rd, 2020. Available at: https://www.cedefop.europa.eu/en/news/coronavirusdistance-learning-increases-dropout-risk-vulnerable-learners Date of Access: 11/12/21

CESIE (2021). *HOPEFUL – Extending teachers' competences in the effective teaching of literacy, numeracy and digital skills to refugee children.* Report. Available at: https://cesie.org/en/project/hopeful/ Date of Access: 11/12/21

Efsyn News Agency (2021, April 15). *Thousands of refugees in legislation captivity.* Available at: https://www.efsyn.gr/ellada/dikaiomata/302498_hiliades-prosfyges-se-nomiki-omiria Date of Access 11/12/21

Elix (2021). *Quality learning and support for children, refugees and migrants in new Lesbos Identification reception center.* News report. Available at: https://elix.org.gr/megala-programmata-elix/koinonika-programmata-stiriksis-evaloton-omadon/mi-typiki-ekpaideusi-prosfigon-kyt-lesvos Date of Access: 11/12/2021

European Commission (2020). *Action plan for inclusion and integration 2021-2027.* European Commission Announcement on 24.11.2020. Available at: https://eur-lex.europa.eu/legalcontent/EL/TXT/PDF/?uri=CELEX:52020DC0758&from=EN Date of Access: 11/12/21

Huffington Post Greece (2020, December 1). *Without computers or help, inside a container. Online learning for students of intercultural schools.* Available at: https://www.huffingtonpost.gr/entry/choris-epoloyistes-e-voetheia-mesa-konteiner-e-telekpaideese-yia-toes-mathetes-diapolitismikon-scholeion_gr_5fc63008c5b63d1b770f9be4?utm_hp_ref=gr-koinonia(Date of access: 11/12/21

Marsh, J., Brooks, G., Hughes, J., Ritchie, L., Roberts, S. & Wright, K. (2005). *Digital beginnings: Young children's use of popular culture, media and new technologies.* University of Sheffield: Literacy Research Center. Available at: http://www.digitalbeginnings.shef.ac.uk/DigitalBeginningsReport.pdf

Ministry of Digital Governance (2020). *Digital skills and competences.* Available at: http://www.opengov.gr/digitalandbrief/?p=2133 Date of Access: 11/12/21

Ministry of Education, Research and Religious Affairs (2017). *The work of the education of children refugees. Report by the scientific committee for the support of refugee children.* Report. Available at: https://www.minedu.gov.gr/publications/docs2017/16_06_17_Epistimoniki_Epitropi_Prosfygon_YPPETH_Apotimisi_Protaseis_2016_2017_Final.pdf Date of access: 10/12/2021

Ministry for Migration Policy (2019). *National Strategy for Inclusion.* Report, July 2019. Available at: https://migration.gov.gr/wp-content/uploads/2020/05/%CE%926.-%CE%95%CE%B8%CE%BD%CE%B9%CE%BA%CE%AE-%CE%A3%CF%84%CF%81%CE%B1%CF%84%CE%B7%CE%B3%CE%B9%CE%BA%CE%AE2019.pdf Date of access: 10/12/2021

Nikou, M. (2014). *The view of migrant parents on their involvement to their children's literacies.* Postgraduate thesis. University of Western Macedonia, Department of Pedagogy for Kindergarten, Florina. Available at: https://ikee.lib.auth.gr/record/136407/files/GRI-2015-14340.PDF

OECD (2015). *Immigrant students at school, easing the journey towards integration.* Report. Available at: https://read.oecd-ilibrary.org/education/immigrant-students-at-school_9789264249509-en#page1 Date of Access: 11/12/21

Office of the Secretary-General of the European Schools (2021). *Syllabuses and attainment descriptors.* Available at: https://www.eursc.eu/en/European-Schools/studies/syllabuses Date of Access: 11/12/21

Paidousi, C. (2020). Digital Transformation-Attention to Digital Gap. Report. *Institute of Labour and Human Resources.* Available at: https://www.eiead.gr/publications/docs/%CE%A8%CE%B7%CF%86%CE%B9%CE%B1%CE%BA%CF%8C%CF%82_%CE%BC%CE%B5%CF%84%CE%B1%CF%83%CF%87%CE%B7%CE%BC%CE%B1%CF%84%CE%B9%CF%83%CE%BC%CF%8C%CF%82_%CE%BA%CE%B1%CE%B9_%CE%A8%CE%B7%CF%86%CE%B9%CE%B1%CE%BA%CF%8C_%CF%87%CE%AC%CF%83%CE%BC%CE%B1__%CE%95%CE%99%CE%95%CE%91%CE%94.pdf

Pedagogical Institute (2008). *Training of primary and secondary education teachers in basic ICT skills.* Report. Available at: http://www.pi-schools.gr/programs/ktp/epeaek/ergo.html Date of Access: 9/12/21

Refugee Support Aegean (2021). *Excluded and segregated. The vanishing education of refugee children in Greece.* Report of April 13, 2021. Available at: https://www.cnn.gr/ellada/story/261937/rsa-se-epipeda-rekor-o-apokleismos-prosfygopoylon-apo-tin-ekpaideysi-stin-ellada Date of Access: 9/12/21

School Education Gateway News Agency (2019). *Combatting bullying and school violence. Critical approaches schools should adopt.* Article. Available at: https://www.schooleducationgateway.eu/el/pub/viewpoints/experts/tackling-school-bullying.htm Date of Access: 11/12/2021

The Press Project (2020, December 12). *Let's defend the refugee child from Afghanistan, Syria, Zefyri, Rethymno, Pyrg.* Report. Available at: https://thepressproject.gr/na-yperaspistoume-to-paidi-apo-to-afganistan-ti-syria-apo-to-zefyri-to-rethymno-ton-pyrgo/#.X9ThizxcwWI.facebook Date of Access: 11/12/2021

Appendix

Questionnaire

1. How would you evaluate the access of refuge children to online learning during the pandemic?
   Excellent
   Very Good
   Good
   Poor
   Inadequate

2. Evaluate form 1 (Poor) to 5 (Excellent) the access of refugee children to the following means of online learning
   Access to data connection (wifi, usb data sticks, landline data etc.)
   Access to digital equipment (laptops, mobile phones, terminals etc.)
   Access to instructions
   Parental supervision-involvement
   Digital Skills

3. How would you prioritize funding needs for future improvement of refugee children's access to online learning? (1= least important, 5= most important)
   Data connection
   Digital equipment
   Interpreters/mediators hiring

4. What is your estimate of the percentage of refugee population aged 5–15 that actually participated in online learning during state school closures in the school year 2020–2021?
   0–20 per cent
   20–40 per cent
   40–60 per cent
   60–80 per cent
   80–100 per cent

5. What is your estimate of the percentage of refugee population aged 5–15 that actually participated in live learning during the periods that state re-schools opened in the school year 2020–2021?
   0–20 per cent
   20–40 per cent
   40–60 per cent
   60–80 per cent
   80–100 per cent

6 How does refugees' state school live participation in the school year 2021–22, just after the schools re-open, compare, in your opinion, to their participation prior to the pandemic?
7 Please give any reasons/explanations you may have about your answer to the previous question:
8 Please give your suggestions regarding the improvement of refugees' access to education during the pandemic
9 Please give your opinion about the obstacles in refugee/migrant student inclusion in class

Part III

Well-being of Children in Migration Processes

Case Studies

Chapter 8

A Profile of Well-Being among Children of Kerala Migrants

Growing Up, Left Behind

S Irudaya Rajan and Ashwin Kumar

Introduction

International labour migration has led to a number of economic, cultural, and societal changes, leading to radical shifts in societal dynamics throughout, especially in developing countries. Increased avenues for migration have led to increasingly varied patterns of individual migration. These varied patterns have also led to the formation of a newer societal – particularly that of the transnational family. South Asia is one of the most important hubs of migration in the world, with a high degree of mobility from the region. Millions of people migrate from the region every year, sending about 20 per cent of all remittances in the world back to their families (World Bank, 2020), making migration one of the major societal trends in the world. The discourse on migration and development in the region has been at the forefront of policy and policymakers for many decades now, and perhaps rightly so. Migration has had tremendous developmental upsides for communities across the region. However, there is a glaring omission when it comes to migration literature within the region – that of the emergence of transnational families and their effects on the individuals within the family. Even less known are the issues of the most vulnerable among those families – children who are left behind.

While the literature has certainly shown the positive aspects of parents' migration, leading to a better life, the effects of migration on children left behind are not uniformly positive. Camacho and Shen (2009) noted that while remittances had the potential to boost household income and increase private educational investments, households that were previously credit-constrained might become able to afford the fixed costs of sending their children to school (e.g., tuition fees and material expenses). Remittances helped migrant households to overcome liquidity constraints which contributed to underinvestment in the education of girls and poor children. Further, remittances reduced the need to rely on income from child labour and hence had a positive impact on the education of children. However, studies on parental migration observed a pattern of both positive and negative implications on

DOI: 10.4324/9781003343141-11

the education of children of migrant households (Koska et al., 2013; Graham et al., 2015; Hoang et al., 2015; Sawyer, 2016). While migration diminished the need for child labour in migrant households, it also increased the workload of these children within the households, as they had to take on the chores of the absent adult household members (Brink, 1991). Studies conducted by Gamburd (2005) state the link between migration, particularly of mothers, and the tendency among children of such households to drop out of school or miss school either to look for work or to help with household chores. Some studies have also shown that in the absence of their parents, a number of negative mental effects were manifested in children left behind in a number of ways depending on their overall living contexts – from feelings of loneliness, anxiety, depression, apathy to even substance abuse and suicidal behaviour (Valtolina and Colombo, 2012). The same was seen in a study from Sri Lanka, which found that two out of five children left behind showed mental disorders – particularly among males (Wickramage et al., 2015).

The transnational households resulting from parental migration certainly pose numerous challenges to the development of close family relations. Children deprived of the intimacy of a normal family set-up can potentially become distant from their parents and fall victim to social pressures from the community, kin, and their peer group to re-create the traditional family and its reorganization. Given the prevailing social norms of parenting, the abandonment and deprivation among children of migrant parent(s) may also have a strong negative bearing on their emotional life. It is also possible that such an emotional disturbance has negative impacts on the well-being of the children of migrant parent(s) even after reunion – for instance, in the case of children who had immigrated to other countries to live with their migrant parents. It is therefore very important to consider how such children endure and adapt to the physical absence of their fathers, mothers, or both, in a way as to rationalize the situation, i.e., how they rationalize the gains against the losses and vice versa. The children of father-away households and mother-away households might have different ways of dealing with them when it comes to confronting problems. Society might also perceive the children of migrant fathers differently from those of the migrant mothers, which would put them under different kinds of social pressures thus resulting in different kinds of resolutions for children of such families. It may well be a social norm of parentage which is deeply gendered that decides the children's preferences – as to whether they prefer the migrant parent to be the father or the mother. The structural factors that cause the formation of transnational households may appear a stark reality in the eyes of children. This perhaps allows them to rationalize the situation, overcome the difficulty of parental separation, and motivate them to resort to feasible ways of mobility particularly through education.

At an individual level, children from transnational households may suffer discrimination from their peers, often stemming from the perception that they are better off because they receive remittances and thus have better access to goods and services, such as education and healthcare. Children left behind may also experience depression and feelings of abandonment at different stages of their life (Camacho and Hernandez, 2007), which can have significant negative behavioural consequences in children transitioning to adolescence. Adolescents whose parents have migrated often experience difficulties in social relations, which can lead to isolation from mainstream society in favour of small groups of peers that share similar experiences, limiting social interaction and development (UNICEF, 2008).

The reunion between migrant parents and their children often becomes the space where the psychological and emotional traumas and displacements linked to migration are played out. Several adolescents reported that when their migrant parents return to their country of origin, they experienced deep conflicts. Some part of their psyche looked forward to their parents' arrival, but after a week of living under the same roof, they were anxious for them to leave. At the same time, most teachers said that relationships between parents working abroad and their children become colder over time. Such situations could be considered as a defence mechanism for children to guard against possible separation from their parents (UNICEF, 2008). In a British study of West Indian children, the reunion was intensely difficult for both the migrant parents and the children (Graham and Meadows, 1967). The children were often denied chances of recognizing their parents and professed a greater attachment to the temporary caregivers (often the maternal grandmother). They were often hostile to their parents for taking them away from their temporary caregivers. Another issue that arose was about how the migration of individual parents disrupts traditional norms when it comes to parenting, especially with regard to gendered norms. Parreñas (2005) finds that maintaining traditional gendered parenting norms in transnational families, and especially mother-away families, ruptures existing dynamics between parents and their children. This is particularly true about societies that have an expectation of close parenting from parents, much like many communities in South Asia.

What is also clear from the extant literature, but perhaps not emphasized enough, on the effects of parental migration on children left behind is that children often are not only passive recipients of any benefits or drawbacks of the migration of their parents. They have to adapt and adjust within an environment in which their parents are away, and as a result, are active agents in building their own worlds. This chapter tries to present that worldview, looking at it primarily through the lens of gender and the type of living arrangements of the children themselves. The study was based in the southern Indian state of Kerala, which has had a long history of emigration from the state over the decades, and whose effect on the overall development of the state has been studied in great detail (Zachariah and Rajan, 2009, 2011, 2016, 2018; Zachariah et al., 2001).

Data

The discourse on migration and development recognizes that migration can help migrants and their families improve their living standards and well-being. At the same time, however, migration introduces new vulnerabilities and costs for migrants, their families, and sending communities. An often-overlooked, yet significant, consequence of migration is the trans-nationalization of households, which affects every individual member of a household in myriad ways. More specifically, within the widely researched topic of migration and its effects on society, one of the most under-researched and overlooked consequences is the effect it has on children whose parent or parents have migrated abroad for work. Such migrations can leave various social, nutritional, and psychological effects on children as they grow up, some negative and some positive. These effects have a direct bearing on their later lives in a variety of ways. It is this phenomenon that the current chapter tries to make an exploration into.

Taking the case of Kerala, the southernmost state of India, which has a significant number of migrants living and working outside India (MEA Annual Report, 2020). From the Kerala Migration Survey of 2010, the first stage in the study is the identification of a sample of households with and without transnational migration through the Kerala Migration Survey 2008 conducted in 15,000 households across the state by the Research Unit on International Migration funded by the Department of Non-Resident Keralite Affairs, Government of Kerala, and the Ministry of Overseas Indian Affairs, Government of India, at the Centre for Development Studies in 2008. These 15,000 households were selected from the 14 districts of Kerala using a stratified multistage random sampling method, with rural and urban areas within each district forming strata. From each stratum, a number of localities (Panchayats or Municipal wards) were selected on the basis of the number of households in the stratum (proportional sampling). The sample of 15,000 households was thus selected from 300 localities. In each locality, 50 households were selected by the systematic random sampling method. A total of 6575 children of both migrant and non-migrant parent(s) in the 12–18 age group were identified and interviewed, of which 14 per cent came from migrant households (Table 8.1)

In addition, a survey among 1,044 children residing in boarding schools in various parts of the state was also undertaken. This makes it one of the very few large-scale datasets in the world focusing on issues of children within the migration process and the largest of its kind in South Asia (Table 8.2).

Compared to the household survey, about 43 per cent of all respondents at the boarding schools came from migrant households. Among these children, 61 per cent came from father-away households, and about 36 per cent of them reported that both parents were migrants (Table 8.3).

After identification and categorization of households into father-away households, mother-away households, both parents-away households, and

A Profile of Well-Being among Children of Kerala Migrants   131

Table 8.1 Migration Status of the Surveyed Children in the Kerala Children's Survey, 2010

Parents Migration Status	Number	Percentage
Father abroad	803	88.5
Mother abroad	10	1.1
Both father and mother abroad	13	1.4
Father in other states	77	8.6
Mother other states	2	0.2
Both father and mother in other states	2	0.2
Children of migrant parents	907	100.0
Children of migrant parents	907	13.8
Children of non-migrant parents	5,668	86.2
Total	6,575	100.00

Source: Kerala Children's Survey, 2010, coordinated by the senior author with financial support from the Rockefeller Foundation, New York.

Table 8.2 Profile of the Surveyed Boarding Schools in Kerala, 2010

District	Schools	Male	Female	Total
Malappuram	Jawahar Navodaya Vidyalaya	69	77	146
	Peevees Public School, Nilambur	96	51	147
Thrissur	Ansar English School, Perumbilavu	203	114	317
	Govt School for Blind, Kunnamkulam	8	4	12
Palakkad	L S N Higher Secondary School	-	14	14
	Mount Seena English School Nagaripuram	143	72	215
Thiruvananthapuram	Viswa Prakash	76	51	127
	Jawahar Navodaya Vidyalaya	33	33	66
Total		628	416	1,044

Source: Kerala Children's Survey, 2010.

Table 8.3 Migration Status of the Surveyed Respondents in the Boarding Schools, 2010

Parents' Migration Status	Number	Percentage
Father abroad	277	61.3
Mother abroad	11	2.4
Both father & mother abroad	164	36.3
Children of migrant parents	**452**	**100.0**
Children of migrant parents	452	43.3
Children of non-migrant parents	592	56.7
Total	**1,044**	**100.00**

Source: Kerala Children's Survey, 2010.

132 S Irudaya Rajan and Ashwin Kumar

non-migrant households, the study embarked on a detailed examination of the problems and challenges of transnational parenting and its consequences on the children among all identified households in the survey with specially developed questionnaires. The survey covered the following broad areas: (1) education, (2) health and nutrition, (3) psychological impact, (4) transnational families: communication and relationships, and (5) children's views on migration. Using the specialized Strengths and Difficulties Questionnaire (SDQ) Assessment, this study also looked to understand the psychological profiles of children in the survey.

Thus, the survey looked at both the objective and subjective well-being of the surveyed children. To gain an understanding of the picture of well-being among children of migrant parent(s), this chapter focuses particularly on three aspects of their well-being, namely, health, educational attainment, and mental well-being. These three, rather interrelated, issues are then seen in the context of future migration, with the study focusing on whether the children of migrants are to become future migrants themselves.

Findings

Health outcomes

The average height across all age groups for almost all groups and across genders was significantly higher among children from migrant households than children in non-migrant households. Moreover, the data also shows that children in migrant households were heavier than children from non-migrant households of comparable ages. This pattern held in both the household and boarding school survey, and was observable among both male and female respondents. This finding suggests that the economic security that can potentially result from migration could easily increase the quality and quantity of foods available to children of migrant households in comparison to those from non-migrant households. However, in order to attempt a more balanced assessment of a child's nutritional status and development, it is not sufficient for us to consider merely height-for-age and weight-for-age; it is also necessary to assess BMI,.

Because the BMI – which is the ratio of a person's weight in kilograms to the square of their height in meters – correlates well with other more accurate measures of body fat and because it is derived from easily obtainable data, this variable is commonly used to define nutritional status. The study found very clearly that children from migrant households had greater access to a wider variety of food choices, which is reflected in the anthropometric data (Tables 8.4 and 8.5).

Based on the anthropometric data collected from the survey, such as height-for-age, weight-for-age, and BMI, the study found that children in migrant households have a higher height-for-age, weight-for-age, and BMI value than children in non-migrant households, which can be a negative

A Profile of Well-Being among Children of Kerala Migrants   133

Table 8.4 Average Height-for-age (cm) of Children by the Migration Status of the Household

| | Migrant | | | | Non-migrant | | | |
| | Male | | Female | | Male | | Female | |
Age	N	Mean (in cm)	N	Mean	N	Mean (in cm)	N	Mean
12	89	143.93	79	142.16	492	140.84	462	141.32
13	77	148.04	71	147.21	370	145.94	393	146.73
14	91	151.75	76	151.41	461	151.07	430	149.99
15	56	157.5	76	152.3	392	156.44	348	152.3
16	52	161	62	153.73	420	158.84	382	154.27
17	48	163.17	49	155.78	378	161.9	376	155.16
18	46	164.74	35	157.14	405	163.59	359	156.54
Total	459	153.86	448	150.51	2,918	153.67	2,750	150.52

Source: Kerala Children's Survey, 2010.

Table 8.5 Average Weight of Children by Migration Status and Gender

Households								
	Migrant				Non-migrant			
	Male		Female		Male		Female	
Age	N	Mean (in kg)	N	Mean	N	Mean (in kg)	N	Mean
12	89	34.93	79	34.08	492	34.42	462	33.92
13	77	38.77	71	38.48	370	37.77	393	37.83
14	91	43.24	76	41.61	461	42.13	430	40.54
15	56	46.5	76	42.71	392	46.23	348	42.64
16	52	50.92	62	46.45	420	48.44	382	45.05
17	48	51.35	49	46.8	378	51.19	376	45.94
18	46	53.54	35	48.29	405	53.58	359	47.55
Total	459	44.03	448	41.73	2,918	44.5	2,750	41.59
Boarding Schools								
12	26	34.31	13	36.38	89	34.93	79	34.08
13	50	40.7	21	41.81	77	38.77	71	38.48
14	37	47.05	25	42.96	91	43.24	76	41.61
15	42	50.1	25	50	56	46.5	76	42.71
16	64	58.05	27	48.96	52	50.92	62	46.45
17	52	62.02	29	52.07	48	51.35	49	46.8
18	25	56.36	16	58.12	46	53.54	35	48.29
Total	296	51.08	156	47.67	459	44.03	448	41.73

Source: Kerala Children's Survey, 2010.

as they are more susceptible to morbidity issues, which is borne out by the fact that children from migrant households show a slightly higher reporting of illnesses, particularly those in boarding schools. The study tried to look at morbidity issues by asking respondents about their general health and health-seeking behaviour. The results were quite pronounced, especially for children in boarding schools (Tables 8.6–8.8).

On looking at the various modes by which migrant children utilize healthcare options, it was found that children from migrant households access private hospitals to a greater degree than their non-migrant counterparts, who still mostly go to government hospitals. Private hospitals, being generally more expensive with more exclusive facilities for services than government services, also show a propensity for remittances to be used towards these more private healthcare services. This finding corroborates with those of Khan and Valatheeswaran (2020), who find that this trend provides children from more marginalized societies the chance to access more private healthcare facilities.

Table 8.6 Proportion of Respondents Reporting any Health Condition Necessitating a Visit to the Health Profession, by Migrant Status of Households and Boarding Schools, 2010

HH	Children of Migrant Parents	Children of Non-migrant Parents	All
Yes	10.1	10.6	10.5
No	89.9	89.4	89.5

Boarding Schools	Children of Migrant Parents	Children of Non-migrant Parents	All
Yes	38.5	37.3	37.8
No	61.5	62.7	62.2

Table 8.7 Health Conditions/Problems Reported by Children among Households by Migrant Status, 2010

	Male	Female	Total	Male	Female	Total
Asthma	1.7	1.3	1.5	2.4	2.5	2.5
Urinary Infections	1.7	2.0	1.9	1.2	2.8	2.0
Eczema/Psoriasis	1.1	0.9	1.0	1.6	1.7	1.7
Stomach pain	3.3	15.8	9.5	4.6	14.6	9.5
Frequent Headaches	9.8	20.5	15.1	9.0	14.8	11.8
Frequent tiredness/ fatigue	1.7	2.0	1.9	3.4	4.0	3.7
Weight gain (>5 kg)	1.1	0.2	0.7	0.7	0.5	0.6
Weight loss (>5 kg)	1.1	0.7	0.9	1.2	1.8	1.5
Sleeplessness/lack of sleep	0.4	0.9	0.7	1.0	0.9	1.0
Too much sleep	1.5	0.4	1.0	1.9	2.1	2.0

Source: Kerala Children's Survey, 2010.

A Profile of Well-Being among Children of Kerala Migrants 135

Table 8.8 Health-Seeking Behaviour among the Children of Migrants, 2010

Site of Treatment	Children in Migrant Households			Children in Non-migrant Households		
	Rural	Urban	Total	Rural	Urban	Total
Government Hospital	32.2	19.2	29.8	51.2	44.8	49.7
Private Hospital	42.6	62.2	46.3	36.4	37.4	36.6
Free Clinic	3.5	1.7	3.2	1.7	1.6	1.7
Private Practitioners	21.0	16.9	20.2	10.3	15.6	11.5
Home remedies	0.5	0.0	0.4	0.3	0.2	0.2
Others	0.1	0.0	0.1	0.2	0.5	0.3
Total	100.0	100.0	100.0	100.0	100.0	100.0
Systems of Medicine	*Rural*	*Urban*	*Total*	*Rural*	*Urban*	*Total*
Allopathy	93.2	93.0	93.2	93.1	90.5	92.5
Ayurveda	1.4	2.9	1.7	2.6	2.8	2.6
Homoeopathy	3.0	4.1	3.2	1.9	4.9	2.6
Unani & Sidha	2.3	0.0	1.9	2.4	1.8	2.2
Others	0.1	0.0	0.1	0.0	0.0	0.0
Total	100	100.0	100.0	100.0	100.0	100.0

Source: Kerala Children's Survey, 2010.

However, a look at the nutritional levels of children in terms of intake of food and how it is affected in the absence of parents indicates that children in migrant households have access to a wider variety of products and brands to choose from. The emphasis of the study was not only on the quantity of nutritional intake but also the quality of nutritional intake, something that can be directly attributed to parental supervision. It is found that children in migrant households, while exposed to a larger variety of food items, consume those of a lower nutritional value. This was borne out by the study which found that at least 17 per cent of children in migrant households reported consuming fast foods daily, compared to 10 per cent of their non-migrant counterparts, perhaps reinforcing the earlier statement.

Educational outcomes

When it comes to educational attainment, Kerala has famously led the way among the Indian states with the highest rates of literacy and broader educational attainment. As we see in Table 8.9, enrolment rates in Kerala across all school-going ages and across rural and urban regions are almost 100 per cent.

This study compared children from migrant households and non-migrant households and analysed these two cohorts over a variety of educational indicators such as enrollment patterns, the various types of modes and institutions, and academic performance, making a special analysis of the gulf between perceived performance and actual performance between children from migrant households and non–migrant households and the impact that has on children's psychological well-being.

When it came to the type of educational institution preferred, it was found that access to larger funds based out of remittances led to children from migrant households accessing education from private institutes (both aided and unaided). Private unaided institutes, in general, have higher fees than the rest of the institutes we looked at, which meant that extra remittances were going to access perceived "better" education. It found that children of migrant parents get access to a wider variety of modes of education, with 24 per cent of children from migrant households enrolled in private schools compared to 14 per cent of their non–migrant counterparts and have generally better academic outcomes than their counterparts (Table 8.10).

However, children from migrant households suffer from the stress of living up to certain expectations of their parents, with more than 13 per cent of children of migrant parents reporting that they did not feel that their performance met their parents' expectations. This became starker within the boarding school cohort, with almost 31 per cent of children from migrant households reporting the same. This adds extra stress and pressure on the children, leading to various mental as well as physical issues (Tables 8.11–8.13).

Table 8.9 Enrolment Rates, Kerala, 2015–2016

School Attendance Rates	Male			Female		
	Urban	Rural	Total	Urban	Rural	Total
6–10 yrs	99.8	99.9	99.9	99.7	99.5	99.6
11–14 yrs	99.8	99.3	99.5	99.5	99.2	99.3
15–17 yrs	92.8	93.1	93.0	95.2	94.4	94.8

Source: NFHS 2015–2016

Table 8.10 Type of Institutions Attended by the Children of Migrant and Non-migrant Households in Kerala, 2010

Type of Institutions	Migrant Households	Non-migrant Households	Total
Government	34.3	44.4	43.0
Private Aided	41.5	41.7	41.7
Private Unaided	24.0	13.6	15.0
Others	0.2	0.2	0.2
Total	100.0	100.0	100.0

Source: Kerala Children's Survey, 2010. All numbers are percentages of the total.

A Profile of Well-Being among Children of Kerala Migrants   137

Table 8.11 Academic Performance Assessment of the Children of Different Households by Migration Status, 2010

	Father away Households	Migrant Households	Non-migrant Households	Total
Academic Performance as per the Child's Expectation				
Yes	54.7	53.9	54.1	54.1
To some extent	40.7	41.8	41.6	41.6
No	4.6	4.3	4.3	4.3
Academic Performance as per the Parents' Expectations Reported by the Children				
Yes	41.2	41.3	41.7	41.6
To some extent	44.5	45.4	46.9	46.7
No	14.2	13.3	11.4[a]	11.6

Source: Kerala Children's Survey, 2010. All numbers are percentages of the total.

Table 8.12 Academic Performance Assessment of the Children in Boarding Schools by the Migration Status of Parents, 2010

	Father Away	Both Parents Away	Children in Migrant Households	CnMH	Total
Academic Performance as per the Child Expectation					
Yes	41.2	31.7	37.4	42.4	40.2
To some extent	38.3	34.8	37.4	38.7	38.1
No	20.6	33.5	25.2	18.9	21.6
Academic Performance as per the Parents' Expectations as Reported by the Children					
Yes	35.7	23.2	30.8	36.1	33.8
To some extent	39.0	34.1	37.4	42.4	40.2
No	25.3	42.7	31.9	21.5	26.0

Source: Kerala Children's Survey, 2010. All numbers are percentages of the total.

Table 8.13 Perceived Impact of Migration on Academic Performance of Respondents Residing in Households and Boarding Schools

Responses	Households			Boarding Schools		
	Male	Female	Total	Male	Female	Total
Yes	50.6	45.5	48.0	46.6	53.2	48.9
No	49.4	54.5	52.0	53.4	46.8	51.1
Total	100.0	100.0	100.0	100.0	100.0	100.0

Source: Kerala Children's Survey, 2010. All numbers are percentages of the total.

The table above shows that girls, in households were more likely than boys to perceive their educational performance to not be up to par with what was expected. However, the opposite was true for children in boarding schools, where more boys felt that their performance was not up to par with expectations. This was borne out by the fact they believed that they needed to live up to the demands of their parents, who were abroad to send in order to send them to "good schools" – which is true especially of boarding schools, where even male respondents did not perceive their academic performance to be at par. This gender- based discrepancy in results between children in households and boarding schools, however, leads to further questions on how expectations are perceived in different circumstances. This corroborates with evidence from elsewhere that while the access to remittances gives certain tangible material benefits to children of migrant parents, it has certain side effects – especially when it comes to their physical and mental health.

Mental health

The study also looked at the very important aspect of how the migration of parents affects children who are left behind psychologically using the Strengths and Deficiencies Questionnaire (SDQ). The absence of parents for children could cause certain problems in the growing phase and can have various negative and even positive effects. On the whole, children both living in households and boarding adjust well psychologically to parental absence, with respondents in both boarding and private schools reporting that they had grown more mature, confident, and economically better off while their parents have been away. However, on the downside, the study also finds increased stress levels due to added responsibilities and the building of self-confidence due to these responsibilities, which interestingly made them anxious when confronted with family reunification as it would significantly alter their lives which they had gotten used to (Table 8.14).

Interestingly, over 70 per cent of children in boarding schools responded that the migration of their parents had made them more independent, compared to just 40 per cent of those living in households. On the other hand, a higher proportion of children living in boarding schools also reported feelings of loneliness and unhappiness than those living in households, which presents a more complicated picture and one that puts into stark context the conflicting emotions that children feel in the absence of their parents. Overall, an overwhelming majority of all children within migrant households reported that they would prefer having their parents' home for good.

With parents' absence, we found that these children were very aware of the weight of responsibilities on their shoulders. A strand of research even found that children may not be comfortable with their parents' return, after having lived all along in their absence. This study, however, showed that most children would welcome their parents' return (Table 8.15).

A Profile of Well-Being among Children of Kerala Migrants   139

Table 8.14 Self-Reported Negative and Positive Aspects of Growing Up Without Parents

Changes Reported Positive Impact	HH children			Boarding School Children		
	Total (n=907)	Male (n=459)	Female (n=448)	Total (n=452)	Male (n=296)	Female (n=156)
I have become more mature.	37.9	43.4	32.4	75.4	78.7	69.2
I am more responsible.	42.4	48.1	36.6	81.6	83.4	78.2
I have become more independent.	19.4	22.0	16.7	49.3	55.7	37.2
I am more confident.	40.5	44.0	36.8	71.7	74.7	66.0
I have greater freedom of movement.	16.9	21.1	12.5	25.7	29.1	19.2
I have improved educational opportunities and social status.	63.0	62.3	63.6	76.3	73.3	82.1
My family has more money.	77.7	77.8	77.7	60.8	60.1	62.2
Other Positive Impacts	9.6	9.6	9.6	2.7	1.4	5.1
Negative Impact	HH Children			Boarding School Children		
I miss my parents.	80.3	79.5	81.0	80.8	78.4	85.3
I am sad/ unhappy.	20.7	21.6	19.9	42.9	39.5	49.4
Too many responsibilities at home	21.5	25.5	17.4	31.0	30.7	31.4
I feel lonely.	6.9	7.8	6.0	26.3	23.6	31.4
I feel angry and frustrated.	7.3	7.6	6.9	23.0	21.3	26.3
I feel insecure.	13.0	10.0	16.1	14.6	13.9	16.0
I have less freedom of movement.	12.1	10.2	14.1	33.8	35.5	30.8
Other Negative Impacts	2.9	2.2	3.6	1.8	1.4	2.6

Source: Kerala Children's Survey, 2010. All numbers are percentages of the total.

140 S Irudaya Rajan and Ashwin Kumar

Table 8.15 Response to Family Reunification among Migrant Children in Households and Boarding Schools

Question: Would You be Happy if Your Parents Returned Home for Good?	Households			Boarding Schools		
	Male	Female	Total	Male	Female	Total
Yes	77.8	80.8	79.3	75.3	84.6	78.5
No	5.7	4.9	5.3	13.9	9.0	12.2
Not sure	16.6	14.3	15.4	10.8	6.4	9.3
Total	100.0	100.0	100.0	100.0	100.0	100.0

Source: Kerala Children's Survey, 2010. All numbers are percentages of the total.

Table 8.16 Response to Family Reunification among Migrant Children by Age in Households and Boarding Schools

Would you be Happy if your Migrant Parents Returned Home Permanently?

Age	12	13	14	15	16	17	18	Total
Boarding School								
Yes	61.5	85.5	80.6	83.6	80.2	73.8	87.5	79.5
No	20.5	11.6	8.1	9.0	8.8	17.5	10.0	11.8
Not sure	17.9	2.9	11.3	7.5	11.0	8.8	2.5	8.7
Total	100.0	100.0	100.0	100.0	100.0	100.0	100.0	100.0
Households								
Yes	83.3	79.7	78.4	81.8	79.8	71.1	76.5	79.3
No	4.8	4.1	4.8	3.8	5.3	8.2	8.6	5.3
Not sure	11.9	16.2	16.8	14.4	14.9	20.6	14.8	15.4
Total	100.0	100.0	100.0	100.0	100.0	100.0	100.0	100.0

Source: Kerala Children's Survey, 2010. All numbers are percentages of the total.

However, male and female interviewees responded very differently to this question. More female respondents reported that they would be happy with the return of their parent(s) than male respondents, from both households and boarding schools. Similarly, it appears that more male respondents were ambiguous, uncertain, or negative about the return of their parent(s) than female respondents. More interestingly, close to 14 per cent of male Children of Migrant Parents in boarding schools and another 5.7 per cent in households were sure that they would not be happy if their migrant parents returned to Kerala and their families were reunited. 9 per cent of female children in migrant households in the boarding schools also reported that their response to family reunification would not be happy. Our study especially showed how as girls mature and go through periods of menarche, the absence of parents, especially in mother-away households, was felt very deeply. With not many people around them to understand and support them through these important changes in their lives, girls often felt lonely and this affected their overall well-being deeply (Table 8.14).

The age of the respondent also influenced the response to this question – younger respondents actually appear more resistant to the idea of familial reunification. More than one-fifth of the 12-year-old respondents reported that they would not be happy if their parents returned permanently and their families were reunited. On the other hand, older respondents appear to report almost uniformly that they would be happy if their migrant parents returned to Kerala and reunited their families. This poses an interesting question as to how children view their parent's absence as they become older and go through more complicated feelings, and perhaps feeling the weight of fulfilling their parents' expectations at an even greater level.

Do children of migrant parents become future migrants?

Overall, the study showed very comprehensively that children of migrant parents think very carefully about the implications that the absence of their parent(s) has on their overall well-being. The question then arises as to, having experienced what they have, would they be the next generation of migrants? When posed this question, the answer was not so unanimous. What makes this survey most important is the implications that this has on the future of migration. Given the high incidence of migrant households in our sampled study, it is imperative to know what children feel about migration to make an estimated guess about the future of migration from the region.

Despite the complicated perceptions of and emotional responses to migration, migration remained a popular future choice and strategy for respondents, who have intimate knowledge of the event and all its consequences. In the boarding school sample, more than three-fourths of all respondents indicated that migration would be an acceptable strategy in adulthood, while 17.9 per cent disagreed and stated instead that they would not migrate. More male respondents answered that they would like to migrate in the future compared to females in the same sample. In fact, a fifth of female respondents felt that they would not like to migrate when they became adults, compared to only 16 per cent of male respondents (Tables 8.17 and 8.18).

Interestingly, there was a stark difference between the responses from children in households and boarding schools, with the latter far more willing to think about migrating in the future.

This became even more clear when we looked at responses between the categories from the perspective of the childrens' ages. In boarding schools, older respondents from migrant households appear less enthused about migration – in

142 S Irudaya Rajan and Ashwin Kumar

Table 8.17 Would You Like to Migrate in the Future? 2010, by Gender

Responses	Households			Boarding Schools		
	Male	Female	Total	Male	Female	Total
Yes	63.6	44.2	54.0	75.7	73.7	75.0
No	15.0	23.9	19.4	16.6	20.5	17.9
Not sure	21.4	31.9	26.6	7.8	5.8	7.1
All Responses	100.0	100.0	100.0	100.0	100.0	100.0

Source: Kerala Children's Survey, 2010. All numbers are percentages of the total.

Table 8.18 Would You like to Migrate in the Future? Responses from Boarding Schools and Households By Age, 2010

Age	12	13	14	15	16	17	18	Total
	Boarding Schools							
Yes	76.9	83.1	72.6	74.6	72.5	79.0	61.0	75.0
No	12.8	14.1	17.7	17.9	20.9	13.6	31.7	17.9
Not Sure	10.3	2.8	9.7	7.5	6.6	7.4	7.3	7.1
All	100.0	100.0	100.0	100.0	100.0	100.0	100.0	100.0
	Households							
Yes	39.9	42.6	45.5	67.4	59.6	73.2	69.1	54.0
No	23.8	23.0	15.6	15.9	21.9	13.4	21.0	19.4
Not Sure	36.3	34.5	38.9	16.7	18.4	13.4	9.9	26.6
All	100.0	100.0	100.0	100.0	100.0	100.0	100.0	100.0

Source: Kerala Children's Survey, 2010. All numbers are percentages of the total.

fact, more than 30 per cent of children in migrant households aged 18 declared categorically that they would not like to migrate in the future. Younger children, particularly those aged 12 and 13, reported in the majority that they would like to migrate. However, we found the opposite trend among children living in households – where younger respondents were far less willing to consider migrating than the older cohort. This clearly shows how differing contexts deeply affect the way children see their overall condition, and hence their future decisions.

If they were to migrate, much like their parents, it was down to mostly financial reasons, with other reasons being a will to travel and encounter new experiences, much like their parents would.

Conclusion

As we have seen so far, negotiating parental absence has its own benefits, but it is not without its negative aspects, which corroborates with studies in other

A Profile of Well-Being among Children of Kerala Migrants 143

areas as well. This chapter, in a very limited way, tried to show a basic picture of how children of migrant parents negotiate the absence of their parents in as much as how they manifest themselves in their health, educational outcomes, and overall mental well-being.

The study was clear in finding that while educational and health outcomes for children of migrant parents were certainly better than those of non-migrants, this was manifested in better anthropometric indicators: better access to healthcare facilities and overall better reporting of health issues. On the educational front, we found that children of migrant parents also gain access to a wider variety of educational institutions, leading to slightly better educational outcomes as well. However, this does not automatically correlate with a better standard of living. When talking about the mental health of children in migrant households, we did find positive feelings when it came to children feeling personal growth in the absence of their parents. However, these positive feelings were juxtaposed with negative feelings and anxieties, particularly with stress on many levels, which was exacerbated by the fact that they could not convey it effectively to their parents.

Finally, when the study enquired into whether these children of migrants are potential migrants themselves, we found a rather clear picture. The fact that most children of migrant parents would consider migrating themselves shows that the economic benefits of migration are apparent to them. Since path dependence is a major factor when it comes to reproducing migration patterns, there is a good chance that these children have seen migration as a path to a better life. They are also aware of the myriad pitfalls of migration as well, as is very clearly depicted in our findings. Whether this migration of parents leads to the migration of the next generation, however, is an important question to ask and to look out for.

References

Brink, J. (1991). The effect of emigration of husbands on the status of their wives: An Egyptian case. *Indian Journal of Middle East Studies, 23*(2), 201–211.

Camacho, C., & Shen, I.-L. (2009). *Public Education for the Children Left Behind and its Implications on Growth and Inequality.* IZA Discussion Paper no. 4833.

Camacho, G. Z., & Hernández, K. (2007). Children and migration in Ecuador: Situation diagnostic. *Centre for Social Planning and Research: UNICEF, Quito.*

Gamburd, M. (2005) "'Lentils there, lentils here!" Sri Lankan domestic labour in the Middle East', in S. Huang, B. S. A. Yeoh and N. Abdul Rahman, (eds.), *Asian Women as Transnational Domestic Workers.* Singapore: Marshall Cavendish: 92–114.

Graham, E., Jordan, L. P., & Yeoh, B. S. (2015). Parental migration and the mental health of those who stay behind to care for children in South-East Asia. *Social Science & Medicine, 132,* 225–235.

Graham, P. J., & Meadows, C. E. (1967). Psychiatric disorder in the children of West Indian immigrants. *Child Psychology & Psychiatry & Allied Disciplines, 8*(2), 105–116.

Guo, L. (2009). Living arrangements of migrants' left-behind children in China. In *Population Association of America 2009 Annual Conference.*

Hoang, L. A., Lam, T., Yeoh, B. S., & Graham, E. (2015). Transnational migration, changing care arrangements and left-behind children's responses in South-east Asia. *Children's Geographies, 13*(3), 263–277.

Khan, M. I., & Valatheeswaran, C. (2020). International remittances and private healthcare in Kerala, India. *Migration Letters, 17*(3), 445–460.

Koska, O. A., Saygin, P. Ö., Çağatay, S., & Artal-Tur, A. (2013). International migration, remittances, and the human capital formation of Egyptian children. *International Review of Economics & Finance, 28*, 38–50.

Ministry of External Affairs, Government of India (2020). *Annual Report 2020–21.* New Delhi: MEA.

Parrenas, R. S. (2003). 'The care crises in the Philippines: Children of transnational families in the mew Global Economy', in B. Ehrenreich and A.R. Hochschild (eds.) *Global Women: Nannies, Maids and Sex Workers in the New Economy.* New York: Metropolitan Books: 39–54.

Parreñas, R. S. (2005). *Children of Global Migration: Transnational Families and Gendered Woes.* Stanford: Stanford University Press.

Sawyer, A. (2016). Is money enough?: The effect of migrant remittances on parental aspirations and youth educational attainment in rural Mexico. *International Migration Review, 50*(1), 231–266.

UNICEF (2008). *The Impact of Parental Deprivation on the Development of Children Left Behind by Moldovan Migrants.* New York: UNICEF Working Paper. www.unicef. org/siteguide/40634.html.

Valtolina, G. G., & Colombo, C. (2012). Psychological well-being, family relations, and developmental issues of children left behind. *Psychological Reports, 111*(3), 905–928.

Wickramage, K., Siriwardhana, C., Vidanapathirana, P., Weerawarna, S., Jayasekara, B., Pannala, G., ... & Sumathipala, A. (2015). Risk of mental health and nutritional problems for left-behind children of international labor migrants. *BMC Psychiatry, 15*(1), 1–12.

World Bank (2020). *Migration data and Remittances.* Available at: https://www.worldbank.org/en/topic/migrationremittancesdiasporaissues/brief/migration-remittances-data

Zachariah, K. C., Mathew, E. T., & Rajan, S. I. (2001). Social, economic and demographic consequences of migration on Kerala. *International migration, 39*(2), 43–71.

Zachariah, K. C., & Rajan, S. I. (2009). *Migration and Development: The Kerala Experience.* New Delhi: Daanish Publishers.

Zachariah, K. C., & Rajan, S. I. (2011). *Inflexion in Kerala's Gulf Connection: Report on the Kerala Migration Survey 2011.* Working paper No.450. Thiruvananthapuram: Centre for Development Studies.

Zachariah, K. C., & Rajan, S. I. (2016). Kerala migration study 2014. *Economic and Political Weekly, 51*(6), 66–71.

Zachariah, K. C., & Rajan, S. I. (2018). *Emigration from Kerala: End of an Era.* Kochi, India: RedInk an Imprint of Nalanda Books.

Chapter 9

What do We know About Migration and the Role of Education in Migration?

The Case of Uzbekistan

Deepa Sankar

Introduction

Migration is a global phenomenon since human history, caused by both "push" factors (social pressures and lack of economic opportunities, fewer jobs and lower wages, forcing people to move to another location outside the areas of their origin) as well as "pull" factors (incentives offered by better jobs, more wages and better living environment in destination countries). The topics related to migration and its impact on the socioeconomic dynamics of host and receiving countries have been studied extensively but received international acknowledgment as one of the powerful drivers of sustainable development only through the 2030 Agenda for Sustainable Development (International Organization for Migration, 2018). Several Sustainable Development Goals (SDGs) and targets recognize migration. For example, SDG target 10.7 (within SDG 10 on Reduce inequalities within and among countries) aims to "facilitate orderly, safe, regular and responsible migration and mobility of people, including through the implementation of planned and well-managed migration policies."[1] Further, SDG targets 10.c aims to "reduce to less than 3 percent the transaction costs of migrant remittances and eliminate remittance corridors with costs higher than 5 percent"; Further SDG 8.8 (Decent work and Economic Growth) talks about "protecting labor rights and promoting safe and secure working environment for all workers, including migrant workers, in particular women migrants"; and SDG 17.18 talks about increase significantly the availability of high-quality, timely and reliable data disaggregated by many parameters, including migratory status.

Migration is a powerful, multidimensional driver of sustainable development for migrants themselves and their communities in countries of origin, transit and destination (IOM, 2018). As per the estimates of the Population Division of the UN Department of Economic and Social Affairs (UN DESA), the estimated number of international migrants worldwide increased in the 20 years between 2000 and 2020, reaching 281 million in 2020 (3.6 percent of the world's population). This figure is up from 248 million in 2015, 220 million in 2010, 191 million in 2005 and 173 million in 2000.[2] In the past

DOI: 10.4324/9781003343141-12

146 Deepa Sankar

two decades, the international migrant stock grew annually by an average of 2.4 percent.

Migration presents both opportunities and challenges for societies, communities, and individuals.[3] International migration—the movement of people across international boundaries—has enormous implications for growth and poverty alleviation in both origin and destination countries.[4] The remittances[5] that flow from host (foreign) countries to the country of origin, mostly low and middle-income countries (LMICs) are often the most direct link between migration and development, play an important role in the economy of several countries, as they offer income to families, facilitate domestic spending and in several cases, offer reliable income for countries experiencing serious economic challenges. The remittance flows to LMICs were $548 billion in 2019, which declined to $540 billion in 2020 due to COVID-19, but the World Bank (2021) estimates projected that the remittance flows to have recovered to reach $589 billion in 2021, registering an increase of 7.3 percent from the previous year.[6]

While migration and inward remittances help receiving families to overcome poverty and unemployment and countries to overcome economic pressures, migration places heavy burdens on the migrating person as well as family members, especially children. Migrants can face harsh living conditions, discrimination and low wages and often lack safety nets and suffer disproportionately in times of economic hardship.[7]

Migration also affects children in different ways: some children are left behind by migrating parent(s); some move along with their migrating parents or even alone, without parents or caretakers; and some children are affected since they stay in communities where large migration take place.[8] *Children left behind* may benefit from having migrant parents (UNICEF, 2004). Remittances sent home by parents can increase consumption, finance schooling, buy health care for children in varying degrees, depending on the household (prioritization of childcare services and other contexts of leaving behind) and child characteristics (such as age, gender). The involvement of substitute care or the lack of care causes difficulties for some children's emotional well-being and psychological development.[9] *Children who migrate with their parents* face different opportunities and challenges, including marginalization, discrimination, and barriers to accessing social services, depending on the host country context.[10]

In this paper, the trends in migration, its impact and the enablers and barriers in benefiting nations, families and particularly children are looked at in the context of Uzbekistan.

Uzbekistan

Uzbekistan is a double land-locked country in Central Asia with a population of 34.9 million. Uzbekistan is also a lower middle-income country, with a

Migration and the Role of Education in Migration 147

GDP per capita of current US$1983 (Ajwad et al., 2014). The country had managed to reduce the proportion of population living below the national poverty line from around 28 percent in early 2000s to around 11.5 percent in 2020.[11] In 2021, about 7.5 percent of the country's citizens lived below the World Bank's lower-middle-income poverty line (World Bank, 2021).

Since its independence from the Soviet Union 30 years ago, the Central Asian countries' population grew rapidly, with around half of the population below 30 years of age and around 45 percent are even below 45 years of age. Uzbekistan is the most populous country in the region and is expected to grow with a relatively high total fertility rate (2.4). The total and working-age population in the country is expected to grow until 2045, while the dependency rates remaining relatively moderate (UNICEF, 2018). As the country is undergoing a steady demographic transition and has reached a phase of 'early demographic dividend' now, the country's youth bulge offers both opportunities and challenges. This will enable the country not only to maximize its chances of a growth and employment spurt in the near future but also to set the base for a more productive, innovative, inclusive and stable society in the longer term. However, a lot of this will depend on human capital development. Boosting its human capital will require that Uzbekistan enhances access and particularly the quality of education, from early childhood to primary and secondary education, tertiary education and job skills development etc. On the one hand, these demographic trends offer the potential to increase domestic production and growth but also increase the pressure on the domestic labor market and push some Uzbeks to migrate to other countries in search of (better) employment and income opportunities (World Bank, 2021).

At present, children in Uzbekistan, by the age of 18 years, are expected to complete 12 years of school. Most of its population of 25 years of age or older have, on average, received at least a decade of formal education. However, factoring in what children actually learn, the expected years of school that a child in Uzbekistan receives are only 9 years (World Bank, 2021). Market demand for graduates of tertiary education is high, yet access to tertiary education is limited. Only 10.7 percent of youth aged 25–34 have a university diploma, while two in three youth have a postsecondary specialized technical diploma, 23 percent have an upper secondary diploma (grade 11), and 2 percent have lower secondary education (grade 9). Uzbekistan has the lowest tertiary attainment rate in the Central Asia region (World Bank, 2021). However, the demand for higher education in the country has been increasing, as the number of applicants for Bachelor's program entrance exams increased fourfold in the last 20 years, whereas those who got admitted into an undergraduate course has increased by only 2.8 times, and the overall intake rate remains less than 10 percent in 2021 (World Bank, 2021).

The unemployment rate, which was estimated to be 9 percent in 2019, had risen to around 10.5 percent in the country (2020), again attributed to the COVID-19 crisis. While there are around 15 million people who are economically active in the labor market within Uzbekistan,[12] it is estimated that around 2 million (UNDESA, 2020) to 2.5 million Uzbeks are working abroad (Sibagatulina, 2021).

Uzbekistan and migration

Uzbekistan presents a unique case of internal and international migration. The evolving socioeconomic and political landscape of the country also impacted migration, particularly international migration. The first phase of migration abroad was during the transformational period of the 1990s, the population of the country, against a background of increasing social inequality and lack of employment opportunities, migrated abroad to support families (Bonderanko, 2021). During the first decade of the millennium, the labor migration from Uzbekistan was due to both push and pull factors, with the formation of "migrant networks" supporting people moving abroad. As a result of country's stagnant economic growth from 2010 to 2015, employment opportunities also began to shrink. However, the "migrant networks" of people of Uzbekistan origin that had already formed abroad facilitated people from Uzbekistan to move to other countries and search for work and livelihood. The new government under President Shavakat Mirziyoyev that assumed power in late 2016 introduced path-breaking reforms to transform the economy into a market economy. While the economic liberalization is yet to transform into increased labor market opportunities, the currency devaluation in September 2018 was a boon to households whose members were working abroad and sending in remittances and hence working abroad remained an attractive option for many households.

Internal migration in Uzbekistan

Internal migration, from rural (and usually poorer regions) to cities, has historically underwritten economic development and poverty reduction.[13] Uzbekistan has one of the lowest rates of internal migration in the world, in part due to its registration system (known as the *propiska* system),[14] a legacy of the former Soviet system. The "propiska" is a compulsory domicile legally tying a person to the address stamped in a passport.[15] Under this system, an individual is required to live and work in the city or town which their propiska indicates and children can receive public education only at the location their parents have their propiska. For many years, Uzbekistan had limited domestic migration by imposing restrictive measures on the ability of citizens to travel to the country's capital.[16] A Presidential Decree (PD-5984) brought out in April 2020[17] introduced new procedures regarding registration and place of residence stipulated under the propiska system. An analysis of data available on the State Statistical Committee (SSC)'s website regarding the number of arrivals or moves within different regions of the country shows that there is an upward trend in the number of people moving within the country, across the provinces or regions, which could be broadly classified as "internal migration". With the relaxation of restrictions on the move to Tashkent city, the share of people moving in and out of Tashkent city has increased in the total internal movement within Uzbekistan.

International migration

International migration is often quantified using the measures of "stock" and "flows". While the migration "stocks" are either the number of *immigrants* settled in a particular country/region or the number of *emigrants* who had left a country of origin to settle in another location, measured at a given point in time, migration "flows" refer to the number of migrants entering or leaving a country or region during a specific period of time.

Migration "stock"

As per the latest data available from International Migrant Stock data (United Nations Department of Economic and Social Affairs, Population Division (2020)), the stock of emigrant population from Uzbekistan living in different parts of the world had risen from 1.42 million in 1990 to over 2 million by 2020. Men account for 52 percent of the emigrant stock from Uzbekistan in 2020. Pitted against the total population of the country, the stock of emigrants account for 6 percent of the population in 2020. This is in fact is a decline from 6.6 to 6.7 percent during the period 2005–2010.

Historically, people from Uzbekistan tend to migrate to Eastern European and Central Asian countries, and as in the case of other Central Asian countries, Russia remains the principal destination for more than two-thirds of all the migrants from Uzbekistan. Neighboring Central Asian countries of Kazakhstan and Turkmenistan are also popular destinations for Uzbek migrants.

It must be noted here that though there is an increase in the number of people from Uzbekistan migrating to Russia, reflecting the overall increase in out-migration from Uzbekistan during the past 30 years since independence, the share of Russia in Uzbekistan emigrant stock has been on the decline, indicating that Uzbekistan people are exploring diverse greener pastures for settling in.

Migration "flows"

The number of people leaving the country in a year has declined from over a 100,000 in 2005 to around 20,000 by 2021. Similarly, the number of people moving into the country has also declined from around 7000 in 2005 to less than 2000 in 2021. The net migration flows in 2021 is estimated to be around 18,000.

The migration flows from Uzbekistan have been declining over the past one and a half decades, but what is also interesting is the decline in the number of youth and young children over the years (World Bank, 2021). A study by the Oxus Society for Central Asian Affairs[18] drawing data collected through the Central Asian Migration Tracker (CAMT) provides interesting insights into the nature of visas available for Central Asians from 2016 to 2019. The study reveals that work visas account for 94.5 percent of all visas issued (by Russia, EU, USA, Canada, South Korea and Japan taken together) for Uzbeks. The share of study visas in total visas issued by the above countries increased from 1.9 percent in 2015 to 2.6 percent in 2019. On the other hand, the share of resident visas in total visas issued for Uzbek nationals by the above countries declined from close to 5 percent in 2015 to 2.8 percent by 2019.

Russia continues to be the most popular destination for Uzbeks for migration—be it for work, or study or permanent move. The number of Uzbek citizens with Russian work visas grew from 1.4 million in 2016 to 2.1 million in 2019. During the same period, the Russian work visas issued for Central Asia had increased from 2.7 million to 3.9 million. Uzbeks accounted for more than half of all the work visas Russians had issued for Central Asians.

During the same period (2016–2019), the number of students from Uzbekistan who had Russian study visas more than doubled from 24,000 to 50,000 and the share of Uzbeks in study visas to Russia increased from 15 percent to almost 20 percent. Kazakhstan accounted for 35–45 percent of the student visas issued by Russia for Central Asians during the period.

The number of Uzbeks with Russian resident visas declined from more than 61,000 to less than 46,000 between 2016 and 2019. Uzbeks accounted for a third of resident visas Russia provided for Central Asians in 2016, but that share also declined to 23 percent by 2019.

Remittances

Remittances are currently the largest source of external financing in the region. Uzbekistan receives the highest amount of remittances among all Central Asian countries. Remittances accounted for more than a fourth of the GDPs in Kyrgyz Republic and Tajikistan and a tenth in Uzbekistan. The personal remittances that Uzbekistan received were US$8,545 million in 2019, and it fell to US$6,979 million in 2020, mainly on account of the reduced employment for migrants on account of the COVID-19 pandemic. However, the remittances are estimated to have reached around US$7.6 billion in 2021, or 12 percent of the country's GDP.

What are the characteristics of Migrants from Uzbekistan?

One of the biggest challenges in studying social issues in Uzbekistan is the dearth of nationally representative data from households. As of now, the most

Migration and the Role of Education in Migration 151

reliable source of primary data to study migration at household level is the "Listening to the Citizens of Uzbekistan (L2CU)" study, carried out by the World Bank together with the Development Strategy Center of Uzbekistan and other partners in 2018. The study covered 4,000 households in its nationally representative baseline survey.[19]

Internal and in-migration

As per the L2CU survey (2018 data), in 2018, 1.16 million people (5 percent of the 15+ years population) in the country moved from a different region or country to their current location in Uzbekistan. Around 4 percent of resident men and 6 percent of resident women had moved from their original location to their current location in the past several years. Among this, 77 percent were people who moved into the current location from another region within Uzbekistan (internal migration), while the rest, constitute in-migration from other countries. Of this, 9 percent came in from Kyrgyz Republic, 6 percent from Tajikistan, 4 percent from Russia and the remaining from other neighboring countries.

The number and share of people who have moved into the region was highest in Tashkent city 270 thousand) in 2018 and the lowest in Samarkhand (12,000+) and Andijan (20,000+). The in-migrants constituted around 14.5 percent of the total population in Tashkent city whereas in Samarkhand, less than a percent of the residents were in-migrants. On the other hand, the people moving out of the region into another region were lowest in Tashkent city (only 0.8 percent of people in other regions had moved there from Tashkent city) and highest in Samarkhand (around 8 percent of the population had moved out of Samarkhand to other places. Through this process, while Tashkent city, Tashkent region, Jizzakh, and Namangan gained more people Samarkhand, Surkhandarya, and Bukhara's net gain of people was negative.

Reasons for in-migration

Among those who moved into the country from other countries or moved across regions within the country, more than half of them had moved for family reasons – while 50 percent moved with family, 21 percent moved in to join the family or after marriage. Eighty six percent of women who moved places had family or marriage reasons to move places. On the other hand, only 46 percent of men moved for family reasons. Overall, a fifth of the people moved places to find or join a job in the current place of residence and 37 percent of the men moved for job compared to only 7 percent of women. Around 4 percent of people moved to their current place of residence for studies—7 percent among men and 2 percent among women. An estimated 220,000 people had moved location for jobs while more than 49,000 people moved for studies. Around 86000 people shifted Tashkent city for jobs and another 35,000 for studies.

Those who moved into their current locations for jobs or finding a job have higher education qualifications than the average population. While 5 percent of such people have a Master's degree (compared to only 1 percent in general population); 37 percent have a Bachelor's degree (compared to only 9.6 percent in the general population) and 35 percent have vocational education (less than the 46 percent in general population).

International migration from Uzbekistan

As per the estimates using the L2CU survey, there were around 1.4 million people who live abroad. The household survey triangulates the official data on international migration from Uzbekistan. These people account for 6 percent of the people in Uzbekistan (of the 15 years old and above). This is in line with the official statistics of the stock of emigrants accounting for 6 percent of the population in 2020. Among men (15 years plus), 11 percent had emigrated while among women, only 1.26 percent had migrated to another country. The country's emigration rate is more than double the world average (3.2 percent) and that of other middle-income countries (2.7 percent), yet lower than that of Europe and Central Asia as a whole (10.7 percent).[20]

Among the emigrated stock, 89 percent were men, and the remaining 11 percent were women. The majority of the male labor migrants are from rural areas (mainly engaged in manual labor), while the majority of women are city-dwellers (their higher level of education and language proficiency allows them to work in the service sector) (Bondarenko, 2021).

More than 91 percent of the emigrants from Uzbekistan were below 50 years of age, and within that 44 percent are young people below 30 years of age. Young people of 20–30 years old constitute 40 percent of all migrants moving to other countries in 2018.

As per the L2CU data, 77 percent of emigrants from Uzbekistan chose Russia as their destination while 15 percent went to Kazakhstan. In a 2013 survey carried out by the World Bank and GIZ, 86 percent of the Uzbek emigrants went to Russia and 12 percent to Kazakhstan.[21] Migration decisions are frequently explained by economic and demographic, political, and social and cultural push and pull factors, and migration results from wage differences between markets, according to the most basic economic models (Mansoor and Quillin, 2006, p. 77). The pattern of immigration between Uzbekistan and Russia, as well as between Uzbekistan and Turkey, is influenced by a variety of economic, historical, cultural, linguistic, and political factors (ERDOĞAN, Zahide, 2021).

One of the reasons that attract the Uzbek migrants to countries like Russia and Kazakhstan is related to the wage differences. While Uzbekistan's per capita income was US$1,983.2 in 2021 (World Bank, 2021), that of Russia was US$10,127, almost five times that of Uzbekistan; the per capita GDP of Kazakhstan was US$9,122 (World Bank, 2020). According to a survey conducted by the Federation of Migrants of Russia (December 2021), the average salary of migrants in Russia is 47,100 rubles (US$869) a month (December 2021). Those who don't speak Russian very well earn 37,000 rubles (US$680), and those who speak it well earn 49,000 rubles (US$900).[22] The average salary of Russian workers with the same level of productivity as migrants exceeds migrants' average salary by 40 percent (Vakulenko, and Leukhin, 2017). As per the statistics from the State Statistics Committee of Government of Uzbekistan, during January-March 2022, the average monthly salary of a person in Uzbekistan had reached 3.5 million soums (around US$323). Clearly, the earnings of those who migrated to Russia, on an average, is at least double that of those who were working in Uzbekistan. Abdulloev et al. (2020) show that the average wage earnings by Tajik, Uzbek, and Kyrgyz migrants in Russia is way higher than that of those who remain in their countries for all education levels and sectors.

As per the MOELR statistics, there are increasing move towards destinations other than the traditional ones like Russia and Kazakhstan in recent years. Some of these are triggered by the policies of the destination countries. For example, In November 2018, Turkey increased the period for visa-free stay for the citizens of Uzbekistan from 30 to 90 days (Bondarenko, 2021), facilitating the migrants to have increased time for searching appropriate employment or even participating in seasonal employment. As a result, as per MOLER statistics, in 2018, 7.8 percent of labor migrants were working in Turkey (compared to less than 2 percent in 2012). While the share of male migrants who were working in Turkey were 4.1 percent, among all female migrants, a fourth were working in Turkey. Among all migrants from Uzbekistan working in Turkey in 2018, the share of women was 57 percent, indicating new countries which are providing opportunities for female migrants as well.

The largest share of emigrant people in the country were reported in Khorezm province, followed by Karakalpakstan. Least share of emigrants was reported in Tashkent city, Noviy province, and Tashkent region. Interestingly, these were the regions that reported the highest in-migration/internal move.

An interesting result that comes out of the analysis is related to the education levels of the emigrants and others. The data from the Ministry of Employment and Labour Relations (MOELR), Government of Uzbekistan, show that the share of migrants who had completed only secondary complete (or less than secondary education) has been declining over the years, and instead, the share of those who had completed secondary specialized education (higher secondary) or vocational education has been increasing. Among those who emigrated out of the country, 2/3rds have a secondary specialized or vocational education (after secondary education). Only 5 percent have a university/higher education (Bachelors' or Masters' or above qualifications) as per the MOELR statistics and only 3.7 percent as per the L2CU survey of 2018. Abdulloev et al. (2020) point out that in contrast to those with secondary schooling levels, the share of people with secondary or vocational (secondary special and technical) among migrants are high, but the share of those with higher education (degrees received from universities) "tend to remain in their home country due to their higher social status and access to higher-income home country jobs". They compare the trends to an inverted-U relationship between education and migration. People at lower and higher levels of education do not migrate, while at middle levels (secondary) more people choose to migrate (Abdulloev et al., 2020).

The reason for the increased share of those with secondary specialized or vocational education is the education policy adopted in 2009 (Decree of the President of the Republic of Uzbekistan no. PP-1157 of July 13, 2009), which mandated all children to have secondary specialized or vocation education. This policy is revised in 2018, with 11 years of secondary education being restored and vocational education being restructured. This may change the structure of the education of migrants in the future.

On the other hand, among those who move internally (from regions to regions/cities), 18.6 percent have a higher education qualification. In the overall population, only 10.5 percent have higher education. This shows that those with higher education were able to find better jobs within the country and hence they moved from region to region or cities, whereas a large number of people with vocational education found it difficult to get a job within the country and hence they moved abroad.

Table 9.1 provides a multivariate regression analysis to understand the characteristics that are correlated with migration and emigration was carried out despite the challenges in detailed data but mainly looking at the education levels. As expected, younger people move within the country and out of the country more than the older cohorts as evident from the age and age 2 variables. In terms of gender, an interesting result comes out. While women move internally within the country (mainly with families and after marriage), men move outside the country (mainly for jobs) more than females.

The first-generation young person tends to move out of the country more than others in the family, but they are not the drivers of move within the country. In other words, internal migration is more driven by household head than young people whereas the first-generation child tends to move outside more than other family members.

In terms of educational qualification of the people, those with higher education degrees tend to move within the country significantly than those with qualifications below that; but when it comes to emigration out of the country, those with secondary specialized education and vocational education have higher probabilities of moving out than those with below secondary education and those with higher education. The higher the size of the family, the lesser the move within the country, whereas people from large families are more prone to go outside the country for better livelihoods.

Migration and the Role of Education in Migration   155

Table 9.1 Multivariate Analysis of the Characteristics of those Migrated within the Country and those Emigrated Outside the Country

	Migrated		Emigrated	
	Coef. *(Std. Err.)*	*t*	*Coef.* *(Std. Err.)*	*t*
age	0.002 (0.00)	88.97***	0.002 (0.00)	220.3***
age2	0.000 (0.00)	−97.26***	0.000 (0.00)	−293.3***
Gender (1=male; 0 otherwise)	−0.019 (0.00)	−205.7***	0.067 (0.00)	974.9***
first_gen (1=first generation child; 0 otherwise)	−0.040 (0.00)	−313.4***	0.023 (0.00)	292.5***
Education				
edu_sec (1=Secondary; 0 otherwise)	0.001 (0.00)	2.05*	0.027 (0.00)	154.6***
edu_sec_spl (1=Secondary specialized/lyceum; 0 otherwise	−0.038 (0.00)	−127.8***	0.058 (0.00)	311.7***
edu_voc (1=vocation education; 0 otherwise)	−0.018 (0.00)	−65.4***	0.061 (0.00)	371.4***
edu_HE (1=higher education; 0 otherwise)	0.013 (0.00)	41.64***	0.013 (0.00)	61.6***
Hhsize (household size)	−0.008 (0.00)	−381.77***	0.003 (0.00)	210.6***
_cons	0.112 (0.00)	285.1***	−0.078 (0.00)	−551.4***

*** significant at 99 percent

Remittances and households

As per L2CU survey, overall, 11.8 percent of the households in Uzbekistan received remittances sent by their family members abroad in 2018. The proportion of households with remittances were high in Khorezm, Bukhara and Samarkhand and were low in Jizzakh, Tashkent city and Navoiy.

To understand the contribution of remittances in households' overall income, the average monthly income of households by emigration status and remittance was analyzed. While the monthly mean income of all households in the country and that of households with no member emigrated outside the country remained similar around Uzbek soum of 22 million, the households with an emigrated member reported an average monthly income of 26 million Uzbek soums. Further, the households which reported receiving remittances sent by the emigrant family member had a monthly income of around 32.5 million Uzbek soums in a month in 2018. Those households with an emigrated member, but not remitting money, had the least income reported: only 15 million Uzbek soums. The inferences that come from this analysis are as follows: remittances contribute to better incomes for the receiving families. People were most likely emigrated from poorer families without much income (and hence not receiving remittance despite an emigrated member made them even poorer than the average households or households where no one had emigrated), and remittances made a difference.

Unfortunately, the L2CU survey did not explore the jobs carried out by the emigrants abroad; hence, it is very difficult to assess the jobs emigrants received, though the official statistics and anecdotal evidence suggest Uzbek nations are mostly engaged in casual labor. In terms of remittances sent by the emigrants, it is very evident that those with secondary specialized education or vocational education remit more money home than those with lesser qualifications or those with higher education. The low levels of remittances by those with below secondary education or only secondary education could be attributed to their overall low wages as these emigrants are most likely to be engaged in low-end jobs. On the other hand, those with higher education were most likely engaged in white-collar jobs with regular salaries, and there could be two reasons for their not remitting as much as the ones with vocational or secondary education: (1) those with higher education were most likely moved out with their families unlike those with lesser education, and they were perhaps spending most of their incomes on the families they live with; and (2) those with higher education perhaps have families back home who were relatively well-to-do, and hence the dependence on remittances for household activities were limited; hence less remittances. By contrast, most of the emigrants with vocational or secondary education work as laborers had left behind their families in Uzbekistan who depend on the remittances for meeting household requirements. Hence, the remittances from those with secondary and vocational education were relatively higher than that of people with higher education.

The results of the multivariate regressions for individual earnings/income and remittances sent home by migrants show that education levels were also significant in explaining the differences, after controlling for age, gender, household size, and other variables. In overall incomes of individuals, with each higher level of education, overall income too increased. On the other hand, as seen with the patterns in absolute volume of remittance, the most significant factor in remittance levels was for those with secondary specialized education and vocational education.

Use of remittances by households

The average remittances received by households and the welfare quintiles that they end up with indicate that higher the remittances, the higher the household being in a better welfare situation. The remittances were used for a range of purposes by households. Overall, 42 percent of the remittances were used for improving housing. Fifty five percent of the richest households (top quintile) spent their remittances on improving houses whereas only 19 percent of the poorest households used their remittances for housing. Around two-thirds of the poorest households used the remittances for food compared to only a fourth of the richest households. Only households belonging to richest quintiles used a part of the remittances for savings. Spending on education and health care accounted for only around 5 percent of overall remittances that households in Uzbekistan received. Clearly, remittances contribute to reducing poverty and housing, but not adequate to invest more in health and education-related matters.

Impact of migration on children left behind

A targeted study by UNICEF (2019c)[23] also confirms these findings. The study reported that most of the households—84 percent surveyed, depended on remittances for paying better nutrition, housing, education, and health. The study further elaborated that many families (of emigrants) did not have other sources of stable income and half of the nonemigrant members were unemployed. The study found that families left behind by migrant workers tend to live in poor conditions. Only 19 percent of the studied households had central heating and only half of the households had access to running water. Around 93 percent of the caregivers of children left behind by emigrating parent(s) stated that expenses on nonessential items (e.g. study materials for children, clothing, and medication) were often not affordable for households with children left behind.

However, what is more serious is the impact of parental migration on the socio-emotional well-being of children. The UNICEF study revealed that half of the children reported worsened moods immediately after the parent(s) migrated, a third of the children experienced emotional problems on a regular basis, with 21 percent of the children suffered from anxiety. Caregivers also reported that young children often became stubborn, whimsical, capricious, and naughty especially when they missed their parents.

The analysis so far reveals the following:

- Uzbekistan, despite its systems of restricted movement within the country (*propiska* system), has a large number of people (around 5 percent) moving within the country (internal and in-migration) for jobs as well as family reasons.

158 Deepa Sankar

- Uzbekistan has a sizeable proportion of people living and working abroad, and the stock of Uzbekistan people living abroad is estimated to be around 6 percent of the population.
- Most of the emigrants from Uzbekistan go to live, work, or study in Russia or Kazakhstan, two former Soviet Republics sharing history with Uzbekistan, and together they account for 92 percent of all emigrants from the country. This also means that the migrants from Uzbekistan have not fully explored labor market available outside the former Soviet Union or had limited success in doing so due to various reasons.
- While those who migrate from one place to another within the country have proportionately more people with higher education (16 percent compared to 3 percent among emigrants), the emigrants from Uzbekistan to other countries have mostly vocational education (60 percent compared to 43 percent among internal migrants), which allows them to mostly work in low skilled occupations, be it in formal or informal sectors in their host countries.
- Uzbeks living abroad send remittances to support their family back in Uzbekistan and this contributes to more than a tenth of the GDP of the country.
- Remittances contribute to improve food and housing among the receiving households and facilitate economic mobility to be among better welfare quintiles
- Despite the benefits that remittances facilitate, studies show that children left behind by emigrating family members have socio-emotional challenges.

Skills and labour migration

One of the insights emerging from the analysis of emigrants and their education levels is that those who emigrate from the country are mostly people with vocational education or secondary specialized (upper secondary) education. While people with higher education tend to move within the country, they are proportionately less represented in people who migrate out of the country. Hence, the highly skilled "brain drain" is limited in the country. However, if more people with higher education get employed abroad, there is a greater potential of raising the perceptions about Uzbek emigrants and thus the overall potential of the Uzbek job seekers abroad. The main challenge in this regard is the limited opportunities available in the country for higher education. Till recently, only a tenth of the young people applying for higher education courses were able to secure an admission (which in reality, translate to less gross enrollment ratios in higher education), though, in the last few years, the situation has improved with the government increasing higher education spaces. Another challenge is related to the expansion of higher education through increasing the spaces for humanitarian and social spheres, with limited enhancements in technical areas.

Migration and the Role of Education in Migration   159

Another issue that hinders emigrants from exploring the potential of migration abroad is related to both "cognitive" and "soft skills." By the time a young person completes his education and enters labor market, it is expected that the person has not only foundational skills (such as literacy and numeracy skills) and job-specific skills (professional or vocational skills), but also transferable and digital skills.

In terms of foundational skills, not much is known about the quality of the school or tertiary education in Uzbekistan as Uzbekistan will be participating, for the first time, in international PISA tests (OECD's Programme for International Student Assessment (PISA) measures 15-year-olds' ability to use their reading, mathematics and science knowledge and skills to meet real-life challenges.) in PISA 2021, to be held in 2022. Uzbekistan has not participated in any other international learning assessment. The country is still in the process of developing its own national assessment systems. A 2019 UNICEF - Ministry of Public Education (MOPE), Government of Uzbekistan study of grade IV students in Math, Language and Science revealed that students in Uzbekistan were able to identify or recall simple and more obvious information and complete clearly set-out, uncomplicated tasks. However, students struggled to identify, interpret, and evaluate more complicated information, solve complex mathematical problems, and respond to questions that required reasoning and application.[24]

A study by Ajwad et al. (2014) of Employers in Uzbekistan revealed a huge gap in transferable skills, particularly socio-emotional skills, and creativity (measured as the difference between the "importance" and "satisfaction" scores assigned by employers).[25] The study further explained that the largest skill deficits were in socio-emotional skills such as "accepting responsibility for one's actions," "self-motivation," and "creativity." The World Bank's Skills Assessment in Uzbekistan showed more than 20 percent of the students reporting various difficulties in engaging with others, suggesting issues with withdrawal, loneliness, and possibly social exclusion at school and future difficulties with teamwork in the labor market.[26] Many of these skills, broadly called as "transactional skills" or socio-emotional skills, need to be cultivated from early years and hence need to be reflected in the early childhood education programs as well as school programs. With this vision, the Government of Uzbekistan, since 2018, have been reforming curriculum, teaching-learning materials and pedagogy to be competency-based rather than just developing theoretical knowledge in subject areas. Many young people in Uzbekistan find it easy to move to countries where Russian is spoken as a link/global language and their access to labor markets in other countries is limited due to limited teaching of other languages such as English in the country.

UNICEF (2020b) study on Youth shows that young people perceive lack of work experience as one of the key factors impeding their employment after graduation.[27] Another UNICEF (2020) study shows huge disparities in young people (10–29 years) in digital skills across location, gender, and economic status of households.[28] In addition, "school-to-work" transition

160 Deepa Sankar

is challenging for most young people in Uzbekistan, resulting in a high rate of young people not in education, employment, or training (NEET). After completion of the compulsory secondary education, 56 percent of young people of 19–24 years of age are NEET[29] -69 percent of young women and 33.4 percent of young men. Most out-migration occurs among people in NEET.

The Government of Uzbekistan has come up with various policies in recent times to facilitate the migration of young people from the country to foreign locations to enhance their jobs and earnings. While the high remittances from abroad is adding around 11 percent to the domestic economy, it must be also noted that the high dependence on remittances is also making the country's economy more vulnerable to external shocks, such as what happened during 2020 with the COVID-19 pandemic or the ongoing Ukraine crisis.

Uzbekistan: Leveraging the benefits of migration

Global evidence suggests that in general, emigration has a positive effect on the sending country (Asch, 1994). The sending country benefits because migration provides employment to the people from the sending country who otherwise would have remained unemployed or underemployed with limited earnings. In the case of Uzbekistan, unemployment rates are already quite high (though the unemployment rate has declined to 9.6 percent in 2021 from 10.5 percent in 2020). School-to-work transition is challenging for most young people in Uzbekistan, resulting in high rate of young people in Uzbekistan being "not in education, employment or training" (NEET). After completion of the compulsory secondary education, 56 percent of young people of 19–24 years of age are NEET—69 percent of young women and 33 percent of young men (UNICEF, 2020). A large proportion of young people in Uzbekistan are employed informally—43.5 percent among 15–24-year-olds (UNDP, 2018). Young men see labor migration as an enticing option—one in 12 young people is temporarily living abroad (UNICEF, 2019a). But one in every six households has a member working abroad. It is expected that with more people migrate, the domestic labor market becomes competitive for the remaining workforce.

An important benefit, as discussed in the paper, is the gain for the sending countries in terms of remittances. The money sent home by the nonresident family members enhances the households' standard of living, particularly spending on social and human development sectors, such as education and health. The remittances also enhance the foreign exchange reserves for the country as well as the enhanced household spending contributes to the domestic growth of the economy. Uzbekistan has been a beneficiary of huge remittances over the years.

However, the recent war in Ukraine is expected to slow down the economic growth to 3.6 percent in 2022 compared to the pre-crisis estimates of about 6 percent. The overall slowdown of the Russian economy because of the war may result in several of the migrants from Uzbekistan losing out on jobs and reduced earnings. It is also anticipated that the remittances will fall by 50 percent due to the weakening of the Russian Ruble. An estimated fall in remittances of 6 percent of GDP will widen the current account deficit to 10 percent of GDP in 2022 (World Bank, 2021).

An important point about Uzbekistan's emigration trends is that the destination or host countries for Uzbek migrants remain predominantly Russia or the former Soviet countries with Russian as the major link language. In order to absorb the volatile global trends and shocks, it is important for the country to diversify its migration patterns. Education has a key role to play here. First of all, teaching and learning an international language other than Russian (mainly English) will enhance the prospects of the migrants to find more diverse markets and host countries. Second, by increasing the opportunities for higher education and skills, including the transactional skills, will make the migrants more competitive in foreign markets in general and will help them to earn more. Some of the challenges in regard, as per a recent World Bank (2021) report, are the following: (1) the mismatch between the technical skills taught at the formal general education system, postsecondary VET, and professional training and the skills demanded by employers; (2) the limited provision of business and entrepreneurial skills conducive to start up successful microenterprises; (3) limited access to higher education; (4) poor labor market information and absence of career guidance at school (with the exception of a handful of schools) to inform education and occupational choices; and (5) strong social stereotypes holding participation of women in the labor force. Overcoming these challenges will not only enable the country to enhance the quantity, quality, and relevance of the jobs created in the domestic sector but also the same for those who migrate outside, by creating a "brain bank" that could help the country to use its soft power better abroad.

Uzbekistan's recent reforms easing the migration process

The starting point for the comprehensive reforms in Uzbekistan was the adoption of the Strategy for Action on five priority areas identified for the development of Uzbekistan during the period 2017–2021. Under the MOELR, an Agency for External Labor Migration was established, which is entrusted with assisting Uzbek citizens in exercising their right to work abroad. It is expected to manage and monitor the processes for organized recruitment as well as the preparation and implementation of adaptation measures and employment abroad. The Agency is further tasked with interacting with the competent authorities of foreign states on the regulation of employment processes for Uzbek citizens abroad and protecting their labor rights (Sibagatulina, 2021). In 2017, the country's internal migration policy was reformed with a view to relaxing the rules preventing the departure of

162 Deepa Sankar

citizens from Uzbekistan, such as the need for a departure visa. Since January 2019, migrants no longer need an authorization to travel abroad.

The Agency for External Labour Migration has also been given responsibility for opening representative offices in destination countries and accreditation of foreign companies for the purposes of recruiting Uzbek migrant workers. A special fund to "support and protect the rights and interests of citizens engaged in labor activities abroad"[30] is also envisaged (Sibagatulina, 2021). Government has also brought in several regulations on the private employment agencies' recruitment of Uzbeks for work abroad. Uzbekistan is also actively advocating for a single interstate mechanism for (reciprocal) the recognition of migrants' professional competencies and qualifications, and medical examinations undergone within the Commonwealth of Independent States (CIS) and developing and adopting Cooperation Programme on Labour Migration. Uzbekistan is actively signing bilateral and intergovernmental agreements with countries hosting large numbers of migrant workers, embedding organized forms of cooperation and allowing support for Uzbek citizens. The Government has launched the online database LaborMigration.uz—which provides information on the rules of stay, working conditions, and social and housing provisions in the prospective country of employment (Sibagatulina, 2021).

Notes

1 https://sdgs.un.org/goals/goal10.
2 United Nations Department of Economic and Social Affairs, Population Division (2020). International Migration 2020 Highlights (ST/ESA/SER.A/452).
3 https://www.unicef-irc.org/knowledge-pages/Migration-and-children/.
4 https://www.worldbank.org/en/topic/labormarkets/brief/migration-and-remittances.
5 usually understood as the money or goods that migrants send back to families and friends in origin countries (https://www.migrationdataportal.org/themes/remittances).
6 https://www.knomad.org/sites/default/files/2021-11/Migration_Brief%20 35_1.pdf.
7 https://www.un.org/en/chronicle/article/help-and-support-migrant-families-around-world.
8 https://www.unicef-irc.org/knowledge-pages/Migration-and-children/.
9 https://www.unicef-irc.org/publications/pdf/sm2004/sm2004.pdf.
10 https://www.unicef-irc.org/publications/pdf/iwp2005_05.pdf.
11 https://stat.uz/ru/ofitsialnaya-statistika/living-standards.
12 https://stat.uz/ru/ofitsialnaya-statistika/labor-market.
13 Bhutia, Sam (2020): Uzbekistan sustains poverty by blocking internal migration; https://eurasianet.org/uzbekistan-sustains-poverty-by-blocking-internal-migration.
14 Putz, Catherine (2020): https://thediplomat.com/2020/02/william-seitz-on-uzbekistans-propiska-problem/.
15 Hashimova, Umida (2018): The Unattainable Uzbek *Propiska;* https://thediplomat.com/2018/12/the-unattainable-uzbek-propiska/.

16 https://www.uzbekforum.org/propiska-uzbekistan-abolishes-soviet-style-residency-restrictions/.
17 https://cis-legislation.com/document.fwx?rgn=127794.
18 https://oxussociety.org/introducing-the-central-asia-migration-tracker/.
19 Please look at https://www.worldbank.org/en/country/uzbekistan/brief/l2cu for more details.
20 Ajwad et.al, (2014): The Skills Road: Skills for Employability in Uzbekistan, World Bank.
21 Ajwad et.al, (2014): The Skills Road: Skills for Employability in Uzbekistan, World Bank.
22 https://24.kg/english/216641__Average_salary_of_migrants_in_Russia_voiced/.
23 UNICEF (2019) Effects of migration on children of Uzbekistan https://www.unicef.org/uzbekistan/media/2936/file/Effects-of-migration-on-children-of-Uzbekistan-EN.pdf.
24 UNICEF (2019): Student Learning at Primary Grades in Uzbekistan: Outcomes, Challenges, and Opportunities: A summary of Uzbekistan National Learning Achievement Study, Grade IV, 2018.
25 Ajwad et.al, (2014): The Skills Road: Skills for Employability in Uzbekistan, World Bank.
26 World Bank (2019): Uzbekistan Education Sector Analysis.
27 UNICEF (2020) "Youth of Uzbekistan: aspirations, needs and risks" report. UNICEF Uzbekistan.
28 UNICEF (2020): "Knowledge, Attitude and Practices of parents regarding education quality and school-based management", UNICEF Uzbekistan.
29 UNICEF (2020) "Youth of Uzbekistan: aspirations, needs and risks" report.
30 Government of the Republic of Uzbekistan (2018). Presidential Resolution On Additional Measures to Further Improve the System of External Labour Migration of the Republic of Uzbekistan, No. PP-3839, 5 July 2018, https://lex.uz/docs/3811333.

References

Abdulloev, Ilhom, Gil S. Epstein and Ira N. Gang (2020). Migration and Forsaken Schooling in Kyrgyzstan, Tajikistan, and Uzbekistan. *IZA Journal of Development and Migration*, 11 (4), 1–27.

Ajwad, Mohamed Ihsan et al., (2014). *The Skills Road: Skills for Employability in Uzbekistan*. Washington: World Bank.

Asch, Beth J. (1994). *Emigration and its Effects on the Sending Country*. Santa Monica, CA: RAND Corporation.

Bondarenko, K.A. (2021). Labor Migration From Uzbekistan: A Family and Community Promoted Big Bang. *Regional Research of Russia* 11, 273–284. https://doi.org/10.1134/S2079970521020039

ERDOĞAN, Zahide (2021). Uzbekistan's Transformation with the New Uzbek Strategy: Shifting Policies towards Mediation of Labor Migration through Migration Infrastructure. *MANAS Journal of Social Studies*, 10 No: SI; ISSN, 1694–7215.

International Organization for Migration (2018). *Migration and the 2030 Agenda: A Guide for Practitioners*. Switzerland: International Organization for Migration.

https://migration4development.org/sites/default/files/2021-09/IOM-EN-REPORT%20WEB.pdf

Mansoor, A. and B. Quillin (2006). *Migration and Remittances: Eastern Europe and the Former Soviet* Union. Washington: The World Bank, cited in Erdogan, Z (2021).

Sibagatulina, Zulfiya (2021). Embracing a Dynamic Future Monumental Shifts in Uzbek Labour Migration Policy, Background Note. Enhancing cooperation among the Prague Process states; https://www.pragueprocess.eu/en/news-events/news/486-embracing-a-dynamic-future-monumental-shifts-in-uzbek-labour-migration-policy

The World Bank (2020). *Uzbekistan*. Human Capital Index 2020.

The World Bank (2021). *Uzbekistan*. https://www.worldbank.org/en/news/press-release/2022/05/18/uzbekistan-systematic-country-diagnostic. Accessed on 29th September 2021

UNDESA (2020) World economic situation and prospects as of mid-2020: United Nations Department of Economic and Social Affairs. https://www.un.org/development/desa/dpad/wp-content/uploads/sites/45/publication/WESP2020_MYU_Forecast-sheet.pdf.

UNDP (2018) *Sustainable employment in Uzbekistan: The Status, Problems and Solutions.*

UNICEF (2004). *Innocenti social monitor 2004.* Florence: UNICEF Innocenti Research Center. https://www.unicef-irc.org/publications/366-innocenti-social-monitor-2004.html

UNICEF (2018). *Generation 2030: Uzbekistan: Investing in Children and Young people to reap the Demographic Dividend.* UNICEF Uzbekistan.

UNICEF (2019a). *Building a National Social Protection System Fit for Uzbekistan's Children and Young People.*

UNICEF (2019b). Student Learning at Primary Grades in Uzbekistan: Outcomes, Challenges, and Opportunities: A summary of Uzbekistan National Learning Achievement Study, Grade IV, 2018.

UNICEF (2019c). Effects of migration on children of Uzbekistan. https://www.unicef.org/uzbekistan/media/2936/file/Effects-of-migration-on-children-of-Uzbekistan-EN.pdf

UNICEF (2020a). "Knowledge, Attitude and Practices of parents regarding education quality and school-based management", UNICEF Uzbekistan.

UNICEF (2020b) "Youth of Uzbekistan: aspirations, needs and risks" report.

United Nations Department of Economic and Social Affairs, Population Division (2020). International Migration 2020 Highlights (ST/ESA/SER.A/452).

Vakulenko, Elena and Roman Leukhin (2017). Wage Discrimination Against Foreign Workers in Russia. *Russian Journal of Economics*, 3 (2017), 83–100.

Chapter 10

African Migrant Children's Experiences in South African Schools

Mariam Seedat-Khan, Aradhana Ramnund-Mansingh, and John Mhandu

Introduction

Pervasive xenophobic violence was rampant in 2017, 2019, and 2020 within a post-apartheid South Africa (SA), affecting migrants' universal human rights and compromising children's access to education. Migrant children's education remains a post-script in SA's education. Prioritising distinctive migrant childhood schooling experiences facilitates a global south analysis of their assimilation into SA society. Espousing a multidisciplinary, legislated, and inclusive approach places teachers, stakeholders, and policymakers at the centre of the solution, which yields an integrated analysis and management of a prejudice-free clinical model.

Migrant children are arguably the most marginalised groups in SA schools. Lived experiences are made more difficult by the co-existence of their migrant status. Intersections of gender, race, class, ethnicity, language, and socio-cultural constructs preserve and complicate differential access and exclusion of children.

With a child-centred approach, rigorous appraisal of multidisciplinary migration unearths intersections, exclusion, education, legislation, access, and marginalisation. Using a sociological framework facilitates a comprehensive understanding of exclusionary school practices and experiences. Scientific knowledge informs the development of a child-centred clinical model that promotes assimilation, integration, and inclusion of migrant children in schools and SA society. The study employs this approach with the primary objective of examining migrant children's school experiences in a post-apartheid context.

The clinical model intends to intensify educational proficiencies, competencies, and dexterities among migrant children to reduce school vulnerability. Interventions rely on stakeholders to execute state-prescribed roles to enhance inclusive education models. The clinical model minimises strains intersecting psychosocial and educational development requirements.

African migrant children

The end of apartheid saw a democratic African National Congress (ANC) state under the guardianship of Mandela. The ANC promoted inclusivity

DOI: 10.4324/9781003343141-13

and tolerance, restoring hope in Africa. A geopolitical framework stabilised SA as an economic leader on the continent, welcoming migrant labour and their children into SA schools. The proliferation of migrants increased the presence of children in SA schools.

The migrant child is "a child born outside of SA and travelled from another country, accompanied or unaccompanied by a parent or caregiver" (UCT Refugee Rights Clinic, 2021, 4). African migrant children come into the country under varying circumstances and care. Traditional family structures may not exist due to the death, abandonment, or imprisonment of their biological caregivers. They enter a new and unfamiliar environment with equally foreign caregivers. The stability and familiarity of family structures are non-existent. There is a correlation between familial support and deviant behaviour and practice variations. Curtis, Thompson, and Fairbrother (2018) confirm that a lack of support from the local migrant community and family leads to alcohol and substance abuse. Although the study is a European study, the relationship is comparable to SA.

SA's dependence on migrant labour is traced to the 19th century, which was instrumental in the country's economic expansion. Migrants sustain cheap unregulated work in SA, which restricts opportunities for children (Vandeyar and Vandeyar, 2017). Crush and Tawodzera (2011) noted colonial exploitation intensified migrant labour in Lesotho, Mozambique, Swaziland, Malawi, and Zimbabwe. Seedat-Khan and Johnson (2018) confirm that colonialism initiated indentured migration producing uneven race, class, and geopolitical development. The dated 2001 statistics only indicate that results for Zimbabwean children's school registration, statistics from Botswana, Nigeria, and other African countries were absent (Sibanda, 2020).

Statistics fail to offer accurate gender figures for legal and illegal migrants (Sibanda, 2020). Migrants in SA are primarily represented by 24 percent from Zimbabwe, 12 percent from Mozambique, 7 percent from Lesotho, and 3 percent from Malawi (Moyo, 2021). Male children are employed to supplement family income at the expense of their education, while female migrants attend school (Murenje, 2020). Sibanda (2020) reported that 64 percent of migrant children include 42 percent orphans and 22 percent with parents who migrate to escape poverty, unemployment, and civil war.

The United Nations High Commission for Refugees (UNHCR) prioritised three intentions for education. First, the school requires attendance, allowing the monitoring of abuse and mistreatment (UNHCR, 2019). Schools offer protection and increase well-being, self-reliance, and self-esteem. Psychosocial development intensifies cognitive development.

A universal human right remains unaffected by migrant status (Kirk and Winthrop, 2007), and in 1951, the Geneva Convention ratified education as a human right. Taylor and Sidhu (2012) established migrant children's exclusion and xenophobia decrease school admission. Roxas (2011) unearthed migrant children receiving inadequate academic support, while Harju (2018) recognised children face social, emotional, and academic challenges. Isseri, Muthukrishna, and Philpott (2018) identified negative experiences were rooted in cultural, social, language, race, prejudice, and xenophobia, producing systemic prejudice obstructing assimilation and child development. Maduray (2014) and Vandeyar and Vandeyar (2012) discovered the extent to which children feel included is informed by familial context, cognitive ability, nationality, and migrant status. Experiences, socio-economic conditions, education, and community support define children's well-being. Crush and Tawodzera (2011) recognise a disconnect between the SA state departments of Home Affairs (DOHA) and Education (DBE), making school registration challenging. The state disconnects adversely compromise the right to education, using migrant status to deny access and protection in SA schools. The absence of synergy between policy and practice dispossesses migrant children of fundamental universal human rights.

The SA DOHA mandates compliance with directives issued in *The Immigration Act 13 of 2002* from school governing bodies. *The Immigration Act 13 of 2002* guarantees inclusive education for all migrants without status prejudice. The failure to implement immigration directives is traced to the ambiguity of stakeholder roles. School administrators do not possess specialised legal proficiencies to include or exclude migrant children. While professional teaching qualifications examine inclusivity, ethics, and universal rights, teachers cannot determine migrant school access. The SA Council for Educators (SACE) statuary body regulates teacher registration and qualification. A review of SACE guidelines has failed to identify specialised legal training to action exclusion from schools. The SA DBE is guided by the Constitution and Bill of Rights, guaranteeing education to children under 15, supported by the SA Schools Act 84 of 1996 (SASA) that pledges access for children aged seven to 15.

Mhandu and Ojong (2018) found that migration decisions are framed within the family. Family migration is impelled by education and employment opportunities, which improve opportunities for generational success (Mhandu, 2020). Significant others socialise migrant children to believe that opportunities outweigh risks. Migration cannot be examined without connecting education, gender inequality, discrimination, forced migration, and marriages imposed on women and girls.

SA schools

SA school system's response impacts migrant children's psychosocial well-being and development, intensifying the failure of inclusive practice and multicultural education to augment universal human rights.

> The psychological well-being of migrant children is affected not only by differences between their country of origin and country of destination

> but also by how well the schools and local communities in their country of destination help them to overcome the myriad obstacles they face in succeeding at school and building a new life.
>
> Schleicher (2015, 6)

Fundamental school integration acknowledges a SA identity. Mhandu and Ojong's (2018) study confirms that the quality of life for migrant children is contingent on satisfaction, self-actualisation, and enjoyment.

A child-centred approach

Child-centred interventions prioritise children's lived schooling experiences facilitating change through connecting policy and practice. Active knowledge dissemination to central stakeholders includes diverse child-focused workshops with real-world toolkits to increase school administration proficiencies, intensifying access and success for migrant children. Innovation and knowledge are directed to the state to exemplify migrant children's voices to synergise policy and practice. The clinical approach is designed to serve migrant communities beyond the academic. Scientific rigour contributes to the recovery and renewal measures of African child migrants in SA. Adopting and advocating a child-centred approach bridges policy and practice. Stimulate social change, promote social cohesion and tolerance, fosters mutual respect, reducing migrants' challenges. The research–policy–practice nexus, examining the SA migrants' school context via examination of 'state infrastructure', delivers an inclusive social contract.

Discussion of methodological approach

The evaluation of empirical migration studies, statistics, policy documents, and universal human rights frameworks underscore migrant children's educational challenges in SA. COVID-19 mandated a secondary approach to sustain fundamental migrant child-centred research in compliance with schools' safety protocols. The failure of researchers to fully capitalise on African migrant children's experiences within SA's inclusive schooling contexts has directed researchers to examine local, national, and international guidelines that promote inclusive universal education. The legal charters and policy frameworks that guarantee education include, among others, the UNESCO (1994) Salamanca statement. Interdisciplinary scientific studies adopted secondary desktop research. Existing knowledge delivers potential bias, mandating a return to critical policy, achievable via a desktop study, strengthening the rigour of the clinical model.

Bias was reduced via interdisciplinary migration, cross-referencing, legal, educational, linguistic, policy, and health scholarship. Using a subject specialist with proficiencies in library science exploited a collection of global academic databases to secure comprehensive historical, visual, and documentary resources. Key thematic searches aligned to qualitative methodology intensified the study's geographical relevance.

Clinical model

A systematic collaborative multidisciplinary child-centred clinical model reconnoitres pervasive challenges influencing migrant children's gendered learning experiences, proficiencies, and dexterities. Schooling challenges intersect cultural, gendered, and socio-economic levels. Offering a gendered constructive model with theoretically applied intervention outcomes reduces prejudice for the boy and girl child's educational outcomes and access. The SA Constitution, Bill of Rights, and universal human rights mandate access to inclusive education. The protection of children is made possible by interrogating pervasive institutional xenophobia, gender, race, language, and cultural inequity. The clinical sociology model is developed by Prof Mariam Seedat-Khan who is affiliated with the Association for Applied and Clinical Sociology. The applied model (Table 10.1) identifies institutional limitations that impede the advancement, well-being, and schooling experiences of boy and girl migrant children in SA schools. The table is based on the body of knowledge and researchers clinical expertise, and offers a preview to challenges, impediments, actions, and solutions.

Key challenges

The fracture between migration, education, and legislation application compromises migrant children's universal right to education. The failure to emphasise and connect stakeholders with legal, universal, and gendered rights prevents cognitive development and well-being, increasing vulnerability, marginalisation, and exploitation. Violation of fundamental human rights against minors contravenes the UN policy. As a UN signatory, SA's contradictions between policy, stakeholder delivery, and access to inclusive education are intensified by xenophobia that excludes the migrant child. Seedat-Khan and Johnson (2018) report that xenophobic attitudes are systemic in SA schools.

Global statistics report that 31 million children of migrants are born in the host country (Allner, 2020). SA reports that 10 percent of children were identified as migrants, displaying a gender balance; African migrants represented 76 percent of the 10 percent (Allner, 2020). Children from SADC countries constituted 80 percent. Seedat-Khan and Johnson (2018) indicated that statistics on documented and illegal African migrants are inaccurate and representative of migrant children. Nonetheless, 40 percent of migrant children from Africa are based in Gauteng and 15.6 percent in Limpopo (Allner, 2020).

Table 10.1 African Migrant Children's Challenges in SA Schools

Key Challenges	Impediments in Context	Action	Solution
Inclusion	• Unwelcoming environment/prejudice • Language challenges/barriers • Trauma • Migration status/outsiders	• Promote inclusion and diverse ethos • Specialised psycho-social skills training. • Sensitivity and multi-culturalism to migrants • Child safety management systems.	• UN child protection and human rights • Teacher training. • Inclusivity and diversity policy • Partnerships
Legal status	• Immigration status and procedures • Access to children in classrooms • Enforcing immigration laws • Education compromised • Documentation demands	• Department of Home Affairs accountability • The State fulfils the immigration role. • Section 39; 42 Immigration Act 13 of 2002 • Permit access to basic education • Immigration documentation not required	• Promote inclusive education policies • Adhere to universal legal frameworks • Fulfil statutory human rights • Eastern Cape High Court Precedent • Education prioritised
Bullying	• 1 in 5 migrants is bullied • Xenophobia intersects • Verbal and non-verbal acts • Social and economic isolation	• Promote tolerance, inclusion, and diversity • Modify lesson plans • Comply with mandates • Implement interventions	• Increase district and provincial support • Prioritise child migrant child education • Transparent reporting systems • Ensure the protection of migrant children.

Familial Status	• Child-male/female headed homes • Teenage pregnancy • Orphans economically marginalised • Unemployment lacks support	• School registration and language lessons • Support via social services • Food, medical access, and temporary shelter • Community protection	• Access to care homes for orphans • Social worker visits and assessments • Food security, housing support, and protection • Education and skills
Xenophobia	• Violence, crime, dispossession • Victims of looting and theft • Verbal abuse and exclusion	• Report criminal cases to police stations • Prejudice-free social service access • Places of safety for children/women	• Mandate to promote and protect human rights • Compliance with SA bodies • International statutory human rights

STAKEHOLDERS

Community	NGO's	Researchers	School administration
School Governing body	Teachers	DOHA	DBE
Social services	Section 27 Stakeholders	Women	Migrants

Source: Author

Approximately, 4.2 percent of migrant children are disabled, increasing the need for child-centred inclusive education and universal human rights. Exclusion compounds challenges with physical, sensory, emotional, cognitive, and psychosocial disabilities, increasing migrant families' vulnerability to living in unfavourable conditions. Food insecurity enhances nutritional deficiency, compromising the cognitive, psychosocial, and physical development of children with disabilities. Migrant status impedes access to public healthcare and is responsible for fatalities among African children with disabilities. While SA's education mandate guarantees access to education to all children without discrimination, African migrant children remain excluded. Exclusion is attributed to affordability and immigration costs (Seedat-Khan and Johnson, 2018). Often the circumstances under which migrants have fled their home does not facilitate essential academic records required for school admission.

Seventy-eight and eight percent of African migrant children in SA live in single female-headed households increasing their vulnerability. Male led child households are pervasive, representing 70 percent of households (Allner, 2020). Ultimately 22 percent of African migrant children between the ages of 7–17 years of age do not attend school. Allner (2020) established that 13 percent of boy migrant children between the ages of 15–17 work or manage a business to supplement the family income. Girl children between the ages of 12–17 account for 14.2 percent of children that have given birth.

Familial status

Dryden-Peterson (2018) contends that a strong relationship exists between the success of a migrant child at school and the role the migrant child's family plays in school communication and activities. The gap herein lies with several debilitating factors. First, families of migrant children lack an understanding of the education system as they may not have had or completed education themselves. Thus, they are unaware of the expectations to communicate or support the migrant learner. Additionally, the host country's curriculum and pedagogy may be vastly different.

Family engagement from the migrant children with the new school is encouraged, as this is said to improve social and emotional well-being, directly resulting in improved academic outcomes (Dryden-Peterson, 2018). However, these actions are not transparently carried out with African migrant children in SA. It should be the responsibility of the school in the host country to foster relationships with caregivers of the migrant child due to the unequal power relationships. Additionally, many migrant parents refuse to send their children to school because they need to start working as early as possible to contribute economically to the family (Tuangratananon et al., 2019).

Inclusion

The most significant challenge is that African migrant children are viewed as *outsiders,* stripping them of human rights. Social interactions such as plays, dance, language, and creative expression reduce migrants' social integration (Marsh and Dieckmann, 2017). Language and competencies intensify differences through labels and xenophobia in schools. Slee and Allan (2001, 178) contend

> Schools are cartographic police. Exclusion proceeds through deep structural and broad cultural mechanisms to invigilate a shifting spectrum of diversity. The boundaries in this sub-map are sharpest along the lines of disability, race, gender, class, sexuality, bilingualism, ethnicity, and geographic position.

Baak's (2019) concept of *othering* is analogous to racism. Othering contrasts with the *in-group*, fortifying exclusion. Migrant children report frequent visual scrutiny in school and outside (Baak, 2019). Tuangratananon et al. (2019) identified migrant children exclusively occupied in learning centres while citizens of Thailand attended public-school systems exclusively.

Bullying

Caravita et al. (2020) and Xu et al. (2020) confirm migrant children are at higher risk of bullying. Tuangratananon et al. (2019) validate claims that migrant children are provoked and alienated for physical differences, appearance, and language. The number of migrant children that experience bullying in school is excessively high. Among a group of six migrant children, five migrant children will experience bullying prompted by their physical difference and foreign status. If a fight occurs, migrant children are identified as instigators. Many migrant children have identified bullying as a reason for leaving school (Tuangratananon et al., 2019). Baak (2019) advances that bullying examined by peers and teachers and notes that migrant children who were victimised based on race, physical appearance, and ethnicity were high on the prevalence list leading to loneliness and social anxiety (Fuentes-Cabrera et al., 2019). They are overtly treated as *outsiders;* often told they should return to their homes. This is problematic as many migrant children have been born in their host country or have fled from their homes for safety reasons (Baak, 2019). This leads to a breakdown in self-esteem from a distorted self-image, which is directly related to academic performance. Despite advocacy efforts for safety and security, migrant children feel unsafe due to prejudice from peers and teachers (Mkhondwane, 2018). Fuentes-Cabrera et al. (2019) posit that first-generation migrant children suffer higher abuse, bullying, and racial and ethnic harassment.

Xenophobia

Xenophobia intensified migrant challenges, making *home* relative and problematic. Upon gaining democratic status in 1994, SA became a land of opportunity for those in other African countries. Racial and xenophobic violence

174 Mariam Seedat-Khan et al.

in SA has gained much media attention. Crush and Tawodzera (2011) found thousands of displaced, homeless, and orphaned migrant children resulting from xenophobic attacks in SA. The bigoted behaviour towards migrant children is violent and aggressive, attempting to exclude them from economic advancement, schools, housing, and healthcare. The shade of skin pigment in terms of complexion was a key factor of exclusion, according to studies by Vandeyar and Vandeyar (2017). The physical, biological, and socio-cultural pieces of evidence are the catalyst for xenophobic discrimination against African migrant children in schools; the social isolation and intellectual alienation are rooted in the behaviour of SA teachers and learners that subscribe to xenophobic ideologies toward African migrants (Isseri, Muthukrishna, and Philpott, 2018). SA refers to them as *Makwerekwere*.[1] They are isolated due to their unusual surname, different from SA surnames. There were specific stereotypes for varying countries, such as impoverished Zimbabweans and Nigerians who are criminals and drug lords. A significantly high percentage of migrant children attended the country's poorly resourced schools. Forms of exclusion are directly related to xenophobic hate and loathing (Vandeyar and Vandeyar, 2017).

Legal status

The legal status of many of the African migrant children comes into question. Reasons for many of their undocumented status include crossing the border illegally, with relatives, or alone. The legal status debate is a painful experience for migrant children and parents. Documents have been destroyed in political unrest, and parents or caregivers must leave their homes in haste. The lack of documentation contributes to their loss of identity in a new town and country. Parents or caregivers undergo immense stress and strain over their undocumented children, and it often prevents them from sending the children to school (Thompson et al., 2019). While teachers have a professional responsibility and legal obligation to promote and undertake inclusive education policies and frameworks, they are forced to take on irregular roles as immigration officers impeding children's fundamental right to education (Crush and Tawodzera, 2011). The status becomes a more significant risk when children have no caregivers and risk various forms of exploitation. These include not attending school, being homeless, taking up odd jobs, and sexual predation. Ncube (2018) confirmed the increase in the migrant teen dropout rate at SA schools. This was a result of a lack of documentation. Not possessing a birth certificate made it impossible to grasp any form of identity or be admitted into the school.

There were an estimated 1.5 million undocumented migrants living in South Africa at the end of 2016, according to a community survey by Statistics South Africa. Around 175,000 of those counted were aged 19 or under. Many more children are born in South Africa to parents without papers. Often these births are not registered because of legislative restrictions on migrant children receiving birth certificates.

Ncube (2018)

Alfaro-Velcamp et al. (2017) blow the whistle on unethical practices in documenting migrant children. The DOHA employees become angry at migrants who attempt to obtain documentation via the legal outlined processes. Unscrupulous government employees demand cash from vulnerable migrants to expedite immigration registration. This resulted in laws that transformed the fate of undocumented migrant children in SA. The Eastern Cape High Court set a precedent that undocumented migrant children cannot be denied access to basic education. The court required an affidavit from the child's guardian facilitating school access (Chabalala, 2019). Section 39 and 42 of Immigration Act 13 of 2002 ratify the admission of undocumented children into schools, providing access to basic education. The migrant child's rights and access to education have remained shrouded in secrecy, escaping migrant parents.

Theoretical framework

The interdisciplinary approach comprehends the relative assimilation of children's experiences into SA schools. An applied sociological lens highlights the scrutiny of familial socio-economic and migration experiences. Lee's (1996) theory of migration and Crenshaw's (2017) intersectionality discourse underscore migrant children's educational experiences in SA.

Lee (1996) delivers an ideal configuration that explicates migration flow patterns from origin to host country and highlights that the relationship between the incentive to migrate and selecting an African destination is influenced by socio-economic and political push and pulls. Lee (1996) and Seedat-Khan and Johnson (2018) conceptualise key intersections of community, opportunity, language, and support that influence migration. Lee (1996) advances that the migration process and resolutions constitute four areas: the area of origin, destination, intervening obstacles, and personal circumstances. Four areas inform the spatial mobility of diverse migratory groups, with socio-economic and political push factors impelling migration on the continent. Pull factors to SA are aligned to socio-political and economic frameworks that offer accessibility from Africa. Employment, educational, and entrepreneurial opportunities are desirable to migrant families and imply the number of migrants is directly proportional to pull factors in SA (Lee, 1996).

Contextualising Lee's (1996) theory of migrant children in SA schools, we advance that migrant families' push and pull factors are a permutation of intersecting elements in their countries. Country-specific conditions and methodically reviewed socio-economic opportunities for a successful migration in schools determine the decision to migrate. Delineated four elements give credence to acts of migration; as much as migrants have extensive knowledge and allegiances to their country, they undertake a significant risk migrating to SA. Migrants' limited knowledge is superficial and imprecise, impacting and impeding assimilation and acculturation. The failure to recognise these processes compromises children's education in the host country. Lee's (1996) theory validates the schooling experiences of African migrant children.

Crenshaw's (2017) intersectional discourse delivers a critical analysis of Lee's (1996) theoretical interpretation of migration. Turan et al. (2019, 6) argue that '*Intersectionality is a lens through which researchers seek to understand the complex nature of identity, health, social relationships, and power that plays out within human interaction and experiences*'. Aligned with this migratory African milieu, an intersectional discourse is of great consequence in exploring the schooling experiences and outcomes for minority migrant children subject to stigmatised xenophobic identities. The SA public school system has been identified as problematic for African migrant children, experienced as an institution that exposes their intersectional differences culminating in their social and academic exclusion. While race, nationality, culture, language, and class are significant in compromising the schooling experiences of African migrant children, conditions of poverty, unemployment, and pervasive inequality among SA's play a substantial role in the exclusionary and xenophobic experiences of migrants (Isseri, Muthukrishna, and Philpott, 2018; Vandeyar and Vandeyar, 2012). The traumatic schooling experiences of African migrant children are best explained via an intersectional lens.

African migrant children's classroom and playground experiences differ from local scholars' experiences (Vandeyar, 2010). Chow (2006), Goyol (2006), and Vandeyar (2010) agree that migrant children experience increased levels of difficulties in the host countries. Significant indicators that compound difficult experiences in schools include communication barriers, ethnicity, diet, religion, and financial position of the migrant family, subjecting the child to a challenging schooling environment.

Key intersections

This chapter has effectively located the concepts of the African migrant child. Significant sociological concepts that emerged as indicators for African migrant children's schooling experience include assimilation, acculturation, adaptation, and care. These indicators are used to advance the analysis of the educational experiences of African migrant children in SA schools.

Assimilation

Examining African migrants' children's assimilation into SA schools provides evidence of their school experiences and challenges. Waldinger (2003) conceptualises assimilation as a process of ethnic change whereby migrants are absorbed into and become part of the host community. Appleton (1983) views that assimilation occurs on two levels: behavioural and cultural assimilation and structural assimilation into a society different from the migrants' home. Appleton (1983) argues that behavioural and cultural assimilation occurs when migrant children adopt the host group's language, values, culture, diet, dress, and lifestyle. Significant cultural traits are acquired during acculturation, facilitating assimilation into social institutions such as schools and universities. Structural assimilation considers the entry of African migrant groups into substantial spaces such as communities, schools, neighbourhoods, and religious establishments in the host country (Appleton, 1983).

Donato's (1997) presumption that migrants are viewed as racial and ethnic outsiders is unlikely to successfully integrate into their host country. The classical standpoint herein considers assimilation a process of cultural subtraction necessary for seamless integration into existing structures. Migrants are forced to surrender their familiar culture in place of a foreign SA culture and language. For African migrant children, attending school, this is, to some extent, is only marginally possible. For the most part, this marginality is due to xenophobia, cultural, linguistic, race, and identity impediments. Drawing on notions of assimilation augments an explanation of how African migrant children are admitted into the SA school. To this effect, specific educational and legal frameworks and practices serve as apparatus of assimilation in SA schools that facilitate the admission of African migrant children influencing how they (re)shape African migrant children's identity as a student.

Acculturation

Acculturation is the ability of African migrant children to integrate with and adapt to the SA school culture. García-Vázquez (1995, 306) conceptualised acculturation as a process *'which occurs as the result of the first-hand contact between autonomous groups leading to changes in the original cultures of either or both of the cultures'*. African migrant children arrive in SA on their own or with their families from an African country to emancipate themselves from gruelling socio-economic and political circumstances compromising their well-being.

Scholars who have successfully established correlations between assimilation and experiences of migrant children provide augmented cultural and structural theoretical acuities (García-Vázquez, 1995). To this end, this chapter draws on both perspectives to understand the relative assimilation of African migrant children into the host country and how they are placed in the socio-economic hierarchies. Acculturation describes the adaptation process of the minority group of migrant children to the dominant SA culture and occurs in three distinct phases: contact, conflict, and adaptation. Berry (1980) opines that conflict and tensions may occur due to a migrant group or individual migrants in the host country counter-attacking the supremacy of another, often local group. This is related to the level of adaptation created by migrant groups in the initial contact phase in the classroom. Although scholars have explored the concept of acculturation, they have failed to capitalise on discussions that prioritise the specific context of African migrant children's schooling experiences. African migrant children must acculturate into academic programmes in SA schools. An illustration indicates that literacy development is prejudiced when migrant children encounter literacy requirements with a multi-faceted acculturation process. Failure of the teacher to identify and determine significant cultural factors that impede literacy demands marginalises and excludes the migrant child. It is, therefore, imperative to consider the success of acculturation on the academic performance of African migrant children.

Adaptation

Alzboon (2013, 63) defines adaptation as the

> individual alignment between his reality, thoughts and the internal culture with his environmental socio-cultural concepts that may be arising from the ideological and the intellectual differences between him and his society.

The individual must adapt and formulate an achievable balance between the self and the new social environment. The concept of adaptation is the core directly linked to the behaviour of African migrant children. At an individual personal level, for the migrant child, it is a reaction of attempts to accomplish synchronisation of motives. It needs to fulfil country-specific requirements to enhance circumstances encountered with ease. Berry (1980) argues that the adaptation process occurs to satisfy members in the host environment. Adjustment of human behavioural and psychological practices is essential to gain acceptance and feel a sense of belonging for the child. While African migrant children are likely to have seamless experiences if they are willing to integrate into schools, schools are responsible for promoting diversity and inclusivity in SA schools, allowing all learners to thrive in their diversity.

Care

The concept of the quality of inclusive care experiences by the African migrant child is of great consequence to the child's cognitive, social, and physical development. The ramifications of optimal care yield positive academic outcomes among migrants. Noddings (1992) underpins notions of care by considering daily interpersonal relationships, emphasising teacher attentiveness and prioritising the emotional well-being of migrant children with specific needs. Caring with a focus on building interpersonal relationships promotes well-being in schools if teachers play the role of including and motivating learners and building self-esteem through diversity promotion and tolerance.

Consequently, an inclusive educational culture and principles promoting tolerance in SA schools are central to positive African migrant children's experiences. Guided by the existing legislature, the SA school should be an enabling, nurturing, protective, safe space where acculturation, assimilation, and identity formation occur. The establishment of an inclusive classroom for African migrant children ought to celebrate and promote diversity to enhance schooling experiences.

Conclusion

The chapter has discussed the experiences of African migrant children in SA schools. They face considerable challenges resulting from pervasive xenophobic violence, hostile school experiences, and limited access to academic support services. Correspondingly, school experiences rooted in cultural, social, language, race, prejudice, and xenophobia create distinctions compromising assimilation and child development. Augmenting migrant children's schooling experiences in SA schools has addressed pervasive institutional challenges intensifying the urgency to adopt principles of Ubuntu to recognise the plight of migrants. Sustained post-apartheid segregation palpable with xenophobic violence, bullying, and exclusion perpetuates 'we-us' and 'them' impacting migrant children.

The clinical sociology approach to mending child migrant's schooling challenges is achieved by adopting a migrant-centred approach to effect practice and policy. The clinical model minimises strains by drawing on an intersecting analysis of psychosocial and educational needs. Ultimately, the clinical model endeavours to promote the integration of child migrants into schools to build inclusion in SA society.

Note

1 Makwerekwere: Derogatory term used by Black South Africans to describe other Africans.

References

Alfaro-Velcamp, T., McLaughlin, R.H., Brogneri, G., Skade, M. and Shaw, M. (2017). Getting angry with honest people: The illicit market for immigrant papers in Cape Town, South Africa. *Migration Studies*, 5(2), 216–236.

Alzboon, S.O. (2013). Social adaptation and its relationship to achievement motivation among high school students in Jordan. *International Education Studies*, 6(10), 63–69.

180 Mariam Seedat-Khan et al.

Allner, A. (2020). *Migration dynamics of women, children, and the elderly in South Africa.* Statistics South Africa. http://www.statssa.gov.za/publications/Report-03-51-04/Report-03-51-042020.pdf

Appleton, N. (1983). *Cultural pluralism in education: Theoretical foundations.* New York: Longman.

Baak, M. (2019). Racism and othering for South Sudanese heritage students in Australian schools: Is inclusion possible? *International Journal of Inclusive Education, 23*(2), 125–141.

Berry, W. (1980). Acculturation as varieties of adaptation. In A.M. Padilla (Ed.), *Acculturation: Theory, models, and some new findings* (pp. 9–25). Boulder: Westview Press.

Caravita, S.C., Stefanelli, S., Mazzone, A., Cadei, L., Thornberg, R. and Ambrosini, B. (2020). When the bullied peer is native-born vs. immigrant: A mixed-method study with a sample of native-born and immigrant adolescents. *Scandinavian Journal of Psychology, 61*(1), 97–107.

Chabalala, J. (2019, December 13). *Victory for foreigners as court rules undocumented children have a right to education.* https://www.news24.com/news24/SouthAfrica/News/victory-for-foreigners-as-court-rules-undocumented-children-have-a-right-to-education-20191213

Chow, H.P.H. (2006). Vietnamese Canadian University students in Regina: Socio-cultural and educational adaptation. *Canadian Ethnic Studies, 38*(2), 2–10.

Crenshaw, K.W. (2017). *On Intersectionality: Essential Writings.* New York: The New Press.

Crush, J. and Tawodzera, G. (2011). *Right to the Classroom: Educational Barriers for Zimbabweans in South Africa.* The Southern African Migration Programme (Migration policy series no. 56).

Curtis, P., Thompson, J. and Fairbrother, H. (2018). Migrant Children within Europe: A Systematic Review of Children's Perspectives on their Health Experiences. *Public Health, 158*, 71–85.

Donato, R. (1997). *The other struggle for equal schools: Mexican Americans during the civil rights Era.* Albany: State University of New York Press.

Dryden-Peterson, S. (2018). Family–school relationships in immigrant children's well-being: The intersection of demographics and school culture in the experiences of black African immigrants in the United States. *Race Ethnicity and Education, 21*(4), 486–502.

Fuentes-Cabrera, A., Moreno Guerrero, A.J., Pozo Sánchez, J.S. and Rodríguez-García, A.M. (2019). Bullying among teens: Are ethnicity and race risk factors for victimization? Bibliometric research. *Education Sciences, 9*(3), 220.

García-Vázquez, E. (1995). Acculturation and academics: Effects of acculturation on reading achievement among Mexican American students. *Bilingual Research Journal, 19*(2), 305–315.

Goyol, A.B. (2006). *Adjustment Problems of African Students at Public University in America.* Lanham: University Press of America, Inc.

Harju, A. (2018). Children practising politics through spatial narratives. *Children's Geographies, 16*(2), 196–207.

Isseri, S., Muthukrishna, N. and Philpott, S.C. (2018). Immigrant children's geographies of schooling experiences in South Africa. *Educational Research for Social Change, 7*(2), 39–56.

Kirk, J. and Winthrop, R. (2007). Promoting quality education in refugee contexts: Supporting teacher development in Northern Ethiopia. *International Review of Education*, 53(3), 715–723.

Lee, E.S. (1996). A theory of migration. In R. Cohen (Ed.), *Theories of Migration* (pp. 47–57). London/New York: Oxford University Press.

Maduray, K. (2014). The geographies of schooling spaces for immigrant children: Vulnerability, belonging, exclusion and power (Unpublished master's thesis). University of KwaZulu-Natal.

Marsh, K. and Dieckmann, S. (2017). Contributions of playground singing games to the social inclusion of refugee and newly arrived immigrant children in Australia. *Education*, 45(6), 710–719.

Mhandu, J. (2020). Navigating the informal economy: Social networks among undocumented Zimbabwean migrant women hairdressers in Durban, South Africa. *Mankind Quarterly*, 61(2), 251–272.

Mhandu, J. and Ojong, V.B. (2018). Virtuous life and enjoyable life: An overview of the well-being of Zimbabwean migrant women hairdressers in South Africa. *Gender and Behaviour*, 16(2), 11678–11694.

Mkhondwane, G.T. (2018). *Protecting the Rights to Basic Education of Immigrant Learners in South African Public Schools* (Doctoral dissertation). University of Pretoria.

Moyo, K. (2021, November 18). *South Africa Reckons with Its Status as a Top Immigration Destination, Apartheid History, and Economic Challenges*. Migration policy institute. https://www.migrationpolicy.org/article/south-africa-immigration-destination-history

Murenje, M. (2020). Ubuntu and Xenophobia in South Africa's international migration. *African Journal of Social Work*, 10(1), 95–98.

Ncube, M. (2018). *Why South Africa's Undocumented Teens are Dropping Out of School*. https://deeply.thenewhumanitarian.org/refugees/community/2018/03/06/deeply-talks-picturing-refugees

Noddings, N. (1992). *The Challenge to Care in Schools*. New York: Teachers College Press.

Republic of South Africa. (1996). *South African Schools Act, No. 84*. Government Printer. https://www.gov.za/sites/default/files/gcis_document/201409/act84of1996.pdf

Roxas, K. (2011). Creating communities working with refugee students in classrooms. *Democracy and Education*, 19(2), 1–8.

Schleicher, A. (2015). *Helping Immigrant Students to Succeed at School—and Beyond*. Paris: OECD. https://www.oecd.org/education/Helping- -immigrant-students-to-succeed-at-school-and-beyond.pdf

Seedat-Khan, M. and Johnson, B. (2018). Distinctive and continued phases of Indian migration to South Africa with a focus on human security: The case of Durban. *Current Sociology*, 66(2), 241–256. doi:10.1177/0011392117736303.

Sibanda, T. (2020). *Crossing the Border: Gendered Experiences of Immigrant Children in South African Schools* (Doctoral dissertation).

Slee, R. and Allan, J. (2001). Excluding the included: A reconsideration of inclusive education. *International Studies in Sociology of Education*, 11(2), 173–192.

Taylor, S. and Sidhu, K.R. (2012). Supporting refugee students in schools: what constitutes inclusive education? *International Journal of Inclusive Education*, 16(1), 39–56.

Thompson, A., Torres, R.M., Swanson, K., Blue, S.A. and Hernández, Ó.M.H. (2019). Re-conceptualising agency in migrant children from Central America and Mexico. *Journal of Ethnic and Migration Studies, 45*(2), 235–252.

Tuangratananon, T., Suphanchaimat, R., Julchoo, S., Sinam, P. and Putthasri, W. (2019). Education policy for migrant children in Thailand and how it really happens; A case study of Ranong Province, Thailand. *International Journal of Environmental Research and Public Health, 16*(3), 430.

Turan, J.M., Elafros, M.A., Logie, C.H., Banik, S., Turan, B., Crockett, K.B., Pescosolido, B. and Murray, S.M. (2019). Challenges and opportunities in examining and addressing intersectional stigma and health. *BMC Medicine, 17*(1), 1–15.

UCT Refugee Rights Clinic. (2021). *Child Rights Manual.* http://www.refugeerights. uct.ac.za/sites/default/files/image_tool/images/248/Practicalguides/14814%20 childrens%20rights%20manual%202021.web2_.pdf

UNESCO. (1994). *The Salamanca Statement and Framework for Action on Special Needs Education.* Adopted by the world conference on special needs education: Access and quality. Salamanca. https://www.europeanagency.org/sites/default/files/ salamanca-statement-and-framework.pdf

United Nations High Commission for Refugees (UNHCR). (2019). *Global Framework for Refugee Education.* https://www.unhcr.org/5dd50ce47.pdf

Vandeyar, S. (2010). Educational and socio-cultural experiences of immigrant students in South African schools. *Education Inquiry, 1*(4), 347–365.

Vandeyar, S. and Vandeyar, T. (2012). Re-negotiating identities and reconciling cultural ambiguities: Socio-cultural experiences of Indian immigrant students in South African Schools. *Journal of Social Science, 33*(2), 155–167.

Vandeyar, S. and Vandeyar, T. (2017). Opposing gazes: Racism and Xenophobia in South African schools. *Journal of Asian and African Studies, 52*(1), 68–81.

Waldinger, R. (2003). Foreigners transformed: International migration and the remaking of a divided people. *Diaspora, 12*(2), 247–272.

Xu, M., Macrynikola, N., Waseem, M. and Miranda, R. (2020). Racial and ethnic differences in bullying: Review and implications for intervention. *Aggression and Violent Behaviour, 50*, 101340.

Chapter 11

A Comparative Study of Language Learning Barriers of German Refugee and Cyprus Migrant Children

Hristo Kyuchukov

Introduction

According to Blanco-Elorrieta and Caramazza (2021), Kroll et al. (2012), Kroll and Bialystok (2013), Kroll and Chiarello (2016) with people who are bilingual, even when they use one language at a time, both of their languages are simultaneously active in their brain. Learning the second language, bilinguals must always pay attention to the communicative situation, and using L2, they must suppress their L1. In many societies, the home language of refugees and minorities (L1) does not have a high prestige and young learners must deal with everyday difficulties at school and in society (Kyuchukov, 2007).

Studies focusing on individual differences in bilingualism-related factors such as language proficiency, the onset of second language acquisition, proportionality of the use of both languages, and duration of second language use have made it possible to provide further insights into the differential structural changes related to bilingualism (DeLuca et al., 2019; Fedeli et al., 2021; Gullifer & Titone, 2020; Stein et al., 2014). According to Kroll and Tokowitcz (2005), bilinguals can control the use of their two languages with relatively high accuracy. This includes frequency of use as well as type of use (Mann & de Bruin, 2021).

Cummins (2021) argued that the process of second language acquisition can be clarified by distinguishing between two dimensions of proficiency that relate in specific ways to determinants of the acquisition process, namely, attribute-based and input-based aspects of proficiency. The author focuses on the role of the cognitive resources that children bring to L2 acquisition, their first language (L1) proficiency. Ohta (2013) proposes the sociocultural theory (SCT) as an integrative approach to human development and cognition built upon the work of Vygotsky, his students and colleagues, and contemporary scholars. Application of SCT to L2 learning focuses on the individual's higher mental processes. Refugee and migrant children have to learn a new language in a new social environment, and they have to adapt themselves and learn the second/third language in a short time in order to be able to function at school and in society.

DOI: 10.4324/9781003343141-14

Genesee, Paradis, and Crago (2004), accepting Cummins' (2000) language proficiency framework, conclude that the minority/migrant student's success at school depends on their 'ability to read about and express abstract, complex ideas without the benefits of past experience or concurrent contextual cues' (161).

Ellis (1997, 1999) suggests observing students to find out what they actually do when they try to learn the language. He thinks that the children 'with well-developed L2 vocabulary will find it easier to infer the meanings of unknown words from context and thus will acquire them more easily and rapidly than those with a more restricted L2 vocabulary' (Ellis, 1999: 53). However, the acquisition of the second language syntax is a more difficult and complex task for the students. The children's L1 should be taken into account when their L2 is analysed because there is always influence from L1 to L2 syntax (Braidi, 1999).

Poverty and the education of traumatised children

Generally, refugee and migrant children grow up in poverty. According to Kaplan et al. (2016), in most cases, refugee children are highly traumatized, and at the same time, they need to acquire a new language. Very often, they are misdiagnosed with learning disorders and must contend with inappropriate placement in schools for children with disabilities. In addition, the refugee child may be semi-proficient in several languages but proficient in none. Lunneblad (2017) writes that many refugee families have been forced to leave their homes under difficult conditions. Coming to a new country, the families and the children have to deal with poverty. The educators use different culturally reflexive and flexible strategies aiming at empowerment of parents so as to teach them to adjust to routines and norms in the new educational system of the receiving country.

It is exactly the same with Roma migrant children. The Roma parents being migrants in different EU countries very often bring their children from country to country and the children actually do not learn any language's full structure; rather they learn some semi-languages, a partial proficiency (Kyuchukov, 2020). Moreover, most West European countries do not have any strategic plan for the integration of Roma (Cools et al., 2017).

In many West European societies, a large number of low-income families and migrants, refugees, and asylum seekers do not have access to good quality education, and migrants and refugee children are more likely than their native peers to be diagnosed as having 'special needs', resulting in their placement in separate institutions providing special education. The lack of adequate education, teachers' low expectations towards them, and stereotypes of a minority cultural group often result in discrimination (Munz, 2010).

Anderson (2001) explains how important it was for the refugee children to have contact with other children in the hostels. They were learning German from other children, and they served as interpreters for their parents when they visited a doctor or local administrative offices. However, the most difficult part for them is the syntax of German. Henley and Robinson (2011) report that the mental health problems among the refugee children are higher than among non-refugees. And their health problems somehow influence the educational process of the children; moreover, the teachers who are not familiar with the trauma of the children miss diagnose them.

The refugee children in Germany as it is described in the literature above live in poverty and they have different motivations for schooling and studying in generally depending on which country they come from. They have also different experiences with schooling in their native countries. The Syrian Arab children usually had experiences with schooling before they left to escape from the war, but it is not the same case with Arab children from Iraq or with Afghan children. The Syrian Arab children in the study are also very motivated to learn German and to continue to study in Germany, because the families plan to stay in Germany.

The situation of Roma children in Cyprus is different. They face double discrimination. Before they came to the Greek part of Cyprus, they were living in the Turkish part of the country. The families lived in extreme poverty because of the parents' low education, and sometimes no education at all, and because of that they cannot find jobs and they live always in the margins of the society. The children usually do not have any experiences with schooling, or if they attend the school usually, they go only to primary school and they do not continue further. From an early age, they start to work in order to support their families.

The load on the shoulders of refugee and migrant children is very heavy: the school and teachers have expectations that they will master the oral and written forms of the new language within a year. At the same time, they have to deal with the poverty and bullying at school due to their different culture and mother tongue. In addition, the expectations of the parents are also high—they expect that the children will learn the language in such a way that they can help the families with translation when visiting different offices.

Are the refugee and migrant children ready to grapple with all these expectations? Are they able to take on such responsibilities, given their weaker knowledge of their second/third language? And what determiners facilitate the acquisition of their second language? These questions are examined in the research discussed below.

Discussion of methodological approach

The motivation for this study is the negative stereotypes in the society, schools, and among many teachers and students towards refugee and migrant children. The problems of the children at school, challenged by learning a new language and having difficulties with reading and writing in the new language, put them in a position where they may seem to be 'mentally retarded' in the eyes of the teachers and classmates. In many European countries, there is still the practice in operation that migrant and refugee children must be administered a psychological test in the official language of the country. And when the children do not understand the tests, they are then to be placed in schools for children with mental disabilities. Germany has a long history of implementing IQ tests specially with Roma children during WWII, using pseudo-scientific methods, in an effort to prove that the children have a low IQ. Because of that, they were deported to the Auschwitz concentration camp and killed there (Kyuchukov & Wieß, 2017).

Two groups of children were involved in the present study: Arab refugee children in Germany and Roma migrant children in Greek Cyprus. The total number of children in the study was 80. They were organized in two age groups: 8 years old (20 children from Germany and 20 children from Cyprus) and 10 years old (20 children from Germany and 20 children from Cyprus).

The Arab children examined in this study are Syrian refugees who came to Germany several years ago from Aleppo. They live in Magdeburg, Germany. The Roma children live in Limassol, Cyprus. They are migrants from the Turkish part of Cyprus and the reason for the migration to the Greek part is the economic situation of the families. All the families from both ethnic groups live in poverty. Most of them are jobless. The children study in mainstream schools in mixed classrooms with majority children.

The working hypothesis upon which the research was based was that the refugee and Roma children are children developing normally, but they are traumatized. The Arab refugee children are war-traumatized, and the Roma migrant children are traumatized by the poverty they live in. The trauma suffered by the children could give rise to various difficulties with education at school and learning the official language as L2.

In order to test this hypothesis, the focus of the included the following tests:

- *Camden Memory Test: Pictural Recognition Memory Test* (Warrington, 1996). The content of the test is as follows. In the first part, the children are shown 30 pictures, and each picture is on a separate page. The second part of the test comprises the same 30 pictures in a mixture with two other pictures, in total three pictures on a page, as shown below.
- *Sentence Repetition Task*—9 items. The child hears sentences, which he/ she then to repeat after the researchers have spoken. The researcher starts with simple sentences containing 2–3 words, and in each next sentence, the number of the words increases. The researcher says: *Repeat after me!* and then says the following sentences:
  The baby cries
  The horse runs fast!
  The boy goes to supermarket, etc.

Language Learning Barriers 187

- *Number Repetition Task*—12 items. The children are given numbers and they must repeat them after the researcher.
  Repeat after me!
  4, 2
  3, 5
  5, 6, 2
  3, 1, 4
  6, 1, 7, 2
  3, 5, 8, 4, etc.

- *Peabody Picture Vocabulary Test*—55 items. The children are shown pictures.
  Nouns—42 items
  Verbs—9 items
  Adjectives—4 items

  The research question which this research sought to address was

  > How do the bilingual traumatized refugee and migrant children perform the tests in their respective mother tongue (L1) and second language (L2)?

In order to answer the research question, I am adapting the Bronfenbrenner's (1979) Development in Context or Human Ecology Theory. According to this theory, the family influences the child development and all aspects of the child development: language, health, beliefs, etc. Children who come to school are a product of the family of which they are themselves a part.

Results

Camden memory test

Presented here are the results of the children performing the different tests. The tests aimed to determine if there is a connection between their short-term memory and the language in which they perform the tests.

As one can see from Figure 11.1, in both ethnic groups, the 10-year-old children perform the test better than the 8-year-olds. The differences between the two age groups are statistically significant ($F_{(1.74)} = 48.946$, $p = .00000$).

Which ethnic group children are better by performing the short-term picture memory test? Figure 11.2 provides an answer.

Figure 11.2 makes clear that the Arab children tested are much better then the Roma children and the differences between them are statistically significant ($F_{(1.74)} = 26.739$, $p = .00000$).

The performance in the short-term memory test was carried out in the children's mother tongue (L1) Arabic, and a variety of Romani. A week later, it was performed in their second language (L2)—German or Greek.

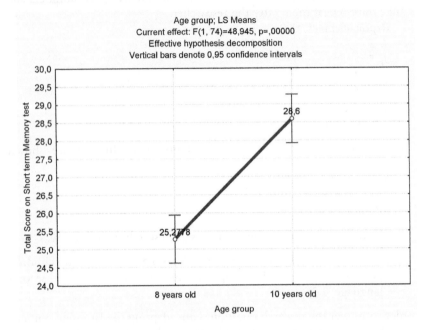

Figure 11.1 Total score of the short-term memory test as a dependent variable. Age group as an independent factor

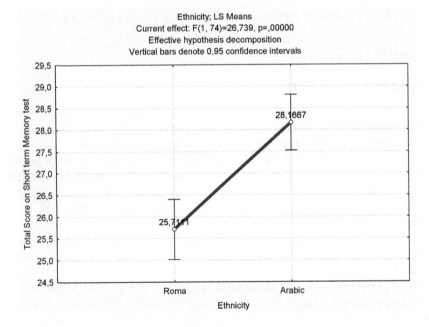

Figure 11.2 Total score of the short-term memory test as a dependent variable. Ethic group as an independent factor

The children perform the test better in their mother tongue (L1) than in the second language (L2). The differences between the performance of both languages are statistically significant (F (1.74) = 8.2827, p =.00523). It means both age groups of children have better memory performance when they use their mother tongue.

However, is there an interaction between the factors of age and ethnicity? That is shown in Figure 11.3.

The results in Figure 11.3 are very interesting. There are differences between Arab and Roma children in the performance of this test at the age of 8 years; however, the differences between the two ethnic groups' children disappear when they are 10-year-olds. Yet, there are statistically significant differences between the two age groups (F (1.74) = 12.154, p =.00083) and the 10-year-olds in both ethnic groups show almost the same results.

Looking at two other factors—language (L1 and L2) and age—we can see that there are again interactions, as presented in Figure 11.4.

Figure 11.4 shows that there are differences between the languages used in performing the test and the age of the children. There are differences between the languages used by 8-year-old children—they are much better in their mother tongue, but the 10-year-olds perform the test almost equally well in both languages—the mother tongue (L1) and the second language (L2). However, there are statistically significant differences between children who are 8 years old and those who are 10 years old (F (1.74) = 4.1438, p =.04537).

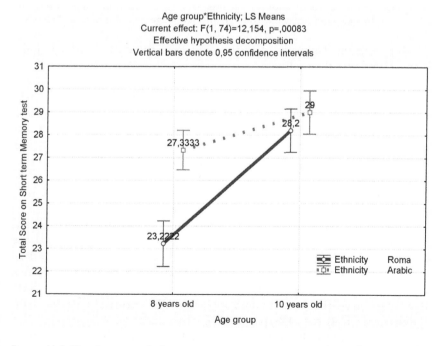

Figure 11.3 Total score of short-term memory test as a dependent variable. Interaction between the age and language as independent factors

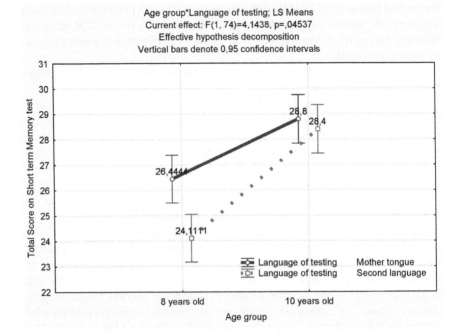

Figure 11.4 Total score of short-term memory test as a dependent variable. Interaction between the age and language as independent factors

Comparing the language of testing and the ethnicity of the children, Figure 11.5 shows the findings.

As can be seen in Figure 11.5, there is an interaction between the factors language (L1 and L2) and ethnicity. The children perform the test much better in their mother tongue (L1). Their proficiency in their second language is not so strong. The differences between the Arab and Roma children are statistically significant (F (1.74) = 8.2827, p =.00523), as Arab children are better in their knowledge of both languages (L1 and L2). The Roma children's proficiency in both languages displays greater differences.

Examining the interaction between the three factors of ethnicity, language, and age, it can be seen that they interact, as shown in Figure 11.6.

Figure 11.6 shows that in mother tongue testing, the Arab children are better than Roma children. The performance of the test in L1 is carried out almost at the same level between Arab and Roma children, and the differences between the two ethnic groups are not very large. Performing the test in the second language (L2), the differences between Arab and Roma children are greater—the Arab children are better. The statistical differences are significant (F (1.74) = 4.1438, p =.04537).

In all comparisons, the children of Arab ethnicity show better results than the Roma children. There are statistically significant differences between the

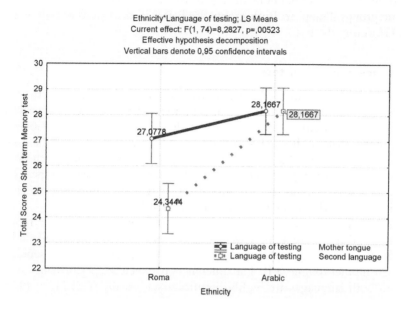

Figure 11.5 Total score of short-term memory test as a dependent variable. Interaction between the ethnicity and the language as independent factors

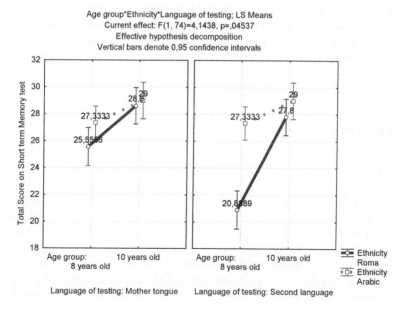

Figure 11.6 Total score of short-term memory test as a dependent variable. Interaction between the age, language, and ethnicity as independent factors

192   Hristo Kyuchukov

children at the age of 8, but by the age of 10, the differences between the two ethnic groups disappear. Both groups are better in their mother tongue (L1) in performing the test.

Sentence repetition test

In the sentence repetition test, the 10-year-old children are much better than the 8-year-olds in both ethnic groups' children. The differences between the age groups are highly significant statistically (F (1.74) = 41.505, p =.00000). This means that children who are 10 years old can repeat not only the simple sentences such as *The baby cries* but also more complex sentences such as *The boy who has a red shirt plays football in the school yard*. The ability to repeat such sentences is very important because it shows that the children possess the vocabulary and the developed structures in their language.

The children were instructed to repeat the sentences in their mother tongue, and after a week, they were asked to repeat them in their second language. Both ethnic groups show better results when they repeat the sentences in their mother tongue (L1). The differences between the performance of the test in both languages are highly significant statistically (F (1.74) = 49.553, p =.00000).

The Arab children are better than Roma children performing this task. This suggests that the Arab children have better developed language proficiency than the Roma children. The differences between the two ethic groups are statistically significant (F (1.74) = 7.0654, p =.00962).

In the performance of this test, the 10-year-olds are better than the 8-year-olds. They perform the test better in their mother tongue than in their second language, and the Arab children's results are better than those of the Roma children. In this test, there were no interactions indicated between the different factors.

Number repetition test

How do the children perform the Number Repetition test? The findings are given below.

Again, in this test, the 10-year-olds perform better. The older children can repeat a much longer series of numbers than the younger children. This indicates that the older children's memory is better developed than the memory of the younger children. The differences between the age groups are statistically significant Figure 11.7 DATA F(1,74) = 9,1672, p = , 00339.

Examining the influence of the ethnicity factor on the performance of this test, we find that the Roma children perform the test much better. This indicates that the Roma children were able to repeat longer digits than the Arab children. The differences between the two groups are statistically significant (F (1.74) = 9.1672, p =.00339).

There is interaction between the ethnicity and the language of testing as shown in Figure 11.8.

Language Learning Barriers 193

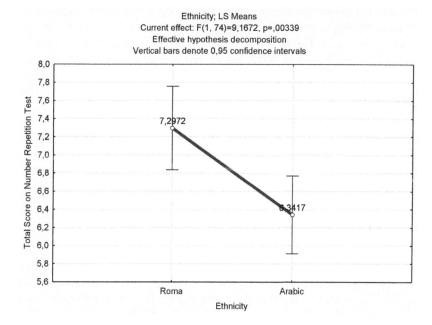

Figure 11.7 Total score of number repetition test as a dependent variable. Ethnicity as an independent factor

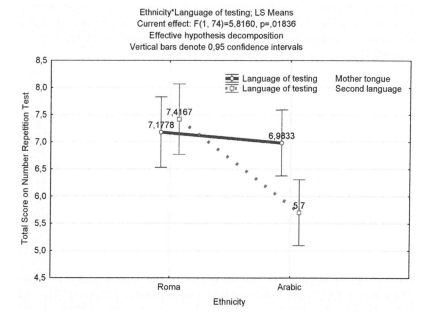

Figure 11.8 Total score of number repetition test as a dependent variable. Interaction between the language and ethnicity as independent factors

Figure 11.8 shows that the language and the ethnicity factors interact. It is clear from the figure that all children perform the test much better in their mother tongue (L1). The performance of Arab children in their second language (L2) is much poorer, while the Roma children show almost the same level of performance in this test in both their languages. The differences between Roma and Arab children in performing the test in their second languages are statically significant (F (1.74) = 5.8160, p =.01836).

In the number repetition test, the Roma children aged 10 are better than the Arab children. The differences between the age and ethnic groups of children are statistically significant. It is quite interesting that the testing in the mother tongue between both ethnic groups does not show any statistical differences. But in testing in L2, the Roma children perform better.

Peabody picture vocabulary test

The Peabody Picture Vocabulary Test for measuring the children's knowledge of L1 and L2 vocabulary was also utilised. Once again, the children were tested in both their mother tongue and the official language of the country. The results of the two age groups show that the children at age 10 perform better than the 8-year-olds. Their knowledge in regard to all 55 items is very high. The statistical analyses between both age groups of children are statistically significant (F (1.36) = 7.6129, p =.00905).

In which language do the children perform the test better, in L1 or L2? Both ethnic groups of children perform all the items in the test better in their mother tongue (L1). The statistical differences between the performance of the test in the two languages are highly significant (F (1.74) = 27.597, p =.00000).

Nouns

Now there will be an examination of the different grammatical categories and the proficiency level of the children in the study. What is the level of the knowledge of the nouns? It is clear that both ethnic groups of children have a better knowledge of the nouns in their mother tongue (L1). The differences between the L1 and L2 nouns are statistically significant (F (1.74) = 14.256, p =.00032). There are not any statistically significant differences between the children's age groups. Both age groups know the nouns in equal measure.

Verbs

What is the knowledge of the children regarding the verbs included in the test? Once more, the 10-year-olds are better in performing this test. The older children from both ethnic groups have a better knowledge of the verbs than the younger children. The differences between the two age groups are statistically significant (F (1.74) = 9.6798, p =.00265).

There is interaction between the age groups and the ethnicity of the children, as shown in Figure 11.9.

It is evident from the figure that both ethnic groups, Arab and Roma, at the age of 8 years have a lower level of knowledge of the verbs, but the 10-year-olds in both ethnic groups have a better proficiency. The differences between the two age groups children are statistically significant (F (1.74) =4.8834, p =.03021). By the age of 10, the Arab children are slightly better than the Roma children, but the differences are not very large.

Adjectives

The three independent factors—age group, ethnicity, and language of testing—do not display an impact on the total score of adjectives and there are no statistically significant differences. The children's knowledge of the adjectives is limited in terms of both age and ethnic group and in both languages.

In this test, once again, the performance in the mother tongue is much better than in L2. The results of 10-year-olds are much better than those of 8-year-olds. Both ethnic groups of children know the nouns and verbs in their L1 but have a poorer knowledge of the adjectives. That is also the reason why their knowledge about adjectives in L2 is likewise weaker.

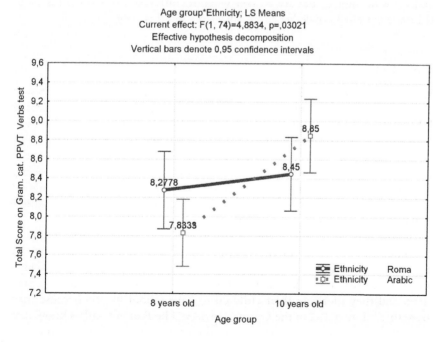

Figure 11.9 Total score of peabody picture vocabulary test. Verbs as dependent variable. Interaction between the age and ethnicity as independent factors

Discussion

The results of the children involved in the study show trends typical for normally developing bilingual children. In all the tests conducted, the children were compared by age, ethnic groups, and language (L1 and L2).

In the short-term memory test and in sentence repetition test, the 10-years-old Arab children show better results than the Roma children. The differences between the age groups and ethnic groups' children are statistically significant. Both ethnic groups are better in their mother tongue (L1) in performing these tests.

In the number repetition test, the 10-year-old Roma children are better than the Arab children of the same age. The differences between the age and ethnic groups of children are statistically significant. It is quite interesting that the testing in the mother tongue between both ethnic groups does not show any statistical differences. But in testing L2, the Roma children are better. The reason for it could be that the Roma migrant children live in Cyprus for a longer period, and very often when the parents are working in the town, the children have to be with parents in order to help.

In the Peabody test, again, the performance of the test in mother tongue is much better than in L2. The 10-year-olders know better the nouns and verbs than children with the age of 8. Both groups of children know the nouns and verbs in their L1 but are weaker when it comes to adjectives. This is the reason that their knowledge about adjectives in L2 is poorer.

Conclusion

In conclusion, the present study although limited in the number of tested children provides new knowledge about the language learning of traumatized bilingual refugee and migrant children. The study shows clear correlation between the short-term memory test and language test. The development of the short-term memory helps the L2 acquisition. With the growth of the age, the children's knowledge on the new language they learn is increasing. The study is also interesting because to date there has not been a comparative study between Arab refugee and Roma migrant children, and the findings collated here give some reason for positive optimism.

Besides the tests, there are some other determiners which influence the educational success of the children. The study proved the theory of Bronfenbrenner (1979) that the family plays an important role in the development of the children. The Arabic refugee families came to Germany to stay here, and they motivate their children to have school success because they have to get integrated in the German society. The Roma families know that even if their children will get higher education still, they cannot find jobs, because of the existing stereotypes in the society in European countries. On the other side, the school environments in Germany and in Cyprus are quite different. In both countries, the schools where the children study have very positive attitudes towards refugee and migrant children. The bilingualism of the children is taken as an asset. In both schools in both countries, the children get a support in their mother tongue. Twice a week, there are mother tongue lessons. The mother tongues of the children are taken as something important. The mother tongue lessons help the children also to strengthen their identity, and how it writes Cummins (2021) the strong knowledge of the children in their L2 is a guaranty for the better acquisition of their L2 for academic (school) purposes. If the Arab children in most of the test show better results, it is due to their better knowledge of their mother tongue (L1). The Roma children speaking a variety of Romani and Turkish at home do not get such a big support in their home languages in the family. Both languages are learned partially and there is no systematic knowledge in the grammar of their home languages (Turkish and Romani), and this is the main reason for the lower results of the Roma children in performing the L2 tests.

References

Anderson, P. (2001) 'You do not belong here in Germany…' On the social situation of refugee children in Germany. *Journal of Refugee Studies, 14*(2), 187–199.

Blanco-Elorrieta, E., & Caramazza, A. (2021). A common selection mechanism at each linguistic level in bilingual and monolingual language production. *Cognition, January*, 104625. https://doi.org/10.1016/j.cognition.2021.104625

Braidi, S. (1999). *The Acquisition of Second Language Syntax*. London: Arnold.

Bronfenbrenner, U. (1979). *The Ecology of Human Development: Experiments by Nature and Design*. Cambridge, MA: Harvard University Press.

Cools, et al. (2017) 'Parity of participation' and politics of needs intervention: Engagement with Roma Migrants in Manchester. *Journal of Social Policies.* doi:10.1017/S0047279417000575

Cummins, J. (2000) *Language, Power and Pedagogy. Bilingual Children in the Crossfire*. Clevedon: Multilingual Matters.

Cummins, J. (2021) *Rethinking the Education of Multilingual Learners*. Bristol: Multilingual Matters.

DeLuca, V. et al. (2019). Redefining bilingualism as a spectrum of experiences that differentially affects brain structure and function. *Proceedings of the National Academy of Sciences of the United States of America, 116*(15), 7565–7574. https://doi.org/10.1073/pnas.1811513116

Ellis, R. (1997) *Second Language Acquisition*. Oxfor: Oxford University Press.

Ellis, R. (1999) Theoretical perspectives on interaction and language learning. In: R. Ellis (ed.), *Learning a Second Language through Interaction*. Amsterdam: John Benjamins Publishing company, pp. 3–32.

Fedeli, D. et al. (2021). The bilingual structural connectome: Dual-language experiential factors modulate distinct cerebral networks. *Brain and Language, 220*(February), 104978. https://doi.org/10.1016/j.bandl.2021.104978

Genesee, F., Paradis, J., & Crago, M. (2004) *Dual Language Development & Disorders*. Baltimore: Paul H. Brookes Publishing Co.

Gullifer, J. W., & Titone, D. (2020). Characterizing the social diversity of bilingualism using language entropy. *Bilingualism, 23*(2), 283–294. https://doi.org/10.1017/S1366728919000026

Henley, J., & Robinson, J. (2011). Mental health issues among refugee children and adolescents. *Clinical Psychology*, 15, 51–62.

Kaplan, I. et al. (2016). Cognitive assessment of refugee children: Efect of trauma and new language acquisition. *Transcultural Psychiatry*, 53(1), 81–109. doi:10.1177/1363461515612933 tps.sagepub.com

Kroll, J. F., & Bialystok, E. (2013). Understanding the consequences of bilingualism for language processing and cognition. *Journal of Cognitive Psychology*, 25(5), 497–514. https://doi.org/10.1080/20445911.2013.799170

Kroll, J. F., & Chiarello, C. (2016). Language experience and the brain: Variability, neuroplasticity, and bilingualism. *Language, Cognition and Neuroscience*, 31(3), 345–348. https://doi.org/10.1080/23273798.2015.1086009

Kroll, J. F., Dussias, P. E., Bogulski, C. A., & Kroff, J. R. V. (2012). Juggling two languages in one mind. What bilinguals tell us about language processing and its consequences for cognition. *Psychology of Learning and Motivation - Advances in Research and Theory*, 56, 229–262. https://doi.org/10.1016/B978-0-12-394393-4.00007-8

Kroll, J. F., & Tokowicz, N. (2005). Models of bilingual representation and processing: Looking back and to the future. In J. F. Kroll & A. M. B. de Groot (eds.), *Handbook of Bilingualism: Psycholinguistic Approaches*. New York: Oxford University Press, pp. 531–553).

Kyuchukov, H. (2007) *Turkish and Roma Children Learning Bulgarian*. V. Tarnovo: Faber.

Kyuchukov, H. (2020). *Socio-cultural and Linguistic Aspects of Roma Education*. Katowice: University of Silesia Press.

Kyuchukov, H., & Weiß, J. (2017). The Roma education in Nazi Germany and its consequences in contemporary Europe. In: Kyuchukov, H. and New, W. (eds.), *Language of Resistance: Ian Hancock's Contribution to Romani Studies*. Munich: Lincom, pp. 326–342.

Lunneblad, J. (2017) Integration of refugee children and their families in the Swedish preschool: Strategies, objectives and standards. *European Early Childhood Education Research Journal*, 25(3), 356–369.

Mann, A., & de Bruin, A. (2021). Bilingual language use is context dependent: Using the Language and Social Background Questionnaire to assess language experiences and test-rest reliability. *International Journal of Bilingual Education and Bilingualism*, 25(8), 1–16. https://doi.org/10.1080/13670050.2021.1988049

Munz, V. (2010). The right to education of migrants, refugees and asylum seekers. *Journal of Human Rights Education*, 2(2), 2–16.

Ohta, A. S. (2013). Sociocultural theory and the zone of proximal development. *The Cambridge Handbook of Second Language Acquisition*, 648–669.

Ohta, A.S (2013). Sociocultural theory and the zone of proximal development. In: Herschensohn, J. Young-Scholten, M. (eds.), *The Cambridge Handbook of Second Language Acquisition*. Cambridge: Cambridge University Press, pp. 648–669.

Stein, M. et al. (2014). Structural brain changes related to bilingualism: Does immersion make a difference? *Frontiers in Psychology*, 5(SEP), 1–7. https://doi.org/10.3389/fpsyg.2014.01116

Warrington, E. (1996). *Camden Memory Test: Pictural Recognition Memory Test*. Hove: Psychology Press.

Chapter 12

Conclusion

Working towards a Hopeful Future through Child-centric Migration Studies Perspectives

This volume underlines the importance of child-centric approaches within migration studies in order to liberate the field from labels, discourses, and terms that continue to marginalise, stigmatise, and pathologise migrant children. We learn from the different studies presented in this volume the need to attend to children's experiences of education and how they navigate the expectations placed on them in relation to language, culture, ethnic belonging, and worldviews. The ultimate goal is to sketch out a hopeful vision for the future; one that accommodates migrant children in ways that care, nurture, and foster them. Central to challenging these discourses, and the practices they produce, is questioning what we mean by 'integration' to whom, into what, for what purposes, by whom, and under what circumstances. As we do this, we take the view that language is critical, absolutely crucial to any discussion about radical hope. We also assert that language is not just a means of describing the world, but it is also a tool for transforming it (Rosa, 2019; Badwan, 2021). The child-centric perspectives we promote here is a step towards changing the language through meeting migrant children where they are. To this end, this volume brings to the fore the importance of re-orienting the focus of existing migrant integration frameworks so we can move from focusing on children's future 'becoming' (as desired adults, citizens, and workers) and attending to children's present 'being' (Gornik and Sedmak, 2021) in order to listen to their experiences, address their needs, and above all else, see them differently. This reframing positions migrant children as different but equally valuable political actors who should be involved in conversations about integration policies. Failing to do so will reproduce existing frames that other migrant children, treat them as voiceless, and fail to see the relevance and richness of their identities, legacies, and different worldviews.

As we prepare for new conversations with new social actors, we can expect new ways of talking about migration taught to us by migrant children. The experiences this volume presents speak of the resilience and perseverance that migrant children exhibit during the process of establishing roots in their new communities. They describe how they developed many footholds in

DOI: 10.4324/9781003343141-15

200 Working towards a Hopeful Future

super-diverse contexts and how such measures have enabled them to develop a sense of belonging which is crucial to their well-being. The children are especially appreciative of the benefits of being part of multicultural communities and diverse schools. In fact, the children advocated for multiculturalism stating its manifold benefits. This resonates with calls for making diversity a lived experience in schools, not just treating it as something to celebrate. And this is a living testimony of the importance of listening to children's views on integration. In what follows, we present summaries of the key arguments and contributions this volume offers.

Challenging 'Deficit Discourses' in Migration Studies

We need to address the 'deficit' discourses that frame how migrants are portrayed in migration studies. This requires key epistemological shifts in how we perceive migration, and who is likely to be seen as a 'migrant'. The epistemological position that continues to direct migration studies is dominated by a uni-directional focus on migration (mainly from the Global South to the Global North), while overlooking the multi-directionality of migration trajectories. This focus produces certain social categorisations that sit at the intersection of race, gender, class, and nationality, and forms the binary of 'us' vs. 'them' while fuelling a framework of difference, leaving migrants (or any individuals of migrant identity) somewhat lost, or at continual risk of being re-othered without agency (Schenk, 2021). What is required to address this epistemological pitfall is a multi-polar axis of our shared planet. This entails putting forward a politics of the commons (Pennycook, 2018) with a renewed focus and a rethinking of the relationship to all those Others who suffered in the construction of the deficit discourses which remain central to who is seen as 'human', and who is not just living but also having a life (Butler, 2009). This will allow the field to critically engage with the biases and inequalities produced by nation-state regimes that operationalise notions of non-recognition, legitimate inequalities, and lack of human rights through processes of border control, and closure which are mainly targeted at those deemed as undesired migrants. By turning these categories on their head, categories key for inclusion and exclusion debates will need to be revisited in ways that protect the visibly racialised individuals from stereotypical labelling and deficit discourses.

From a theoretical perspective, multiculturalism is a useful concept as it has been found to promote inter-ethnic and co-ethnic ties and positive attitudes towards others (Werbner, 2013: 416). For example, Agirdag et al. (2011) found that ethnic minority pupils who attended schools with large composites of minority pupils reported less peer victimisation. Indeed, our research showed that children were empathetic towards migrant pupils and certain children relied on their ethnic ties for social and emotional support.

However, a problematic aspect of these settings is that individuals tend to cluster around those with whom they have shared characteristics sometimes leading to ethnic enclaves (Danzer and Yaman, 2013), thereby, defeating the purpose of promoting interethnic ties. To address this challenge, there is a need for schools to focus more on cultivating interethnic ties, communications, and conversations amongst their diverse populations. This needs to be done with the view that multiculturalism is as a social and cultural asset to be utilised for the integration of everyone in the school, not just for the Others. This reframing places the task of integration on everyone in ways that pushes for integration to be seen as discursive and collaborative work.

Challenging adult-centric migrant discourses

Children are a valid source of information when it comes to expressing themselves and communicating about their worlds (Mayeza, 2017). Encouraging migrant children to take space, speak about their experiences, and make their voices heard would contribute to the creation of more inclusive societies. Migrant children typically are viewed as passive subjects with little input towards the decision to move elsewhere. However, this is not always the case. If these situations are interpreted through a child centred lens, we realise that migrant children are autonomous agents fulfilling their own decisions. The concept that migrant children are completely dependent on their parents further rids these children of their agency, especially because independent child migrants (those who leave without their parents) are only reliant on their own skills (Huijsmans, 2011). This lack of agency is mirrored into migration policies as several documentary requirements, legal barriers, and delays culminate into prevention of these migrant children being able to join their family in the country of destination. Similarly, these same policies result in a large number of deportations for unaccompanied migrant children back to their country of origin (Muraszkiewicz, 2015), further taking away agency from them. Often in research centring migrant and displaced children, the children themselves are the sole participants, and for such studies to be as representative as possible of the very different migration experiences and trajectories, they should strive towards involving groups from different backgrounds and circumstances (Doná, 2006). This allows for a plethora of measures of social inclusion as the children get to frame and also portray their own narratives.

Allowing migrant children to be involved in the research study itself gives the children further autonomy over their actions by allowing their perspectives to influence the direction of the study rather than having an imposed idea of their experience from an external researcher. Attempting to transcend the processes of marginalisation and othering 'requires reflection on the ways in which one is always implicated in the processes of othering, whether by overcoming or reproducing them' (ibid: 42). Foremost is the importance of

202 Working towards a Hopeful Future

the relationship between the researchers and gatekeepers and the attention to how different educational settings have their own individual educational cultures and values. In addition, being reflective and reflexive on aspects related to researcher positionality and they influence the construction of research affordances remain very important. That is to say, it is necessary to be aware of how multiple aspects such as researchers' personal characteristics, theoretical and personal standpoints, and research methods, interact with the fieldwork and influence researcher positioning, the research process as well as the research participants (Khawaja and Mørck, 2009).

We would like to conclude this point by calling for de-Occupying of Migration Studies from its adult-centric views, values, and ways of thinking and describing the lived realities of migrant children. This radical act requires moral commitment to listen differently to what children say. This, however, requires another act of liberation; once that is linked to de-colonising the methodological and conceptual lenses through which academic scholarship on migration is constructed. This is the point to which we turn our attention next.

De-colonising our path ahead

What does liberating migration studies from the White gaze look like? This question guides our thinking as we sketch out a hopeful future for the field, one that challenges, resists and advocates, while wrapping arms around those who need care and recognition. We start by the need for cognitive recognition, or what Santos (2014) refers to as 'epistemic justice'.

We argue that we need to challenge conventional truths and worldviews by bringing to the table 'unconventional' epistemic subjects. To clarify, there is nothing inherently unconventional about listening to children; it is a paradigm that goes back to a few decades in many social science fields. But this listening is typically associated with acts of consulting or desires to be curious about what children know and do. These approaches, while claiming to be child-centric at heart, do not always attempt to decentre the adult in the process of knowledge production. As we aspire to de-colonise the path ahead for migration research, we need to start with questioning the sources of knowledge we rely on, and the role of the non-typical epistemic subject in bringing to light different worldviews and ways of theorising and conceptualising the social world.

This process is stubbornly linked with challenging the White gaze, a generative space that Tony Morrison (1998) describes in an interview as

> As though our lives have no meaning and no depth without the White gaze. And I have spent my entire life trying to make sure that the White gaze was not the dominant one in any of my book…This was a brandnew space and once I got there, it was like the whole world opened up, and I was never going to give that up

Our hope is that this volume acts as a window into what this brand-new space looks like or can be like. Throughout the different chapters, we maintained the focus on the need to listen to children in order to create a fair and just school environment, with the ultimate target of making them 'empowered by and through the school' (Badwan et al., 2021: 707). We emphasise that a shift away from Eurocentrism through attempting a holistic representation of the world where the western imperial gaze is minimised (Heleta, 2016). A field shaped by mobile individuals and groups, it is crucial to ensure that they are seen as active agents and crucial epistemic subjects, rather than passive ones subjected to top-down, national-centric integration expectations or theories that maintain the European supremacy and the White saviour narrative. As previously mentioned, this academic and epistemic shift will take great amounts of effort, reflexivity, and discomfort especially as colonisation and therefore de-colonisation are so closely linked with severe internalised trauma (Ramani, 2011). Taking such an approach to the study of migrant children's experiences is important and timely given the ubiquity of migration levels around the world and the dominating adult-centred discourse.

When we talk about de-colonisation, it is worth pausing to think of this term that has gained currency over the past few years. It is a buzz term often used in different ways to push different research agendas and approaches. We take the position that we need to be careful when it comes to academic slo-ganisation (Pavlenko, 2019) so that this term does not end up being a mere slogan. We see in de-colonisation a movement that aims at bringing to the fore the long-term legacies of colonialism that sometimes go unnoticed and argue that these legacies are far from gone. Rather they are deeply engraved in the local and global practices and in the production of knowledge (Tuley, 2020). Legacies that strive to represent Western norms and knowledge as universal, value-neutral, and 'better'. In San Paulo, we see models of good practices in intercultural education and integration through a de-colonial critical intercultural pedagogy framework.

As Markowska-Manista & Liebel (this volume) draw attention to the need to adopt a non-Euro-centric approach, indicating that this research rarely incorporated the non-western epistemologies, de-colonial approaches, local knowledge production, and children's participation in childhood studies (which has to be also understood from below). They note that this research needs to be situated within the understanding that the globalisation of child-hoods produces not a single, uniform 'global childhood' but many 'global childhoods' that are highly interdependent on the unequal power structures surrounding them. They consider the reality that the attempt to de-colonise child research is fraught with challenges, particularly given that concepts of children's voice, agency, and participation have emerged in specific historical and geopolitical contexts, and the meanings and assumptions underlying them interact with other concepts in complex ways. To combat this would require deep reflections by social science researchers on how post-colonial patterns of relationships are getting reproduced. Further, we should consider

204 Working towards a Hopeful Future

the possibility of applying ethical symmetry in research about children, searching for the topography of ethics that would be proper in the type of research conducted. The general principle underlying this attempt is to challenge the power asymmetries of the adult–child relationship that stems from an undervaluation of children and their abilities, and to consider them as co-researchers instead of subjects. As they stress, the ethical dilemmas of participatory research with children of the Global South cannot be overcome by establishing ethical principles alone. Instead, they require researchers to critically self-reflect on the persisting inequality of power in the globalised post-colonial world and between adults and children. This requires that childhood studies not only expand knowledge about children but also contribute to policy interventions that lead to greater equality and social justice. We see a fundamental condition for this in strengthening the social position of children and giving more attention and support to the ways of thinking, seeing, and acting of children of the Global South (in a changing environment of global migration processes).

Digital inequalities and the challenge of inclusion

With alarmingly low levels of school and university enrolment among applicants from refugee backgrounds, in a new report,[1] the UNHCR, the UN Refugee Agency, have called for an international effort for ensuring a good future for this generation of refugees. According to data gathered by UNHCR in 40 countries, the gross enrolment rate for refugees at secondary level in 2019–2020 was just 34 percent, trailing behind local populations. In this volume, we find that refugee and migrant children were disproportionately affected by the remote learning systems brought on by the COVID-19 pandemic in Greece. It introduced new challenges to the digital inclusion of refugee/migrant children in education; problems that are likely to remain in the future. Policies that tackle the digital divide are key, such as the provision of adequate equipment, free data, and accessible learning for all pupils, including refugee groups. The online learning platforms could also be used to bridge the gaps in schooling, during the time spent by refugee children on a long waiting list for registration to a school.

During the pandemic period in the UK, schools' closure and the shift to online learning reshaped the practices of everyday life, education, and social life for all children. Research with migrant pupils shows their struggles both in their education and their social life during the pandemic, and they accentuated the role of schools in children's socialisation and integration processes for newly arrived children particularly. During the lockdown, the day-to-day practices of migrant children and young people changed and many of them experienced feelings of isolation and lack of support. Such social isolation has an impact on how migrants form meaningful, nurturing social bridges and bonds in the host country (Barker, 2021: 37). According to Barker (2021), successful social integration for newcomers requires the fostering of meaningful social bonds (ties to co-ethnic, co-religious, and co-national communities), social bridges (ties to the different, diverse groups in the community), and social links (links to the structures of the state). The formation of such social connections is essential for migrants in order to build trust and shared values in the host society to function effectively. For newly arrived children and young people who are yet to form such social connections, schools are an important resource and space where social bridges, bonds, and links can be built and maintained. Thus, schools' closure and forced social isolation may leave severe and long-lasting impacts on children's social integration.

In line with our plea to re-construct the framings of migration studies to tackle such issues of migrant integration within the Global North, Morris (2021) points to the post-colonial 'logics' and colonial legacies underpinning the European national state which continue to construct and frame the study of refugees. This problematises how life-long learning is incorporated and conceptualised in global policies, moving away from a nation-state-based discourse and North–South binaries, which create desirable and undesirable migrants. Essentially, this requires a coordinated international effort that recognises and protects the right to education for all children and young people, especially those from migrant backgrounds.

De-othering: A provocative approach

Social scientists use provocations as an approach to initiate critical reflection amongst participants on issues that are often otherwise overlooked, obscured, or accepted as naturalised practice (Pangrazio, 2017). As provocateurs, stimulators, and/or agitators, we, as social science researchers, ask if we can interrupt the flow of migration discourses that normalises the language of national supremacy, privilege, and othering. The simple questions of 'who is a migrant?' or 'should internal movements within national borders be termed as migration?' are telling testimonies of the ontological and epistemological pitfalls that surround the term 'migration'. Evidence from Albanian children in Slovenian educational settings shows that the othering discourses and practices point to the hierarchically characterised in-group and out-group binary opposition, the exclusion and segregation practices and social distancing based on the stigmatisation, symbolic degradation, and stereotyping, as well as the existence of discursive violence. This perception of the Albanian ethnic community points to the definitive Other or the subordinate where the existing exclusionary practices and discursive violence significantly affect the integration of migrant children and youth.

To turn these othering mechanisms on their head, we add our voice to Nail (2019) who calls for a new paradigm shift that centres mobility and motion, rather than fixity and statis. He maintains that 'the expectation that the world of mobile bodies will conform to static models of states, borders

206 Working towards a Hopeful Future

and political behaviour is causing millions of people around the world to undergo immense suffering' (Nail, 2019: 2). This volume has opened a window into the different types of sufferings that migrant children and young people experience as they navigate multiple national expectations and try to survive what Badwan (2021) refers to as 'language blocks' with reference to the ever-changing expectations that marginalised individuals have to survive in different places and at different times. The survival mode indicates the potential violence and disruption that these national expectations and gate-keeping mechanisms create. Will they ever disappear? Badwan (2021) doubts this saying, 'Can these language blocks ever melt given the very cold and stubborn macro socio-political contexts that create and sustain them? (2021: 222). This is a question that we cannot answer with certainty but we continue to invoke it here in line with our provocative approach to de-other those who have remained historically marginalised in the construction of migration studies and relevant discourses.

Framing of north-south migration in economic terms

For a long time, migration theories, focussing on push and pull theories (de Haas, 2014), have often examined the structural barriers that motivate migration pinpointing to the economic value of migration to home and host countries either through remittances or addressing skills shortages. The pandemic also revealed the fault lines of migration, in terms of the preponderance of migrants who were frontline workers in the global north, and also who faced the wrath of pandemic through both health impact, but also were less shielded through social security schemes through and citizenship rights. Evidence from two contexts shows the role of education and well-being of children and youth in economic migration. First, Uzbekistan remittances are considered the highest amount of remittances among all central Asian countries and the largest source of external financing in the region. This economic return from migration is mainly used for improving the houses, housing, and food; however, these remittances are not enough to invest in health and education as the remittances spent on them are only around 5 percent. More importantly, parent migration has a significant influence on their children; for example, half of the children have worsened mood after parent(s) migration, a third of them suffer from emotional problems, and 21 percent suffer from anxiety. Similarly, among a group of children Left Behind in southern India, evidence from a large-scale survey shows that while economic remittance does indeed improve the financial situation of the household, there may be disadvantages to the children in other aspects.

The study deployed specially designed questionnaires targeting children of both migrant and non-migrant households in Kerala, India, and reported on three different measures of well-being. With regards to physical health, children from migrant households score lower on measures such as BMI. Even though they have greater access to a wider variety of foods and brands, they tend to consume foods with lower nutritional value as compared to the foods consumed by children from non-migrant households, perhaps owing to the lack of parental supervision. In terms of education, a greater percentage of migrant-household children are enrolled in private schools as compared to non-migrant households, which is largely considered as 'better education'. However, a large portion of these children report feeling extreme stress from living up to their parents' expectations as a consequence. With regards to mental health, employment of the Strengths and Deficiencies Questionnaire (SDQ) revealed that while children from migrant households report feeling more independent and mature as a result of their parents being away, particularly among boarding school children, they also report feelings of loneliness and unhappiness to a greater extent. Contrary to previous research, majority respondents said that they would be happy if their parents returned home from their migration. Female pupils were more likely to report as such compared to males, and older respondents are more likely to do the same than the younger ones. Finally, children from migrant households report that they themselves would consider migration as a possible future choice for themselves, showing the continuity of migrant routes in life and identity formation.

These studies provide new arguments to counter the neoliberal narratives that stress migration-related prosperity. They highlight that what might appear to the world of adults as a prosperous life might not necessarily offer children the same perceived levels of prosperity, well-being, and success. We need more child-informed studies to address the fallacy of push and pull factors from familial, children, and young people-orientated perspectives.

A social justice approach to migrant education studies

The language of migration in the era of migration, one of the most pressing issues of our times (Castles et al., 2013), exposes the dangers of deeper, newer, and often less visible forms of exclusion both in the global north and in the south. For example, in the rainbow nation of South Africa that has seen many forms of racialised mobilities within and from other regions of Africa, migrants are often criminalised and seen as a 'problem' through discriminatory discourses and with strong anti-immigration voices within the state apparatus, media and public (Ruedin, 2019) with danger of not just xenophobia, but also, Afrophobia—of discrimination against Black Africans from other countries (See Neocosmos, 2010; Hanna, 2022). Often 'White' migration from outside of the African continent is mostly considered to be for economic or lifestyle reasons whilst black migrants are seen to be associated with poverty, unemployment, and criminalisation. Thus, in sites of education, understanding of racialisation and privilege is significant for how we mould our children's' futures and to shape methodological and analytical approaches in migration studies. Issues of 'discrimination, xenophobia and

208 Working towards a Hopeful Future

racism are often invisible in migration studies, calling for new methodological approaches to understand these narratives' (Hanna, 2022). In this volume, the experiences of African migrant children in South African schools demonstrate challenges resulting from pervasive xenophobic violence, hostile school experiences, and limited access to academic support services, where school experiences rooted in cultural, social, language, race, prejudice, and xenophobia create distinctions compromising assimilation and child development.

Similarly, the experiences of Zimbabwean diasporic children show how they are caught up in discourses of social exclusion that migrants face in diaspora countries through scapegoating, isolation, and bio-cultural hypotheses which affects social cohesion, assimilation, and a sense of belonging affecting the well-being of children as in nation building discourses of inclusivity, the community. and the institutions may exclude migrant groups in society on the basis of their legal status (legitimacy) and level of assimilation (belonging). This then borders on racialisation and may question the "morality" of laws legitimately constituted but bordering on exclusion.

In the field of migration, discourses of hierarchies and othering create a binary categorisation that pits desirable migrants against undesirable migrants. Children are then caught up in this socio-legal chasm and their development is strictly curtailed thus affecting realistic chances for them to attain full self-actualisation. All this calls for multitudes of approaches as a way forward to broaden understanding and empathy of children's identities as part of a social justice approach to education. More importantly, to address migration as a 'global challenge', it is timely that we transcend the traditional North–South division in a global society, as countries in the north and the south of global face similar sets of challenges related to migration, such as structural barriers and systematic exclusions as in education (See Morris, 2021). A universal frame of reference of the United Nations Sustainable Development Goals (SDGs), which mark a radical shift from the Millennium Development Goals' exclusive focus on "developing" countries in the South (See Horner, 2020), will help towards "converging divergence" and shared learning for global justice (Horner and Hulme, 2019).

We finally conclude by arguing that if we are serious about a social justice approach to migrant integration, we need to re-imagine integration at different levels: global (north-south); national (policies and practices on inclusion, race, class); local (resourcing, networks, including institutions such as schools); epistemological (de-colonisation), among many others. Maybe then we can unlearn the habits of oppression and othering that continued to inform how we name and label different mobile individuals differently.

Note

1 The 2021 Education Report, **Staying The Course: The Challenges Facing Refugee Education** highlights how young refugees have been disproportionally affected by the disruption by the COVID-19 pandemic.

References

Agirdag, O., Demanet, J., Van Houtte, M., & Van Avermaet, P. (2011). Ethnic school composition and peer victimization: A focus on the interethnic school climate. *International Journal of Intercultural Relations, 35*(4), 465–473.

Badwan, K. (2021). *Language in a Globalised World: Social Justice Perspectives on Mobility and Contact.* Cham: Palgrave.

Badwan, K., Popan, C., & Arun, S. (2021). Exploring schools as potential sites of foster-ship and empowerment for migrant children in the UK (Exploramos las escuelas como posibles centros de acogida y empoderamiento de los niños migrantes en el RU). *Culture and Education, 33*(4), 702–728.

Barker, M. (2021). Social integration in social Isolation: Newcomers' integration during the COVID-19 pandemic. *New Horizons in Adult Education and Human Resource Development, 33*(2), 34–45.

Butler, J. (2009). *Frames of war.* London: Verso.

Castles, S., de Haas, H., & Miller, M. J. (2013). *The Age of Migration: International Population Movements in the Modern World.* 5th ed. Basingstoke: Palgrave Macmillan.

Danzer, A. M., & Yaman, F. (2013). Do ethnic enclaves impede immigrants' integration? Evidence from a quasi-experimental social-interaction approach. *Review of International Economics, 21*(2), 311–325.

de Haas, H. (2014). Migration theory: Quo vadis? International Migration Institute. Available from: https://ora.ox.ac.uk/objects/uuid:45aacf94-8f24-4294-9c74-cbc8453fcbfb

Doná, G. (2006). Children as research advisors: Contributions to a 'methodology of participation'in researching children in difficult circumstances. *International Journal of Migration, Health and Social Care, 2*(2), 22–34.

Gornik, B., & Sedmak, M. (2021). *The Child-Centred Approach to the Integration of Migrant Children: The MiCREATE Project.* Available from: https://www.researchgate.net/publication/352019076_The_Child-Centred_Approach_to_the_Integration_of_Migrant_Children_The_MiCREATE_Project [accessed Sep 08 2022].

Hanna, H. (2022). Being a migrant learner in a South African primary school: Recognition and racialisation, *Children's Geographies,* DOI: 10.1080/14733285.2022.2084601

Heleta, S. (2016). Decolonisation of higher education: Dismantling epistemic violence and Eurocentrism in South Africa. *Transformation in Higher Education, 1*(1), 1–8.

Horner, R. (2020). Towards a new paradigm of global development? Beyond the limits of international development. *Progress in Human Geography, 44*(3), 415–436.

Horner, R., & Hulme, D. (2019). From international to global development: New geographies of 21st century development. *Development and Change, 50*(2), 347–378.

Huijsmans, R. (2011). Child migration and questions of agency. *Development and Change, 42*(5), 1307–1321.

Khawaja, I., & Mørck, L. L. (2009). Researcher positioning: Muslim "Otherness" and beyond. Qualitative Research in Psychology, 6(1 & 2), 28–45.

Mayeza, E. (2017). 'Girls don't play soccer': Children policing gender on the playground in a township primary school in South Africa. *Gender and education, 29*(4), 476–494.

Morris, J. (2021). Colonial afterlives of infrastructure: from phosphate to refugee processing in the Republic of Nauru. *Mobilities, 16*(5), 688–706.

Morrison, T. (1998). Interview with Tony Morrison. Online. Available from: https://www.youtube.com/watch?v=SHHHL31bFPA

Muraszkiewicz, J. (2015). Child migration and human rights in a global age. *International Journal of Refugee Law*, 27(3), 515–519. https://doi.org/10.1093/ijrl/eev040

Nail, T. (2019). *Being and motion.* Oxford: Oxford University Press.

Neocosmos, M. (2010). *From Foreign Natives to Native Foreigners. Explaining Xenophobia in Post-apartheid South Africa: Explaining Xenophobia in Post-apartheid South Africa: Citizenship and Nationalism, Identity and Politics.* Dakar: African Books Collective.

Pangrazio, L. (2017). Exploring provocation as a research method in the social sciences. *International Journal of Social Research Methodology*, 20(2), 225–236, DOI: 10.1080/13645579.2016.1161346

Pavlenko, A. (2019). Superdiversity and Why it Isn't: Reflections on Terminological Innovation and Academic Branding. In B. Schmenk, S. Breidbach, & L. Küster (eds.), *Sloganization in Language Education Discourse* (pp. 142–168). Bristol: Multilingual Matters.

Pennycook, A. (2018). *Posthumanist Applied Linguistics.* London: Routledge.

Ramani, S. (2011). Decolonising knowledge systems. *Economic and Political Weekly*, 46(30), 17–19.

Rosa, J. (2019). Contesting representations of migrant 'illegality' through the drop the I-word campaign: Rethinking language change and social change. In N. Avineri, L. Graham, E. Johnson, R. Riner, & J. Rosa (eds.), *Language and Social Justice in Practice* (pp. 35–43). London: Routledge.

Ruedin, D. (2019). Attitudes to immigrants in South Africa: Personality and vulnerability. *Journal of Ethnic and Migration Studies*, 45(7), 1108–1126.

Santos, B. (2014). *Epistemologies of the South: Justice against Epistemicide.* London: Routledge.

Schenk, C. (2021). The Migrant Other: Exclusion without Nationalism? *Nationalities Papers*, 49(3), 397–408. Doi:10.1017/nps.2020.82

Tuley, M. (2020). Taking decolonising seriously – the problem with migration studies. PhD Blog. Available from: https://www.researchgate.net/profile/Marie-Tuley/publication/353121561_Taking_decolonising_seriously_-_the_problem_with_migration_studies/links/60e824bc0fbf460db8f30df7/Taking-decolonising-seriously-the-problem-with-migration-studies.pdf

Werbner, P. (2013). Everyday multiculturalism: Theorising the difference between 'intersectionality' and 'multiple identities'. *Ethnicities*, 13(4), 401–419.

Index

Note: **Bold** page numbers refer to tables; *italic* page numbers refer to figures and page numbers followed by "n" denote endnotes.

Abdulloev, Ilhom 153
"Active Search" 61
adultism 21
African migrant children's experiences: acculturation 177–178; adaptation 178; African migrant children 165–167; assimilation 176–177; bullying 173; care 178–179; challenges 169, **170–171**, 172; child-centred approach 168; clinical model 169; familial status 172–175; inclusion 172–173; intersections 176; legal status 174–175; methodological approach 168–169; SA schools 165, 167–168; theoretical framework 175–176; xenophobia 173–174
African National Congress (ANC) 165
Agenda for Sustainable Development (2030) 145
Agirdag, O. 200
Åhlund, A. 12
Ajwad, Mohamed Ihsan 159
Albanian ethnic origin: methodological approach 78–79; others and process of othering (*see* Othering)
Alfaro-Velcamp, T. 175
Allan, J. 173
Allner, A. 172
Alzboon, S.O. 178
Anderson, P. 184
Andrew, A. 90
Appleton, N. 177
"Appropriate School" 62
Armus, D. 37
Arun, S. 4

Baak, M. 10, 173
Badwan, K. 206
Barker, M. 103, 204
Berry, W. 177, 178
Bhabha, J. 21
Bialystok, E. 183
Black, Asian and Minority Ethnic (BAME) 6
Blanco-Elorrieta, E. 183
Blundell, R. 90
Bronfenbrenner, U. 187, 196

Camacho, C. 127
Camden memory test 186; age group as independent factor 187, *188*; ethic group as independent factor 187, *188*; interaction between age and language as independent factors 189, *189*, *190*, *191*
Candau, V. M. 55
Cannella, G.S. 28
Caramazza, A. 183
Caravita, S.C. 173
Catalano, T. 75
Cavicchiolo, E. 40
Cèsaire, Aimé 54
Charter on Ethical Research with Children 21, 22, 24, 28
Chiarello, C. 183
child-centred migration studies 3–4; challenging adult-centric migrant discourses 201–202; challenging 'deficit discourses' in migration studies 200–204; de-colonising our path ahead 202–204; de-othering,

Index

provocative approach 205–206; digital inequalities and challenge of inclusion 204–205; framing of north-south migration in economic terms 206–207; methodological, conceptual, and ethical considerations in 5–8; social justice approach to migrant education studies 207–208

child migrants: decolonisation 30; and educational experiences 2–3; importance of 21; participatory research 30; role of informants or respondents 22; symbolic participation 2

children's voice 25–27
civil society organisations 24
colonial genocide and revolt 25
coloniality of power 28
Constitution and Bill of Rights 167, 169
Convention on the Rights of the Child 40
COVID-19 pandemic 9; inequalities 53; and learning 41; MiCREATE project 5–6, 12n1, 74, 87n1, 96–97; migrant children in times of crisis 92–94; online learning 91–92, 95; outbreak of coronavirus 9; safety restrictions and social distancing 91; São Paulo City during (*see* São Paulo City during COVID-19 pandemic); socio-economic status on children's schooling 90
Crago, M. 184
Crenshaw, K.W. 175, 176
critical decolonial interculturality (ICD) 54–56
Crush, J. 166, 167, 174
Cullinane, C. 92
Cummins, J. 183, 184, 197
Curtis, P. 166
Cussiánovich, A. 25

Dahinden, J. 1
Davies, M. 37
decolonising debates 5, 7, 30
Dennis, B. 97
de-othering 73, 76, 87, 205–206
De-othering politics and practices of forced migrants in modern society (Kutsenko) 76
Digital Education Action Plan 109
discrimination of migrant pupils 8–9
Donato, R. 177

Dryden-Peterson, S. 172
Duffy, K. 38
Durkheim, E. 38
Dussel, E. 25

Educacion Popular 25
education: access to 111, 115–116, 119, 136; Albanians 77; better education 207; Brazilian 65; career of professionals 57; debates on interculturality 7; digital 110; distance 120; elementary 54, 58, 61; ethno/eurocentric 55; experiences 2, 5; formal 111, 115–116, 118, 120, 147; Greece 9; higher 147, 152–154, 156, 158, 196; inclusive 169, 172, 179; indigenous 55; inequalities 90, 104; institutions 3, 7, 74, 136, 143; intentions for 166; intercultural 7, 67, 203; investments 127; legal status 45; for migrant children 2–3, 54, 65, 94, 110, 127–128, 207–208; and migration, inverted-U relationship 154; non-formal 111, 117–118; online **113, 114**, 117–119; outcomes 135–138, 143; parental involvement 119; perception and racist behaviour, distinction between 8; primary 147; private 127; public 57, 148; quality of 60, 65, 95, 147; refugee 9, 109–111, 115–116; remote learning 90, 109; secondary 111, 147, 153, 154, 156, 160; Slovenian 8, 73, 86, 87n2, 205; South Africa 165, 172; of students 23, 91; tertiary 147, 159; of traumatised children 184–185; UK 9, 91; university 153; vocational 152–154, 156, 158
educational setting experiences 2–3, 10, 12, 200, 207
education for youth and adults (EJA) 54
Ellis, R. 184
English as other Language (EAL) 6
epistemic violence 27
Ethical Research with Children (ERIC) 19
ethnicity 5, 39, 73–75, 79, 111, 165, 173, 176, 189–195

Fairbrother, H. 166
Fanon, F. 39, 54
feminist-oriented research 29
Fielder, G. E. 75
foster-ship 1

Index   213

Freire, P. 25, 57, 65
Fuentes-Cabrera, A. 11, 173

Gamburd, M. 128
García-Vázquez, E. 177
gender 10, 26, 39, 156, 159, 165, 169,
   173, 200; equality 59; inequality 66,
   167; intersectionalities 67; minorities
   55; norms 129; and violence 59, 64;
   weight of children **133**
Genesee, F. 184
Geneva Convention 166
German refugee and Cyprus migrant
   children: Camden memory test
   187–192, *188–191*; comparative study
   of language learning barriers 183–197;
   methodological approach 185–187;
   number repetition test 192, **193**,
   194; peabody picture vocabulary test
   194–195, *195*; poverty and education
   of traumatised children 184–185;
   sentence repetition test 192
Global North, educational
   setting experiences 2–3, 10, 12, 200,
   207
Global South: children's voice and
   silence 25–28; decolonisation of
   childhood studies 28–30; educational
   setting experiences 2–3, 10, 12, 200,
   207; importance of social place and
   epistemological environment 23–25;
   migrant children from countries
   of the global south 20–23
Goyol, A.B. 176
Greece: access mindset 117; comparison
   of refugee in-person attendance after
   pandemic 111, **113**; digital skills 118;
   estimates of refugee population 111,
   113; in-person attendance before
   school closures and after school
   re-openings 111, **114**; literature
   review 109–110; malfunctions 118;
   methodological approach 110–111;
   obstacles in refugee/migrant student
   inclusion in class 111, **115**; online
   education access 117–119; online
   learning during pandemic 111, **112**;
   parental involvement 119; physical
   access 117–118; prioritization of
   funding 111, **112**; refugees' access
   to online education 111, **112**, **114**;
   socio-emotional reasons 118–119;

suggestions 111, **114**, 120; 'zerorating'
   Internet connections 120
Grosfoguel, R. 39

Harju, A. 166
Harris, B. 39
Henley, J. 185
human capital 23

ICT resources 109–110
The Immigration Act 13 of 2002 167
indigenous or horizontal epistemologies
   29
integration 94; of migrant children
   94–95; and migration 1, 11
Inter-Censal Demographic Survey
   (ICDS) 36
interculturality 55, 59; critical decolonial
   54–56; debates on 7
international migration 149–150
intersectional inequalities 8–9
Isseri, S. 167

JEIF 57, 58, 61
Jensen, S. Q. 74–76
Johnson, B. 166, 169, 175
Jonsson, R. 12
José, M. 24

Kaplan, I. 184
Kellett, M. 26
Kerala migrants: academic performance
   assessment 136, **137**; children of
   migrant parents 141–142, **142**; data
   130, 132; educational outcomes
   135–136; emergence of transnational
   families 127–128; enrolment rates 135,
   136; growing up without parents 138,
   139; health conditions/problems 134,
   134; health outcomes 132–135; health-
   seeking behaviour 134, **135**; mental
   health 138–141; migration status and
   gender 132, **133**; migration status of
   household 132, **133**; migration status
   of surveyed children 130, **131**; patterns
   of individual migration 127–129;
   profile of surveyed boarding schools
   130, **131**; proportion of respondents
   134, **134**; respondents residing in
   households and boarding schools 136,
   137; response to family reunification
   138, **140**; type of institutions 136, **136**

214 Index

Khan, M. I. 134
Komulainen, S. 26
Kroll, J. F. 183
Kumar, Ashwin 10
Kutsenko, O. 75, 76, 86; *De-othering politics and practices of forced migrants in modern society* 76
Kyuchukov, H. 9

language 2; acquisition 87, 183; Albanian 77, 80; barriers 9, 80, 91, 94, 95, 101; blocks 206; challenges 9; classrooms 104; colonial legacies of 12, 29; of communication 24; context of decolonisation 12; difficulties 63; English 94, 101, 102, 104; first 183; Greek 117, 120; host 41, 46, 177; as independent factors *189, 190, 191, 193*, 194; of migration 207; non-official 7; official 186, 194; Polish 45; Portuguese 63; primary 7; proficiency 152, 183–184, 192; of refugees and minorities 183; second 183–185, 187, 189, 190, 192; skills 26, 46, 94, 101, 104, 110; Slovenian 77, 78, 82; social exclusion/inclusion 39; of testing 192, 195, 196; third 183, 185
learning guides (LGs) 56, 58, 60
Lee, E.S. 175
liberation pedagogy 25
Liebel, M 5, 203
low and middle-income countries (LMICs) 146
Lunneblad, J. 184

Maduray, K. 167
Major, L. E. 92
Markowska-Manista, U. 5, 203
McLeod, A. 26
Memmi, Albert 54
Mhandu, J. 167, 168
migrant child, defined 166
Migrant Children and Communities in a Transforming Europe (MiCREATE) project 5–6, 12n1, 74, 87n1, 96–97
migrant education studies: methodological and ethical considerations in 5; social justice approach to 207–208
migrant networks 148
migrants: hosts function 20; second- and third-generation 6

migration: decolonisation movement 3; experiences of children 4; and integration 1, 11; international migration 149–150; 'matters of concern' 3; monolingualising discourses 7; plurilithic experiences 2–3; and research 1; Uzbekistan 146–149
Mirziyoyev, Shavakat 148
Modernity/Coloniality (MC) 54–55
Montacute, R. 92
Morrison, T. 202
multiculturalism 200, 201
Muthukrishna, N. 167
Mutsvara, Shepherd 6

Nail, T. 205
Ncube, M. 174, 175
NGOs 24
Noddings, N. 178
Not in Education, Employment, or Training (NEET) 10

OECD 109; Programme for International Student Assessment 159
Ohta, A. S. 183
Ojong, V.B. 167, 168
'one nation, one language' European model 7
orientalism 74
Othering 73–74, 173; discursive violence 84–86; exclusion and social distancing 81–84; and migrant children 79–86; and others 74–78; 'us' and 'them' 73, 79–81; *see also* Albanian ethnic origin
Ozan, J. 4

Palaiologou, Nektaria 9
Paradis, J. 184
Parreñas, R. S. 129
participatory ethics 23
patterns of individual migration, Kerala migrants 127
Philpott, S.C. 167
Piekut, A. 77
practical ethics 23
procedural ethics 23
propiska system 148
pupils with migrant backgrounds: digital inequalities 204; ethnic minority pupils 200; intersectional inequalities, racism, stereotypes, and discrimination of 8–9;

online learning period 111; through EAL 6, 104

quality of inclusive care experiences 178

race 5, 38, 40, 44, 67, 165–167, 169, 173, 176–177, 179, 200, 208
racism 7–9, 45, 74, 79, 173, 208
Rajan, S. I. 10
Redmond, P. 91
Refugee Education Coordinators (RECs) 111, 117
refugee education in Greece 9, 109–120
Refugee Hospitality Centres (RHCs) 9, 109, 111, 120
refugeeism 21
Reid, S. 91
research methodologies 29
Reyes, R. 66
Robinson, J. 185
Roger, K. 97
Roxas, K. 166

Said, E. 74
Salinas, C. 66
Sankar, Deepa 10
Santos, B. 202
São Paulo City during COVID-19 pandemic: final considerations 65–67; methodological description and critical interpretative analysis 56–65; theoretical dialogues 54–56
SA Schools Act 84 of 1996 (SASA) 167
SA state departments of Home Affairs (DOHA) 167
Save the Children (2002) 22–23
Sedmak, M. 8
Seedat-Khan, M. 166, 169, 175
severe acute respiratory syndrome coronavirus 2 (SARS-CoV-2) pandemic 41
Shen, I.-L. 127
Sibanda, T. 166
Sidhu, K.R. 166
Silva, Lucas Rech da 7, 60
Silver, H. 39
Sime, D. 95
situated knowledge 25
Slee, R. 173
sociocultural theory (SCT) 183
socio-legal exclusion/inclusion (SLEI) 6, 37–40, 48
Spivak, G. C. 74, 75

Spyrou, S. 26
stereotypes 8–9
Strengths and Difficulties Questionnaire (SDQ) Assessment 132, 138
Sustainable Development Goals (SDGs) 145

Taibi, Hadjer 9
Tawodzera, G. 166, 167, 174
Taylor, S. 166
Thompson, J. 166
Tokowicz, N. 183
transactional skills/socio-emotional skills 159
Tuangratananon, T., 173
Turan, J.M. 176

Ubuntu, principles of 11
UN CRC 19
UN Department of Economic and Social Affairs (UN DESA) 145
UNESCO 7, 54, 90
UNICEF 157; Innocenti Research Centre 19; Ministry of Public Education (MOPE) 159; "school-to-work" transition 159–160
United Kingdom (UK): approaches for integration of migrant children 94–95; challenges of online learning 99–102; education system 9, 91; grappling with forced social isolation 98–99; migrant children in times of crisis 92–94; online learning during COVID-19 91–92; principle of researcher 104; study 95–98; tackling pandemic's challenges: children's perspectives 102–103
United Nations High Commission for Refugees (UNHCR) 166
unwanted migrant 55–56
Uzbekistan 146–148; characteristics of migrants 150–151; impact of migration on children 157–158; internal migration 148–149, 152–154; leveraging benefits of migration 160–161; migrant networks 153; and migration 148; migration flows 149–150; migration stock 149; multivariate analysis **155**; NEET 10; *propiska* system 10; reasons for in-migration 151–152; recent reforms easing migration process 161–162; remittances 150; remittances and

households 155–156; skills and labour migration 158–160; unemployment rate 147–148; use of remittances by households 157

Valatheeswaran, C. 134
Valenzuela, A. 24
Vandeyar, S. 167, 174, 176
Vandeyar, T. 167, 174, 176
Vezovnik, A. 75
Vižintin, M. A. 77
Viruru, R. 28

Waldinger, R. 176
Walsh, C. 56, 65
well-being of children in migration processes of the global south 10–11
World Bank 146

xenophobia 166
Xu, M. 173

Youth and Adult Education 65

Zimbabwean child in diaspora: age of accompanying child *44*, 45–48; bio-cultural theorem 40; country of arrival *44*, 45–48, *46*, *47*; demographic features of survey 42, **43**; effect of culture and peer interaction on social inclusion 45–46, *46*; inclusive framework for children 40–41; influx of Zimbabweans 37; isolation hypothesis 39–40; limitations 41–42; methods 41; migration status *47*, 48; reasons for migration **43**, 43–45; sense of belonging and identity 38, 39; socio-legal exclusion/inclusion discourse 37–41; undesirable migrants 39; writer's ZEP permit *36*, 36–37
Zimbabwean Exemption Permit (ZEP) 35, *36*